Golf Course Design

*An annotated
bibliography with highlights
of its history and resources*

*Books in all their variety
are often means by which civilisation may be
carried triumphantly forward*

Winston S. Churchill

EIGCA

Golf Course Design

*An annotated
bibliography with highlights
of its history and resources*

Compiled and Edited by

Geoffrey S. Cornish
ASGCA

Michael J. Hurdzan
Ph.D. ASGCA

With contributions by
Bob Labbance, Editor, Golf Collectors Society

Peer Review
Gil Hanse, ASGCA

Foreword by
Paul Fullmer and Chad Ritterbusch

Grant Books, Worcestershire 2006

Golf Course Design
An annotated bibliography with
highlights of its history and resources

Copyright © Geoffrey S. Cornish

All Rights Reserved

ISBN 0 907186 58 9

Titles in the Series

Aspects of Golf Course Architecture 1889-1924, *F.W. Hawtree* ★

Aspects of Golf Course Architecture 1924-1971 (not yet published), *F.W. Hawtree* ★★

Eighteen Stakes on a Sunday Afternoon, *Geoffrey S. Cornish* ★★★

Golf Course Design: An Annotated Bibliography, *Geoffrey S. Cornish, Michael J. Hurdzan* ★★★★

Series Editor
H.R.J. Grant

Typeset in 11 on 13 point New Baskerville
and printed in Great Britain by
Hughes & Company
Kempsey, Worcestershire

A Grant Books Publication
The Coach House, Cutnall Green
Droitwich, Worcestershire WR9 0PQ. United Kingdom
www.grantbooks.co.uk

Frontispiece and title page: The 11th Hole, the Red Course at The Berkshire
Photograph by Dr. P. Sievers

Golf Course Design

*An annotated
bibliography with highlights
of its history and resources*

First Trade Edition

Grant Books, Worcestershire, UK 2006

Geoffrey Cornish has written or co-authored six books on course design. Co-authors include celebrated golf writer Ron Whitten who was a practicing attorney when he collaborated with Cornish, Robert Muir Graves, ASGCA, and Bill Robinson, ASGCA

Dr. Hurdzan has written four exceptionally important works on design and construction One was co-authored by his partner Dana Fry. Golf Course Architecture was re-published in 2005 in a largely re-written form

Contents

Acknowledgements

Both Authors have dabbled in writing. In doing so, we have observed the interrelationship between designing and writing. Indeed, we suspect that the creation of golf courses, as described by the enthusiasm of those that produce its glorious literature may be part of the answer to why our species is on this earth. At the same time, we comprehend that the evolution of the royal and ancient game of golf and its playing fields, for over half a millennium, has paralleled the progress of Western civilization.

In preparing this bibliography, we sought help from the contemporary and exceptionally creative generation of course designers as to the literature that has influenced, guided and educated them. We acknowledge, and deeply so, the contributions of all who penned the books included in this compendium. Yet we hasten to add that, although not documented here, there are countless important essays on the subject that warrant acknowledgement.

Several bibliographers have laboured over the years to compile a broad record of all aspects of the literature of golf. Our work is limited to course design and subjects closely related. Nevertheless, in our effort to compile information, we found prior bibliographies to be pertinent: those by Donovan and Murdoch; Grant; and, more recently, Daniel Wexler, deserve special mention and our thanks.

Others have also helped to produce and shape this bibliography. The Foreword was penned with great insight by Paul Fullmer and Chad Ritterbusch, former and present executive secretaries of the ASGCA, respectively. Gil Hanse, ASGCA, reviewed our work and performed "far beyond the call of duty". Bob Labbance, president of Notown Communications in Montpelier, Vermont and editor of *The Bulletin* of the Golf Collectors Society, assisted us from start to finish. His partner at Notown, Patrick White, writer on course issues for several trade journals, reviewed sections for us, while Kim Hatch of Postal Connections in Amherst, Massachusetts photographed the book covers. Susan Richardson, the amazingly helpful high-tech person of Amherst, saw to it this bibliography was electronically organised before it was sent to the celebrated British publisher, H.R.J. "Bob" Grant, who graciously crossed the pond to consult with us and lend his expertise throughout the publication process.

Finally, we thank members of the American Society of Golf Course Architects and kindred organisations in Australia, Europe and Japan, for the assistance they provided us. Paraphrasing Winston Churchill: we wonder if so much has ever been owed to so many by two course architects who dabble in writing.

Michael J. Hurdzan, Ph.D., ASGCA

Geoffrey S. Cornish, ASGCA

Dr. Michael J. Hurdzan

Geoffrey S. Cornish

Foreword

GOLF ARCHITECTURE is an under-appreciated art form. Yet, thousands of avid golfers around the world want to learn more about its deep, dark secrets. This book, by Geoffrey Cornish and Dr. Michael Hurdzan, will provide the research needed to delve into the history and evolution of golf course architecture through the years.

Literature is the core of understanding. This bibliography will help the story unfold – from the beginnings of the game of golf to today. The authors even use their crystal ball to look ahead at where golf and architecture are heading.

The compilers of this bibliography are the foremost golf architects/authors in North America, and their interest and enthusiasm are readily apparent in this Herculean endeavor. Geoffrey Cornish has long been regarded as the premier golf architecture historian, and his talks and books on the subject are legendary. Michael Hurdzan also is a prolific writer, with scores of articles and books on the subject. They are simply the best resources in golf course architecture. Both have served with distinction as president of the American Society of Golf Course Architects, continuing to be most active participants in the largest golf architect organization in the world.

Here you'll find a short history of golf course architecture from before World War I, through the Golden Age and the Dismal years, into the era of Robert Trent Jones and modern golf course architecture.

Those interested in golf will find the sections on literature, by golf course architects before 1960, fascinating and somewhat prophetic. Since that time, course architects have written extensively about their profession, their work and the art form itself. Readers will find their theories and strategies following many divergent paths.

Geoffrey Cornish and Michael Hurdzan have even presented a primary source of books on design, construction and maintenance and the environment, which should be mandatory reading for students, lovers of the game and avid golfers interested in improving their golf course.

Of particular interest to students of the game is the "rare treasures" section, which unearths some real gems.

You'll find this book to be a lifelong friend and companion. Most importantly, it will direct you to many hours of enjoyable reading about the mysteries of golf course architecture.

Paul Fullmer   *Chad Ritterbusch*

Executive Secretary Emeritus   Executive Secretary 2005

American Society of Golf Course Architects

Devil's Elbow in South Carolina. George Fazio, ASGCA, and nephew, Tom Fazio, ASGCA, created modest but attractive bunkers. Later Tom developed his own distinctive style

Introduction

Golf has a playing field like no other in the world

From *Golf by Design* Robert Trent Jones Jr.

FOR SHEER size, golf courses dominate sports landscapes. But massive scale is not their most noteworthy characteristic. Thanks to the masterful hand of mother nature, as well as the genius of their designers, the playing fields of the game outshine other landscapes and sporting venues in terms of artistic magnificence and variety.

In the early centuries of golf, the game was played on links land, the sparsely vegetated thin ribbon of sand and plants between high tide and solid ground, that almost encircles the British Isles. This natural links land, with its unpredictable terrain and magnificent settings, provided a home for golf's beginnings and an inspiration to course architects when they later constructed courses on countless terrains around the globe.

As golf courses evolved from natural sites, grazed by livestock and maintained superficially, into today's multi-million dollar layouts, often meticulously groomed, so the field of course architecture has grown. The profession has been transformed to an era when computer-assisted design, environmental and construction permits, advanced earth moving equipment and engineering expertise are all needed to build a course. Still, the common bond between contemporary course architects and their predecessors is artistic dedication to producing inspired creations. Part of the chain connecting past to present is a remarkable literature that charts the evolution of this extraordinary profession. Those accounts helped shape the profession and continue to do so.

This bibliography brings together a century or more of literature pertaining to course architecture, from entire books by practicing architects and professional writers covering the subject, to single chapters in books. To a lesser extent we include a few of the many outstanding club histories and guidebooks that devote space to design or designers. Additionally, publications on related topics such as golf course environment, construction and maintenance, irrigation and drainage are included. Course design and maintenance are so closely interrelated it is not possible to separate them when trying to comprehend the overall picture. Therefore we have listed turfgrass texts that deal completely or in part with course maintenance. An early example would be the 1895 book by H.J. Whigham, *How to Play Golf.* It had a chapter on "The Making of a New Course" including design and maintenance suggestions. This set an example and, as late as 2002, when Dr. James Beard released his revised edition of *Turf Management for Golf Courses,* he also included design information by practicing course architects.

Together this literature tells the story of the evolution of course architecture and forms a base of knowledge for students of course design and those numerous golfers with a more than casual interest in where golf courses come from.

A wealth of information on course design is also to be found in golf periodicals and newspapers, also dating back over one hundred years. Time and resources do not allow us to explore their value in detail. Interest in course architecture and book collecting is increasing. Still many of the publications are not readily available or affordable and many important seminal texts are rare. Fortunately many have been reprinted and are more common and affordable. To help those interested in making a collection of books on course architecture, we provide dollar values for various books based on prices in the year 2005. Yet a word of advice to a starting collector is to be careful about fakes and forgeries for books of high value. Deal with established dealers or book collectors and consult with them before purchasing an expensive book. A partial list of sources is found starting on page 174.

To focus a reader's collecting efforts, we include a check list, for personal use, that divides the bibliography into categories based upon each publication's main content. Then, within a category, we establish our personal priority of the importance of each entry. This allows cross-referencing of the same book or entry in all categories that we believe are pertinent.

Photocopies of books may not have the same prestige and value as the actual publication, but if one's goal is to amass knowledge and not necessarily a collection, a copy imparts the same information as the original. In the past, when our funds were limited for purchasing books, we were thrilled by a photocopy of the book. Then we passed it on to another "impoverished" collector, once we found an original copy we could afford. With the game growing in popularity worldwide, golf is increasingly becoming part of all societies and environments. A reading of the literature concerning the architecture of its playing fields is therefore important. Fascinating, it adds a dimension to the game and links golfers and designers across generations. This book endeavors to assist collectors. Yet the authors yearn to assist those whose libraries include only a few books on course design, and to help even those seeking a single book.

Billions of our species roam the globe seeking meaning for their lives. Is it possible that in some small way, the Royal and Ancient game, its playing fields and its literature are providing part of the answer?

Geoffrey S. Cornish

Michael J. Hurdzan

The Country Club of Detroit. British architects Colt and Alison created bunkers with eye appeal

18th Hole, Red Tail Golf Club, Ayer Massachusetts by Brian Silva. Grass, sand, trees and water are the architects media

Waverley Oaks Golf Course, Plymouth, Massachusetts, by Brian Silva exemplifies the practice of adapting styles from previous eras

Part I

The Architecture of Golf Courses

A Chronology

*Golf was not formed by a single incident;
a long process over generations, centuries and
revolutions was needed. When civilisation was on
the march, golf was too …*

Fred W. Hawtree – Golf Course Architect and Author

Innisbrook Country Club, Florida, by Larry Packard, ASGCA. Packard created bunkers reminiscent of his mentor's, Robert Bruce Harris, ASGCA, but enhanced

Westmoreland Country Club in the Chicago area. Arthur Hills, ASGCA, recognised that bunkers add accent to a golf hole

The Architecture of Golf Courses

A Chronology

FROM ROMAN days, stick and ball games similar to golf have been popular in Europe. They included *paganica* or *cambuca, pall mall* or *jeu de mail, chole* or *soule* and *koluen*. Scholars continue to debate whether the most likely forerunner of golf was jeu de mail, a French game that migrated from indoors to the open links of Scotland, or a Dutch game, kolven, played on ice. While these other games held a strong attraction for participants for brief periods, no game before golf involved man and nature to such a degree, and none made them as passionate about their playing fields.

For several centuries, probably starting about 1400, golf was played in open spaces, with little done to refine them or define individual holes. Rules were made by the players and a round included no set number of holes of prescribed distances. Still the game grew in popularity. Gradually it became mandatory to play in a more organised and controlled fashion, to designated points or holes; eventually standard layouts emerged. Yet there was no standard number until 1764 when the Society of St Andrews Golfers consolidated the first four holes into two, resulting in an eighteen hole round, considered "standard" today. British course architect Fred W. Hawtree said this was "the first tiny seed of course design".

Late 1700s – Early 1800s

Golf spreads to Ireland, as far south as Dublin, and follows the path of the British Empire. It was played along the banks of the St Lawrence River in Canada during the War of 1812 and shortly after on links land in Australia, with one inland course in Tasmania still in existence that dates to 1822.

In the late 1700s, two golf clubs, in Charleston, South Carolina and Savannah, Georgia were formed. Canadian golf historian and author Jim Barclay has discovered some evidence of a seven hole course in play around 1840 at the Hudson Bay's Fort Steilicom, in what is now the state of Washington.

British armed forces establish two private clubs in India, Royal Calcutta, 1829, and Royal Bombay, 1842.

By the last decades of the eighteenth century, the game is relatively widespread. Wherever Scottish explorers, soldiers, traders or settlers traveled, they would use clubs to hit balls on open fields, having brought the implements from their homeland.

1840 – 1850

Five important developments occur in this critical decade:

Allan Robertson, the leading golfer of his day, is induced by the Provost, Sir Andrew Playfair, to upgrade the course at St Andrews.

The gutta-percha ball is introduced and supplants the more costly and less durable "featherie".

The rapid spread of the British railway system makes it possible for wealthy Londoners to reach the links in hours, not days, to watch widely publicized matches between famous professional golfers.

In 1848, David Robertson, brother of Allan, emigrates to Australia where he establishes the Australian Golf Society and lays out early links.

Following widening of the fairways on the Old Course at St Andrews, players find they can take less dangerous but longer routes around the frightening bunkers. Strategic golf is born and the game becomes even more exciting.

1850 – 1898 in Great Britain

By 1857, there are seventeen golf clubs in Scotland, all playing on ancient links. Probably there were many informal links with few defined holes.

By 1888, there are seventy-three golf courses in Scotland, fifty-seven in England, six in Ireland and two in Wales, with at least one in France in addition to informal links.

Allan Robertson, the pioneer course designer who had laid out several links courses, all in Scotland, passes away in 1859. His protégé, "Old" Tom Morris, is soon active in course design in Scotland, England, Ireland and Wales.

Before his death in 1902, Tom Dunn claims to have laid out 137 courses in the British Isles, the continent and distant Canary Islands. All are somewhat primitive and involve little or no construction, but they satisfy the multitudes that are taking up the game.

Canadian born Charles Blair Macdonald, future "father of American course architecture" attends St Andrews University starting in 1872. He is introduced to golf and plays with "Old" and "Young" Tom Morris together with other leading golfers. He gains an abiding passion for the game and venerable links courses.

Photograph: Courtesy of Dr. P. Sievers

5th Hole, the Red Course at The Berkshire, England, a heathland layout

1899 – 1914 The Heathland Era in Great Britain

Sunningdale, by Willie Park, set in the heathlands near London, opens in 1901. Its construction involves tree clearing, earth moving and grassing of open soil. Golf course architecture is born. Prominent heathland architects, in addition to Park, include Harry Shapland Colt, Herbert Fowler and J. F. Abercromby. All except Abercromby eventually cross the Atlantic to lay out courses in North America.

The rubber core ball is introduced in the United States around 1900. Its use soon spreads to the homeland of the game.

1870 – 1900 in North America

The first authentic golf clubs in North America are formed, all in Canada. They include Royal Montreal, 1873, Royal Quebec, 1874, Brantford, 1880, Toronto Golf Club, 1881 and Niagara on the Lake, 1881.

The first organised golf clubs in the United States are the Dorset Field Club in Vermont, 1886, Foxburg Country Club in Pennsylvania, 1887 and St Andrew's Golf Club in New York, 1888. The Country Club, in Brookline, Massachusetts, is the oldest country club in the United States, but without a golf course until 1893.

The first organised golf club in Mexico is San Pedro, 1899.

Willie Davis, a Scot, arrives from Royal Montreal to lay out Newport Country Club in Rhode Island, 1894. The next year he lays out Shinnecock

Hills on Long Island, a layout soon modified by "Young" Willie Dunn, younger brother of prolific designer Tom Dunn.

Before 1900, most designers practicing in North America were Scottish born. These designers, Scottish born unless otherwise noted, included: Tom Bendelow, Willie Campbell, John Duncan Dunn and Seymour Dunn, Tom's sons, Dev Emmet and Arthur Fenn, both American born, Alex Findlay, James and Robert Foulis, J.H. Gillespie, the American Herbert Leeds and C.B. Macdonald, Canadian born, Charles Maud, born in England, Maurice McCarthy, Ireland, Willie and Mungo Park, Robert Pryde, the renowned Donald Ross, Willie Smith, Walter Travis, Australia, William Tucker, England, Herbert Tweedie, England, Lawrence Van Etten, US, Willie Watson, "Bert" Way, England, H.J. Whigham, Robert White, Charles Worthington, US and George Wright, US.

By 1900, there are more courses in the United States than in the United Kingdom; nearly all are modest. Exceptions, where more sophistication is evident, include Myopia Hunt Club in Massachusetts by Leeds; Ekwanok in Manchester, Vermont, by John Duncan Dunn and Travis; Oakley County Club in Massachusetts by Ross; the Island Golf Links on Long Island by Devereux Emmet and several layouts in the Chicago area.

Americans demand better playing fields, with writer and course designer H.J. Whigham, soon to become Macdonald's son-in-law, authoring a scathing and ongoing literary tirade concerning the quality of American courses.

1900-1914 – The Landmark Courses in North America

The clamor for better American layouts soon results in courses of distinction. These include, but are by no means limited to, Oakmont Country Club near Pittsburgh by W.C. Fownes, 1903, Merion East near Philadelphia by Hugh Wilson, 1912, Pine Valley Golf Club in New Jersey by George Crump and H.S. Colt (not completely opened until 1922), the Toronto Golf Club by H.S. Colt, 1912, the Hamilton Golf and Country Club, Ontario and the Country Club of Detroit, both by H.S. Colt and both opening in 1914. Architects including Donald Ross and A.W. Tillinghast see their reputations grow.

Notwithstanding the increased quality and integrity of courses opening in the first two decades of the 1900s, it is the opening of the National Golf Links of America in 1911 that sets the standard for American courses. That layout, on the eastern end of Long Island, by C.B. Macdonald, is a collection of adaptations of the finest holes in Europe. It is so magnificent that it leads to the remodeling of many established courses and inspires excellence in those yet to be built.

In 1902 Charles Blair Macdonald coins the title "golf architect".

In 1912 British greenkeepers form an association.

In 1913 Francis Ouimet, a nineteen-year-old American, defeats renowned British golf professionals Vardon and Ray to win the United States Open

Championship. This victory, a milestone, symbolizes the transfer of wealth and power that followed World War I to the United States from the British Empire. Author Herb Graffis says that Ouimet's victory is the second time in history that shots fired near Boston were heard around the world.

By the outbreak of war in 1914, golf had been played on natural sandy links land and coastal dunes, and primitive man-made layouts, many of them inland, the heathland layouts near London, where course architecture was born, the landmark courses in North America and increasingly elaborate layouts around the world.

World War I – 1914-1918

With World War I underway by 1914, new course construction came to a halt in Europe and the British Empire, though it continued in the United States even after it entered the conflict in 1917.

Developments in golf are limited:

1915 The size and weight of balls are regulated with standards differing across the Atlantic.

1916 The Professional Golfers Association of America is formed.

1917 C.V. Piper and R.A. Oakley's *Turf for Golf Courses* is published in America.

The Roaring Twenties – "The Golden Age" of Course Design

The Roaring Twenties, perhaps the most glamorous period in America's history, was a time of extravagance and jubilation, a coming out for America and golf. Course development was soon flourishing in North America, Europe, South America, Japan and South Africa. Architects such as Macdonald, Ross, Tillinghast and others, who had become widely known before the war, were still on the scene and would experience their most creative years. A talented group of newcomers joined them, including Canadian Stanley Thompson, William Flynn, who partnered Howard Toomey, Seth Raynor and Charles Banks, both Macdonald protégés, Willie Park Jr., who had crossed the Atlantic in 1916, and other Britons, H.S. Colt, C.H. Alison and Alister Mackenzie. Herbert Fowler, although based in England, worked on both sides of the pond. Fred G. Hawtree, father of Fred W. and grandfather of contemporary architect Dr. Martin Hawtree, two prominent architects of the future, also became active and was soon to be joined in partnership with J.H. Taylor. Taylor, like the two other members of the great British golfing triumvirate, Harry Vardon and James Braid, was a prolific architect. Other prominent British architects included but were by no means limited to Tom Simpson, C.K. Hutchison, Sir Guy Campbell and S.V. Hotchkin.

Unlike earlier eras, the construction of courses now involved an increasing degree of earth moving, including the creation of artificial bunkers and somewhat elevated greens together with grading for visibility and landing areas. Still, the prevailing style was one that followed existing contours. Donald Ross said "God created golf holes; it is the duty of the architect to discover them". Generally, this approach resulted in natural, graceful lines.

One major exception was the work of Charles Blair Macdonald, along with protégés Seth Raynor and Charles Banks, who favored massive greens with steep drop offs and huge bunkers. By adapting the classic holes of the British Isles and elsewhere and exaggerating their features, this trio's work attracted attention and helped to maintain interest in course architecture in the lean years that lay ahead. During the golden years, a third style also became apparent. Sometimes known as the "grand style", it was epitomized by Banff and Jasper, two creations by Stanley Thompson in the Canadian Rockies and the Royal York, now St George's, in far less spectacular surroundings near Toronto. Thompson strove for the awesome and impressive, whatever the surroundings.

The era saw changes in construction technology including more sophisticated steam shovels and the advent of primitive bulldozers. Yet most of the earth moving was still done with mule and horse-drawn scrapers although even they had evolved into more effective rotary scrapers. Early shapers, or "teamsters", would on occasion use the knowledge they gained in sculpting courses to become architects themselves. Also helping to drive the industry full-steam was the availability of reasonably priced land that was well suited to course development and close to urban areas.

The Roaring Twenties saw unheard of advances in playing interest, beauty and turfgrass quality. They helped to define the golden age of golf architecture.

1919   Charles Worthington introduces a golf course tractor.
1920   The Green Section of the USGA is formed.
1920s Matched sets of numbered clubs are introduced, and steel shafts are legalized.
1926   The National Greenkeepers Association, soon to become the Golf Course Superintendents Association of America, is formed.
1927   Professor Lawrence S. Dickinson establishes the first school for greenkeepers at Massachusetts Agricultural College, to help greenkeepers understand the abundant research data that had begun reaching the field and to comprehend the discipline of management.
1929   The British Board of Greenkeeping Research is formed.
1920s Fairway irrigation (manual) becomes widespread.
1920s Strategic, as opposed to penal, design asserts itself.

The Depression, World War II and the Aftermath 1929-1953 – The Dismal Years
If the Roaring Twenties was the golden age for course architecture, the next quarter century can be described as dismal. Not only did course

construction diminish with the stock market crash in 1929, but maintenance budgets for existing courses were slashed. "Extravaganzas" of the 1920s, including daring new bunker styles, or "features with character" as the architects called them, were hard hit. The lesson was learned that even the greatest course was not great for long without adequate maintenance.

There were a few silver linings to this despair. One was a renewed respect for links courses, where interest is less dependent on grooming. The Works Progress Administration in the United States, together with an equivalent program in Canada, produced several hundred publicly owned courses. What is more, a number of high quality layouts were unveiled even in these dismal years. Augusta National opened in Georgia in 1933; the first nine of Prairie Dunes in Hutchinson, Kansas, was unveiled in 1937; and a rebuilt and expanded Crystal Downs opened in Michigan in 1933. North of the border, Stanley Thompson's Capilano in British Columbia was in play by 1937, while his Highland Links in Cape Breton, Nova Scotia was near completion when World War II erupted in 1939. In the depths of the Depression, the No. 2 Course at Pinehurst was converted from sand to grass greens under the direction of Donald Ross.

From 1929 to 1953:

1930 The Stimpmeter, a device for measuring the speed of putting surfaces, is invented by Edward Stimpson, though it would not be widely used until modified in 1978.

1931 Gene Sarazen introduces a straight-faced sand wedge.

1936 The National Golf Foundation is formed by Herb Graffis.

1930s A limit of fourteen clubs is established and ball velocity is limited.

In the years immediately following World War II, many new chemical pesticides are introduced. The gas powered golf car appears.

1950 The first edition of Burton Musser's *Turf Management* is published, with a chapter devoted to course design written by course architects Robert Bruce Harris and Robert Trent Jones.

Following the end of World War II, the increased might of earth moving equipment becomes apparent.

Despite these advances, the span from the beginning of the Great Depression through to the end of the Korean War in 1953 can be described as disappointing in terms of golf and its playing fields. While a few world-class courses were unveiled, many existing courses saw their maintenance standards plummet.

Yet even before the Korean War, a rebirth was on the horizon signaled by the phenomenal rise of Robert Trent Jones, who would dominate course design for years to come and influence the profession and art form far into the future.

The Age of Robert Trent Jones – 1953-1980

Optimism was in the air. Buoyed by the fruits of the G.I. Education Bill and an equivalent program in Canada, millions of servicemen and women who had taken advantage of those programs, had an impact on society, including all those responsible for the creation and upkeep of golf courses.

The recovery years were still with us in the early 1950s. Robert Trent Jones, a protégé and partner of Canadian Stanley Thompson, and "the eternal optimist", even in the depths of the Depression, had created several courses on his own before the War. In the few years of peace from 1945 to 1950, his work began to earn true recognition. In those years, three projects of importance to his career and the field of course architecture were:

The creation of Peachtree Golf Club near Atlanta in 1948, in collaboration with Robert Tyre Jones Jr.

Major revisions to Augusta National, also with Robert Tyre Jones, between 1946 and 1950. (Hole #16 received worldwide renown when President Eisenhower painted a watercolor of the view from its tee).

Startling revisions to Oakland Hills in Michigan for the 1951 US Open.

Jones' style included: long, flexible teeing areas; narrower landing areas for long hitters; yawning fairway and greenside bunkers; immense expanses of water; and massive greens, often compartmentalized with a variety of pin positions. Jones dubbed any layout he built that satisfied his standards a "signature course", a designation that entered the lexicon. In summary, Robert Trent Jones brought revolutionary changes to course design. Dr. Brad Klein, a student of course design, later opined that Jones' style, along with universal fairway irrigation, changed the game itself as the era of power and aerial golf was ushered in.

Course architecture changed in other ways from 1953 to 1980, not all of which were good for golf or its architecture. It was a time that saw the introduction of "celebrity" designers, many of whom were accomplished golfers but not necessarily adept in the art of course architecture. It also became a time when the look was more important than the play of the course, and money seemed to be no object to many course developers, often with dire consequences because the truth was that it was not always available. The emphasis was on higher quality courses, despite construction budgets that were rarely adequate. In fact, most courses, private and daily fee, opened for play before they were ready in order to generate revenue. Many layouts that eventually reached top quality were actually constructed under what was known as the "work in progress" method, whereby some planned features were omitted initially and added later when funds became available. During this period, several thousand new courses came into play world-wide, though the oil embargo of the 1970s and resulting "stagflation" temporarily reduced course openings in the United States from some 400 to fewer than 100 annually.

The Links style of Robert Trent Jones at Spyglass Hill in California. His inland style had an impact on course architecture worldwide

Century World near Milwaukee. Robert Trent Jones Jr. produced golf holes with ultimate eye appeal

Photograph: Courtesy of William Roberts

In the shadow of Jones, several little known individuals contributed mightily to the field of course architecture, although their contributions were often unheralded. Two less well-known figures who had an impact on the profession were:

Lawrence Packard, course architect and president of the ASGCA, converted the organization from an exclusionary group to one that accepted all qualified people and he drew up Society policies for the future. Paul Fullmer, executive secretary of the ASGCA, worked beyond the call of duty in the interests of recognition of course design and the Society.

Harry C. Eckhoff, with the title regional director of The National Golf Foundation, but often serving from coast-to-coast, encouraged innumerable groups and individuals to develop courses and provided tireless advice on their organization and finance.

Despite Eckhoff's heroic efforts, many a new course was forced to file for bankruptcy, with subsequent owners purchasing the property inexpensively and reaping the rewards. It seemed that many golfers, including those with adequate resources, were not willing to pay a membership or green-fee that assured a profit or even a breakeven for the owner. Nevertheless the game grew dramatically.

From 1953 to 1980:
Club and ball developments threaten course design.

Turfgrass management becomes a science as contrasted to an art.

An increasing number of course superintendents are college educated.

The might and sophistication of heavy earth moving equipment is enhanced.

Complete automatic irrigation becomes almost universal.

Powered golf cars are accepted in North America and continuous paved paths are often provided for their use.

The USGA method of green construction, introduced in 1960, is followed by the California and other methods. Yet the USGA method predominated by the turn of the century.

In 1970, the Golf Course Builders of America forms. Later, this group of contractors becomes the Golf Course Builders Association of America.

In 1978, the stimpmeter is revised. Its increased use accelerates rivalry for ever faster putting surfaces. Soon this had an impact on green design.

Renowned golf professionals re-enter the field of course design. They had been on the scene on both sides of the pond in its early days on the links and in the Golden Age.

By the early 1970s, environmental awareness becomes important in the development and maintenance of courses, most apparent in the arrangement of holes in relation to wetlands. Regulations now had to be met on the drawing board because architects' plans were submitted to regulators for approval. High-tech equipment begins to play a role in course planning by the 1980s.

With ever increasing space devoted to golf, its playing fields exert an ever larger role in the environment and society. The age sees increasing interest in course remodeling and restoration. Master plans are prepared and entered in club bylaws. Often only a portion of the plan is executed, but the master plan helps to prevent tinkering by future green committees.

Though Robert Trent Jones was still very active in the late 1970s and early 1980s, changes in the game and profession of course architecture signaled that a new era was at hand.

The Contemporary Age, circa 1980 – Present

The Contemporary Age begins after a dormancy in course construction caused by the 1974 Oil Embargo and subsequent shortages in everything petroleum based or powered. By the early 1980s, however, the industry was in full swing, driven in part by the National Golf Foundation's study that claimed the market needed one new course per day. Course architects Pete Dye and his wife Alice had made an extended visit to the links of Scotland in the 1960s. Returning home, they planned several layouts, notably Harbour Town Golf Links, with a links touch including extensive mounding and abundant grass and sand bunkers, sometimes with railroad ties lining them. Yet, the greensward was lush and dictated aerial golf in contrast to the sparse turf of links land and its unpredictable bounces. Whatever, the Dye style was a links style with a North American flair. It was spectacular and was characterized by heroic carries that placed a premium on risk-reward considerations, while innovative features including island greens helped to generate both eye appeal and playing interest. Golf writers and photographers admired it but it was somewhat controversial among the tour players who had never seen courses like those of the Dyes. This shone a spotlight on that style, and for a decade or more, many copied it. Eventually it seemed to give way in part to courses with more classic lines and looks.

With some forty protégés, including Jack Nicklaus, the Dyes created landscapes that supplanted those of Jones. Leading architects such as Tom Fazio, Arthur Hills and others eventually adopted this style, but each with their own touch. Yet during the 1980s, there were not always opportunities to design and build new layouts. Course development was sporadic. Nevertheless the overall result was solid growth until the economy slowed at the end of the decade. By then, the North American links style was predominant, even on inland terrain.

During the mid-1990s economic prosperity, on a scale never before equaled, led to a golfing boom. Everything came together for golf including demand for new playing fields and the rebuilding of established layouts. This coincided with adequate budgets, new computer planning technologies, miraculous earth moving equipment, sophisticated soil mixtures and a new generation of grasses cared for by college-trained superintendents. Amidst this "perfect storm", an immensely creative generation of courses designers seized the opportunity to produce the most magnificent courses since golf had spread from Scotland. Indeed, some feel that the work of contemporary course architects has produced the most creative landscape endeavors in the history of our species.

Yet not everyone admired contemporary North American course architecture and some said so. Soon some of those critics gained a following and emerged as arbitrators of good taste. They wrote books, spoke on national panels, formed societies in the name of dead designers, and developed websites to discuss good and bad course architecture. Nevertheless it was the case they made by research-ing and publishing books and articles on classic golf courses and designers that lead to the "restoration movement" in the United States. Soon course architects were specializing in modernizing layouts designed by past masters. They endeavored to capture the original design intent. This led to architecture litera-ture becoming rich in content and details. It had an impact on public opinion concerning what is good course architecture. Not surprisingly, a few of these former and present critics are now trying their hands at designing. By associating themselves with established designers, the results have been impressive.

Creation of many masterpieces of the 1990s involved moving immense quantities of earth. On the other hand, natural layouts emerged that needed a minimum of earth moving. They too met with wide acclaim. Examples in the US are Sand Hills in Nebraska by Coore and Crenshaw and three courses in Oregon, namely Bandon Dunes by Briton David Kidd, Pacific Dunes by dynamic American Tom Doak, and the newly opened Bandon Trails by Coore and Crenshaw.

Describing the courses in Oregon, their owner Mike Keiser quotes from Wordworth's *Tintern Abbey*, "…and I have felt a presence that disturbs me with the joy". Keiser adds "Let us be serious about the poetry of a well wrought course". (Daley, Paul. *Golf Architecture, A Worldwide Perspective*). Keiser's essay strikes a chord with course architects.

Until the 1990s, rebuilding of established layouts included preparation of complete plans, but was often followed by partial and selective execution only. In the last decade of the twentieth century, however, after planning was complete, the entire course was often rebuilt. Plans were based on what the original designer might have done if contemporary miracles, financial resources and know-how had been available. Yet a major objective was to preserve the genius of the original designer. Controversial as this may be, the results of major changes were accepted by golfers with enthusiasm.

As in other periods, but even more so, designers in the Contemporary Age are challenged by improved clubs and balls together with young golfers that are physically stronger than their predecessors. This is met, but only in part, by longer and denser roughs together with narrower landing areas for long hitters. The challenge to architects is immense and ongoing. Indeed the game itself is threatened.

In the Golden Age and previously, the interchange between North American and British architects was one-sided, with many a Briton working on this side of the pond but no Americans on the other. Since the end of the Korean War, this has been almost reversed with Trent Jones followed by his sons, Robert and Rees and protégé, Roger Rulewich, working worldwide. Other North American course architects working in Europe and around the world include but are not limited to Bill Amick, Bernard Von Hagge, Gary Baird, Graham Cooke, Ron Fream, Cornish, Silva and Mungeam, Inc., and Cabell Robinson. Some golf courses in Europe market themselves as "American style" and attract a following. British born Fred W. Hawtree and Dr. Martin Hawtree created Mount Mitchell in North Carolina and before them Sir Guy Campbell was responsible for one nine at the Tides Inn in Virginia. The 1990s saw an increase in this interchange: British in North America and Americans in the United Kingdom. Examples are:

> Donald Steel – Red Tail in Ontario, Carnegie Abbey in Rhode Island, Vineyard Golf Club on Cape Cod
>
> Gil Hanse – Craighead Links, Crail, Scotland
>
> Clive Clark – Belgrade Lakes in Maine
>
> Jay Morrish with Tom Weiskopf – Loch Lomond, Scotland
>
> David Kidd – Bandon Dunes in Oregon
>
> Kyle Phillips – Kingsbarns and Southern Gailes, now Dundonald Golf Club, Scotland
>
> Howard Swan, with American Ron Garl – Eagle Creek Golf Club, Orlando, Florida
>
> Arnold Palmer and Ed Seay – Tralee and other layouts in Ireland.

Following the 11 September 2001 attack and war in Iraq, profound changes in travel and security resulted. Economic stability and public opinion towards America have also changed. Moreover the world economy has slowed. This was soon reflected in course development, which went from a boom period of over 500 golf courses opening annually in the United States to about 300 in 2003. On the other hand, new books and articles appear. Course architects have more time to write. They are doing so.

What of the Future?

In retrospect, we see that as golf spread from the links, its playing fields were created in parks, prairies, valleys, mountain sides, mountain tops and on innumerable other land forms. This varying terrain, together with the diverse imaginations of designers, have added to the variety of golf. Still, sufficient financial resources have helped. Famed course architect Tom Fazio and writer Cal Brown in their superb work, *Golf Course Designs*, provide a look at construction costs per hole by decade.

Photograph by John and Jean Henebry

Four holes at the famed Devil's Pulpit and Devil's Paintbrush courses in the Toronto area show the style of course architect Michael J. Hurdzan and Dana Fry

1960s	$10,000 to $20,000
1970s	$30,000 to $60,000
1980s	$70,000 to $200,000
1990s	$200,000 to $400,000

These figures are startling and have been of intrinsic importance to the design and redesign of courses because they determined what was possible.

Course architects have long known that the principles of design, when embodied in the landscape, provide golfers with a sense of well-being in addition to the excitement and absorption of the game itself. Until recently, however, it was never known why. Dr. William Zimmerman of Amherst College says the answer likely lies in a paper by Orians and Heerwargen* on evolved responses to landscapes and the "Savannah Hypothesis". Though this academic work makes no mention of golf, the landscapes described, namely the savannahs of East Africa where our species evolved over tens of thousands of years, indicate why a sense of well being comes over one as he or she tours a golf course. The hypothesis is that we yearn for features that allowed our ancestors to survive. These include close-clipped, lush green grass, which showed them that game animals had been present and would return; scattered trees and forest areas together with distant vistas that allowed the hunter to hide and see prey at a distance; fresh water ponds

---

* Orians and Heerwargen's work was recommended to the writers by Dr. William F. Zimmerman, Professor of Biology at Amherst College.

Photograph by Doug Ball

The Devil's Pulpit: this feature epitomises contemporary styles

and scars (bunkers) in the landscape to provide landmarks. Remote as Orian's and Heerwargen's paper may be from golf, it points to the relevance of evolved responses to the art of course design. It is no exaggeration to say that an inland course is a miniature savannah, as is a links course, with shrubs instead of trees. This academic knowledge may impact on course design in the future.

We also postulate that, as environmental regulations become increasingly rigid, golf courses and the vast area they occupy will work still more for the betterment of society. One change in contemporary or future courses, brought about by increasing environmental concerns, will be a shift in maintenance to use less water, fertilizer, pesticides and fossil fuels. In fact, we posit that courses of the year 2020 will be closer in maintenance inputs to the classic courses of the 1920s, but with far better playing conditions.

Golf will continue to flourish if "lessons learned long ago on the links of Scotland are not forgotten"* and if the literature surrounding course design is valued as a precious resource and available to all who love the game and its playing fields. Surely over the course of written history, literature has helped breathe life into design and define its soul.

Finally "what is the role of the course architect?" The answer could come from a title of a treatise by Kenneth Donovan, historian of Fortress Louisbourg in Nova Scotia: *Imposing Discipline on Nature.*

* Sir Guy Campbell

17

Pine Valley Country Club, Clementon, New Jersey by Crump and Colt features bunkers similar to those on the heathlands of England

Photograph: courtesy of William G. Robinson

Plainfield Country Club, Plainfield, New Jersey has one of Donald Ross's few elaborate bunkers

Part II

The Literature of Course Design

A thing created is loved before it exists

Preface to Dickens' *Pickwick Papers* – G.K. Chesterton

Geoff Shackelford, a prolific and eloquent writer, has written nine significant works in a decade and co-authored another

The Literature of Course Design

THE FIRST written reference to the game of golf, according to Donovan and Murdoch, is by King James II of Scotland, when he tried to outlaw the game in his kingdom by an Act of Parliament. These two distinguished bibliographers follow this statement in their bibliography with *A Brief History Of Golf Literature In The Featherie Era, 1620-1850*.

Course Design before World War I

In step with the growth of the game, its literature flourished in the late 1800s and early 1900s; yet little was devoted specifically to course design. What was published concerning design was found mostly in periodicals and newspapers. According to British architect and author Fred W. Hawtree, many of these pieces at best cover the subject of design briefly and superficially. Nevertheless articles and books were written by golfers such as C.B. Macdonald, who paid close attention to the details of classic golf holes and wrote equally detailed descriptions. British authors, including Horace Hutchinson, John Low, professional golfer and course designer Willie Park Jr., Bernard Darwin and seedsman Martin H.F. Sutton, all with golf construction experience, were also contributing to the literature of its playing fields.

According to Joseph Murdoch, "the first real book published in America on golf" was *Golf in America, A Practical Manual* by James L. Lee in 1895. This ground-breaking work included references to several courses of that early period but paid little attention to their designers, although it stated correctly that Willie Davis, not William Dunn, was the original designer of Shinnecock. By 1896, H.J. Whigham, scion of a famous Scottish golfing family and later, 1909, the son-in-law of C.B. Macdonald, was residing in America. He launched a literary and literal tirade against courses in America with a piece in *Scribners Magazine* in 1897. He wrote at length of how poorly the courses of America compared to those in the British Isles. Other writings were more positive. In 1900 Willie Tucker, who had arrived in America from England in 1895, published *Laying Out and Care of a Golf Course* that appeared in *Outing*

Five landmark books of the 1920s found a receptive readership

Magazine, June 1900. By 1901, Walter Travis, who hailed from Australia, had written *Practical Golf,* followed by *The Art of Putting* in 1904.

Down under, as early as 1906, Daniel "Des" Soutar, transplanted Carnoustie golfer and course designer, wrote *The Australian Golfer* with descriptions of renowned courses in the southern hemisphere. A Travis piece on course architecture that appeared in *The American Golfer* in March 1909 was a milestone in the literature of course design.

Articles such as these, and single chapters in golf books, provided fairly abundant literature on course architecture in the United States, the United Kingdom and other parts of the English speaking world. Still, at the beginning of World War I, the only book devoted almost entirely to course design was Aleck Bauer's *Hazards* in 1913. It also included papers by several prominent course architects.

The Golden Age

Like the blossoming field of course architecture, the 1920s was a landmark era in the literature of the profession. Several books, including *Golf Architecture* by Alister Mackenzie and *Some Essays on Golf Course Architecture* by H.S. Colt and C.H. Alison, both published in 1920 in Great Britain, found receptive audiences. In America, in 1926, Robert Hunter's *The Links* was released to dismal sales, though the next year *Golf Architecture in America* by

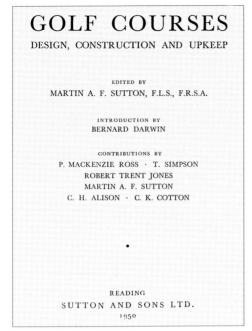
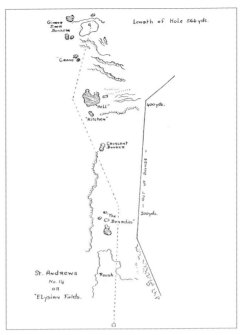

GOLF COURSES

DESIGN, CONSTRUCTION AND UPKEEP

EDITED BY
MARTIN A. F. SUTTON, F.L.S., F.R.S.A.

INTRODUCTION BY
BERNARD DARWIN

CONTRIBUTIONS BY
P. MACKENZIE ROSS · T. SIMPSON
ROBERT TRENT JONES
MARTIN A. F. SUTTON
C. H. ALISON · C. K. COTTON

•

READING
SUTTON AND SONS LTD.
1950

Martin A.F. Sutton's inflential 1950 book followed two similar works by Martin H.F. Sutton

George C. Thomas generated more interest, as did *The Architectural Side of Golf* by H.N. Wethered and course architect Tom Simpson, published in the United Kingdom in 1929. C.B. Macdonald's *Scotland's Gift – Golf* was released in 1928 with many passages related to design. Any number of periodicals and newspapers, on both sides of the Atlantic, also allotted abundant space to course architecture with the latter often written by course architects. In America, the two major golf publications, *American Golfer* and *Golf Illustrated*, were edited by course architects of renown, the former by Walter Travis, also its founder, and the latter by course architect Max Behr, Wilfred "Pipe" Follett and A.W. Tillinghast, in that order.

The eloquence and dynamic efforts of British architect – writers have been the foundation for design literature in North America. Nevertheless the eloquence of American course architect Max Behr, 1884-1955, ranks among the greatest. His essay, Art in Golf Course Architecture, appearing in *The American Golfer*, August 1927, includes some of the most beautiful passages in golf literature.

The Dismal Years
The fate of the literature of course architecture suffered alongside the profession as the Great Depression deepened. In the United Kingdom, writers continued to provide essays on course design, and in 1950,

23

Martin A.F. Sutton's monumental *Golf Courses, Design, Construction and Upkeep* was published. It was a greatly revised form of previous Sutton works (H.F. and A.F.) and included articles by several British architects and the American, Robert Trent Jones. In North America it was quieter, with Herb Graffis serving as the "voice crying in the wilderness" through his pieces on course architects that often appeared in his *Golfdom* magazine. The National Golf Foundation, also his creation, continued to assist in promoting new courses by providing timely articles and booklets. H.B. Martin's *Fifty Years of American Golf* that appeared in 1936 included a chapter on course design, that was referred to by Herbert Warren Wind and other writers for years to come.

Robert Trent Jones, the subject of several influential articles and an author himself, was propelled to ever increasing fame when Wind, whose own renown was also escalating, authored a piece on Jones in *The New Yorker* of 4th August 1951. This followed an article in the *Saturday Evening Post*, 8th June 1946, by John Lacerda, with its protagonist, the Canadian Stanley Thompson and significant references to Jones. Lacerda's piece was the first major American reference to course designers following the war. Jones' influence was further increased by the chapter he wrote in Herbert Warren Wind's 1954 book, *The Complete Golfer*. In that chapter Jones provided an overview of course architecture and described eight world-class courses with text and color prints.

The Age of Robert Trent Jones
This age was ushered in with *A History of Golf in Britain*, by Bernard Darwin, et al., published in 1952, with three chapters by golf architect Sir Guy Campbell. Robert Trent Jones, a future legend in the profession, was also an author, with numerous essays published as chapters in books and as articles in periodicals. In 1974, his son Rees followed in his father's footsteps by writing the Urban Land Institute publication, *Golf Course Development*, with Guy Rando. In 1976, Bill Davis and the editors of *Golf Digest* produced *Great Golf Courses of the World*, while *The World Atlas of Golf* by Ward-Thomas and others was released with immense significance to course design. The British publication, *Shell's Encyclopedia of Golf*, by course architect Donald Steel, et al., appeared in 1975. It included numerous references to course designers.

Oxford educated course architect Fred W. Hawtree's essay, *British Golf Course Architecture*, appeared in *Golf Course Superintendent*, now *Golf Course Management*, on January 1975. This eloquent and graphically illustrated piece helped revive an interest in the ancient links among an important group, namely the superintendents that maintain and enhance the playing fields of the game. It may also have encouraged club officials to make the pilgrimage to the links.

Throughout this period and later, the renowned Herbert Warren Wind published countless pieces describing golf courses. His multi-part series on course design, appearing in *Golf Digest,* was widely read. Finally in 1981, *The Golf Course* by Cornish and Whitten appeared. Intrinsically a book on architects and their courses, it was heralded as the first book devoted exclusively to course design or designers since the Golden Age.

The Contemporary Age

As early as the 1970s, course architect Donald Steel was writing a regular column in *Country Life,* as well as producing several books. Similarly, course architect Fred W. Hawtree was providing insight into the subject with his essays and books. The appointment of Ron Whitten, student of course design and co-author of *The Architects of Golf,* as architectural editor of *Golf Digest,* in the late 1980s was another milestone.

Since the 1980s and the appearance of *The Golf Course* by Cornish and Whitten, an outpouring of design literature has been obvious. Authors have included recognized course architects as well as interested students of the profession who may themselves have gone on to do some design work. Several names stand out. Two are John Strawn, whose *Driving the Green* and Robert Trent Jones, Jr.'s *Golf By Design* introduced concepts familiar to course designers, but not previously discussed in literature. The eloquence of Tom Doak and Fred W. Hawtree, both course architects, rivaled that of their predecessor Max Behr and is perhaps unrivaled even by professional writers. Some say Dr. Michael J. Hurdzan's *Golf Course Architecture* is intrinsically a long overdue and much needed update of George Thomas' classic, *Golf Architecture in America.*

Paul Daley, the Australian author, prepared a study of links courses in the British Isles and another concerning the sandbelt courses of Australia. In 2002 and 2003, his *Golf Architecture, A Worldwide Perspective* appeared in two volumes with essays by people from many nations. It is an amazing collection.

It is difficult to argue with the statement that Ronald E. Whitten had become the "dean of architectural writers" by the end of the last century. Yet he has many illustrious peers, including but not limited to the erudite Dr. Brad Klein, editor of *Golfweek's* "*Super News*" and Geoff Shackelford, who writes a column in *Golfdom* and has authored many widely read books, all superbly illustrated; they have filled a void. Bob Labbance and his partner Patrick White at Notown Communications in Vermont have produced papers galore on course design and related subjects, while Labbance's biography of Walter Travis was a milestone. Two Canadians, Jim Barclay and course superintendent Gordon Witteveen, have produced several books on designers and greenkeeping and there have been others dedicated

Aleck Bauer's Hazards *published in 1913 may have been the first book exclusively on course design while John Strawn's* Driving the Green *1991 was stranger than fiction*

to superb writing on the subject. One example is course architect Desmond Muirhead, a respected cult-like figure, who wrote monthly articles for the *Executive Golfer*. They attracted wide attention within and outside the profession, while his book on playing the Old Course at St Andrews appeared shortly before his sudden death in 2001.

Contributions from those outside the English speaking world should not be overlooked. Books on course design have been published but not translated into English. Japan is the prime example, with author Sato and long-time course architect Takeaki Kaneda being particularly productive.

In retrospect, we see that authors of golf literature have been recognized course architects while others have been professional writers, and still others, students of the profession who have gone on to design. This literature first arose in Britain in the late 1800s and soon spread to America and the English speaking world.

Landmarks in the Literature of Course Design

Before 1900

1889 How to Layout Links and How to Preserve Them. Horace G. Hutchinson, *Golfing Annual 1889*. A twelve page essay. It heralded the abundant literature of course design that was to follow.

1895 *Golf in America; A Practical Manual* by James Lee. This work included limited references to course design and designers. It was important to the early growth of golf in America.

1896 *The Game of Golf* by Willie Park Jr., included an influential chapter on course design.

1897 *How To Play Golf* by H.J. Whigham, had one chapter, "The Making of a New Course".

The Heathland and Landmark Period (1898-1914)

1901 *Practical Golf* by Walter J. Travis, with one chapter entitled "The Construction and Upkeep of Courses".

1906 *Laying Out of Golf Courses and Putting Greens* by Martin H.F. Sutton.

1906 *The Australian Golfer* by Daniel Soutar devoted space to describing courses "down under".

1910 *Golf Courses of the British Isles* by Bernard Darwin.

1912 *The Book of the Links: A Symposium on Golf* by Martin H.F. Sutton.

1913 *Hazards. The Essential Elements in a Golf Course Without Which the Game Would be Tame and Uninteresting* by Aleck Bauer with essays by H.S. Colt, W. Laidlaw Purves, of Royal St George's fame, Ted Ray, the great professional golfer, Alister Mackenzie and others. This may be the first book exclusively on course architecture.

1914 Weeks before the outbreak of World War I, the magazine *Country Life* announced in July that Alister Mackenzie had won first prize in its competition for a great hole. As conceived by Mackenzie, the hole was described and illustrated. Several periodicals around the world had published and were to continue to feature essays on golf holes, many featuring classic holes of the British Isles. C.B. Macdonald and other designers were students of these influential essays.

1917 *Turf for Golf Courses* by Charles Piper and Russel Oakley.

The Golden Age (1920-29) and the Lean Years (1929-53)

1920 *Golf Architecture: Economy in Course Construction and Greenkeeping* by Dr. Alister Mackenzie.

1920 *Some Essays on Golf Course Architecture* by H.S. Colt and C.H. Alison, with a chapter by Dr. Mackenzie.

1926 *The Links* by Robert Hunter.

1927 *Golf Architecture in America: Its Strategy and Construction* by George C. Thomas Jr.

1927 *Art in Golf Course Architecture* by Max H. Behr, an essay in *The American Golfer*, August 1927. Authored by a course architect, the essay ranks among the most eloquent in the literature of course design.

1928 *Scotland's Gift – Golf* by Charles Blair Macdonald.

1929 *The Architectural Side of Golf* by H.N. Wethered and T. Simpson.

1936 *Fifty Years of American Golf* by H.B. Martin. One chapter, "Golf Architects and Famous Courses", helped keep the traditions of the profession alive during Depression and war.

The Contemporary Age (1953 - present)

1946 "He Drives Golfers Crazy on Purpose" by John Lacerda. A whimsical essay concerning the Canadian, Stanley Thompson, in the *Saturday Evening Post,* 8 June 1946, was the first on course architects following the war. With abundant references to the up-and-coming Robert Trent Jones, Thompson's former partner, it refers to what had gone on before and heralded what lay ahead.

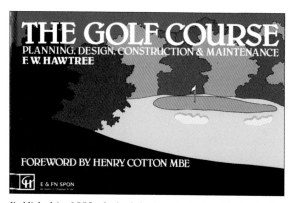

Published in 1983, the book had an impact on the profession as did his later works

1950   *Turf Management* by H. Burton Musser included an influential chapter by course architects Robert Bruce Harris and Robert Trent Jones.

1950   *Golf Course Design, Construction and Upkeep* by Martin A.F. Sutton. This monumental work included essays by British architects Mackenzie, Ross, Tom Simpson, C.H. Alison and C.K. Cotton and the American Robert Trent Jones.

1951   An essay in the *New Yorker* 4 August, by H.W. Wind, heralded Robert Trent Jones' ever increasing fame and enhanced the author's.

1952   *A History of Golf in Britain* by Bernard Darwin, et al. contains three chapters by course architect Sir Guy Campbell, including a memorable passage on the geological formation of links land.

1954   *The Complete Golfer* by Herbert W. Wind contained an illustrated chapter by course architect Robert Trent Jones on the layouts of celebrated courses.

In earlier years, Herbert Graffis, founder of *Golfdom* magazine and the National Golf Foundation, continued to be the "voice crying in the wilderness" concerning course design, as he had been during Depression and war.

1974   *Golf Course Developments* by course architect Rees Jones and landscape architect Guy Rando became the first book, since the Golden Age, devoted entirely to course design.

1974   *100 Greatest Golf Courses and Then Some* by William H. Davis and the editors of *Golf Digest*.

1975   *Encyclopedia of Golf* by Donald Steel, Peter Ryde and Herbert W. Wind included descriptions of the layouts of renowned courses worldwide. Steel later became a leading course architect and author of influential books.

1975   Course architect Fred W. Hawtree's "British Course Architecture: An Illustrated Essay", appearing in *Golf Superintendent,* now *Golf Management,* in January, served to re-introduce links courses to an important group, namely course superintendents and club officials. Descriptive color photographs provided the reader with the feeling of links golf. In 1983 Hawtree published his influential *The Golf Course* and then followed it with other books that provided meaning for the profession.

1976   *The World Atlas of Golf* by Pat Ward-Thomas, H.W. Wind, Charles Price and Peter Thomson with a Foreword by Alastair Cooke described courses and their architects worldwide. It also provided a vivid history of course architecture.

1981   *The Golf Course* by Geoffrey Cornish and Ronald Whitten heralded a surge in the literature of course design. Whitten, an attorney, became architectural editor of *Golf Digest* and one of the most influential and best known writers on golf design in history.

1991   *Driving the Green* by John Strawn acquainted readers with the problems, some stranger than fiction, encountered in developing a new course in the age of environmental awareness.

1992   *An Environmental Approach to Golf Course Development* by William R. Love, ASGCA, 1992, revised 1999, became a definitive text on course development and the environment.

       The Anatomy of a Golf Course by Tom Doak, 1992. For several years Doak, a course architect, was part-time architectural editor of *Golf Magazine* and in 1996 wrote *The Confidential Guide to Golf Courses*. Despite a heavy design load, he continued writing.

1994   The Architect's Vision by Tom Doak, an essay in the USGA's *Golf, the Greatest Game*, rivals Max Behr's *Art in Golf Course Architecture* for vision and fluency.

1995   *The Course Beautiful*, the first volume of Tillinghast's essays, compiled by R.C. Wolffe, Jr. and Robert S. Trebus, with library and pictorial research by Stuart F. Wolffe, was followed by *Reminiscences of the Links* in 1998 and *Gleanings From the Wayside* in 2001. The trilogy, unique in itself, provides superb text concerning Tillinghast's philosophy and achievements.

1996   *The Captain: George C. Thomas, Jr. and His Architecture* by Geoff Shackelford became the first published book by this brilliant and prolific writer. Enlightening works, concerning courses and their designers, have flowed from his pen since then.

1996   *Golf Course Architecture: Design, Construction and Restoration* by Dr. Michael Hurdzan, ASGCA, soon became one of the most important works since Thomas' *Golf Architecture in America*. It seemed to reflect the importance of Thomas' work.

1998   *Golf Course Design* by R.M. Graves and G.S. Cornish was the first effort to create a textbook at college level on design and construction.

2000   *The Missing Links* by Daniel Wexler described renowned courses that have disappeared forever. A second volume soon appeared.

2002   *Golf Architecture: A Worldwide Perspective, Volume I* by Australian Paul Daley provides opinions of course designers worldwide. Volume II and III followed.

Despite a heavy design load, course architect Tom Doak continued writing brilliant books and essays

2003 *All Courses Great and Small* by James W. Finegan is a treatise on layouts in England and Wales including many mentions of their architects, many of whom had pioneered the process.

2003 *Building a Practical Golf Facility* by Michael Hurdzan. The profession of course architecture seeks to create them and golfers yearn to play them. Yet the message of the Hurdzan book is that "affordable", "accessible" and "sustainable" layouts are urgently needed and can be built.

Biographies

Course Architect	Biographer
H.S. Colt	F.W. Hawtree
Alice Dye	Alice Dye with Mark Shaw (autobiography)
Pete Dye	Pete Dye with Mark Shaw (autobiography)
Robert Trent Jones	Robert Trent Jones with Larry Dennis (autobiographer)
Joe Lee	Ron Whitten
C.B. Macdonald	George Bahto
C.B. Macdonald	C.B. Macdonald (autobiography)
Alister Mackenzie	Tom Doak, James Scott, R.W. Haddock
Mick and Vern Morcom (Australia)	John Scarth
Tom Morris	Robert Kroeger
Larry Packard	Mickey Rathbun
Willie Park Jr. & Family	John Adams
Donald J. Ross	Donald Grant
Donald J. Ross	Bradley Klein
George Thomas	Geoff Shackelford
Stanley Thompson	James Barclay
Walter Travis	Bob Labbance

Over the years, many important biographies concerning course architects have been published. Philip Young has recently had his biography of A.W. Tillinghast published by Classics of Golf. The writing of two more is well advanced. They include one by Stuart Bendelow concerning his grandfather pioneer course designer Tom Bendelow. The other written by Bob Labbance and Kevin Mendik covers the life of Wayne Stiles, course architect of the 1920s.

Architects Who Were Authors

By Bob Labbance *

An idea is of little value unless communicated or expressed, to allow it to be utilized. Traditionally architects have communicated their concepts in many ways, ranging from arm waving to detailed plans and specifications. Because the focus of this book is bibliographic, this essay highlights those who could best convey their ideas by the written word. Admittedly there are course architects whose names appear on books as the authors, but those books were in reality the work of ghostwriters. It is difficult to know the story behind every written work. Yet in this essay, I attempt to name those who could turn a phrase, illustrate a point and spread their ideas by written word.

Most architects wrote something about their work. Yet to consider those who penned one article as writers is to consider those golf writers

Bob Labbance

of today, who consult on one course, to be golf architects. That does a disservice to both professions, especially those involved in the life long study of the art and science of course architecture. Nevertheless, some architects have written so eloquently and often they can be called writers. Of these Walter J. Travis was one of the first, and one of the most prolific. From one hundred love letters in elegant flowing prose, written to his future bride Ann Bent in the 1880s, to his twelve years of writing monthly columns and features as editor of *The American Golfer* magazine from 1908 to 1920, Travis was as much a wordsmith as he was a deadly putter.

Even before he published his first book, the ground breaking *Practical Golf* in 1901, Travis had written for *Country Life in America* and *Golf* magazines. While he wrote his share of instruction, Travis found that magazines were interested in his opinions and therefore wrote of courses in America and the United Kingdom. His *Practical Golf* collected some of these pieces, adding primers on course architecture, green construction and maintenance, balls and clubs, handicaps and hazards.

As his competitive career wound down, Travis concentrated on course design and publishing. He established *The American Golfer* as the premier golf

* Bob Labbance is editor of *The Bulletin* of the *Golf Collectors Society* magazine, golf editor of *Turf Magazine*, author of the definitive biography of Walter J. Travis, together with three golf travel books, a score of club histories and innumerable essays.

publication in the country and wrote dozens of articles for it, covering a range of topics touching on every aspect of golf. He offered insight and opinion on rules, golf terminology, amateurism, stymies, housing developments on courses and course agronomy. He never stopped updating and improving his understanding of turfgrass.

The ideal putting green is covered with a close sward of very fine grass, with a thick matting of roots. The blades should be fine and slender, silky yet tenacious – entirely different from the ordinary first-class lawn. A coarse, large-bladed grass, the product of undue fertility, is not what is wanted – quite the contrary.

Of the same era as Travis, though more geared to editing than writing, Tom Bendelow was also one of golf architecture's most literary members. When Bendelow arrived in America in 1892, he found a job as a typesetter with the *New York Herald,* laying out the classified advertising section. It was from that position he answered an ad for a golf instructor to teach the game to a Long Island, New York family. When that family, the Pratts, needed golfing grounds on their estate, Bendelow designed the first of his many courses.

Bendelow's efforts caught the attention of Albert Spalding, owner of A.G. Spalding and Brothers, America's most active sporting goods purveyor. He moved to Chicago in 1902 and by 1907 started a decade long position as editor of *Spalding's Official Golf Guides.* These annual compendia of information recounted descriptions of numerous championships in every section of the country, profiled the best players in each region, detailed the spread of the game and its playing fields and offered basic advice on laying out courses, conducting events and playing techniques.

Bendelow never wrote a book on golf, though after his involvement with Spalding ended, he contributed regularly to the Chicago-based *The Golfers' Magazine* and completed a booklet entitled *Golf Courses by the American Park Builders.* While building a case for aeration and top dressing Bendelow wrote:

The ground must be opened up in some way to allow the making available of the food content which is already there, but which because of the lack of porosity and caking is not available. Don't imagine that fertilizers will take the place of the tillage that is necessary, for it will not.

As prolific as Travis and Bendelow, but directing the vast majority of his writing specifically to course design, Albert W. Tillinghast wrote volumes of material between 1914 and 1937, primarily for *Golf Illustrated,* though his byline also appeared in *The American Golfer, Pacific Coast Golfer, The Golfers' Magazine, Country Club Life* and the *Professional Golfer of America.* Tillinghast's compositions covered every aspect of design, singling out the virtues of par 3 holes, the strategy of par 5's, the use of water hazards, bunkering, proper teeing grounds, trees on the course and every nuance of course planning imaginable. His discourses wandered into blind shots, boomerang holes, punch bowls, practice areas, the double dogleg and the Redan. When he had thoroughly covered design details, he turned his attention and talents to caddies, course construction and maintenance, turfgrasses and even miniature golf. He also wrote about contemporaries, including Donald Ross, Thomas Turner, Ben Sayers, Willie Anderson, Tom Morris, David Herd and the Smiths of Carnoustie. On his own, and as a consultant for the PGA of America, Tillinghast traveled nearly every inch of the country. During his travels, he wrote about Shawnee-on-Delaware, Merion, Winged Foot, the San Francisco Golf Club, Five Farms, San Antonio, Puget Sound, Oakland Hills and Mexico. Few courses, people or topics escaped his attention. Tillinghast also wrote two works of fiction, *Cobble Valley Golf Yarns* and *The Mutt*. Both are still highly collectible in their original printings.

Many, perhaps the majority of Tillinghast's abundant essays have been compiled into a fascinating trilogy by Rick and Stuart Wolffe with Bob Trebus

In a 1920s article cleverly titled "The Fetish of Length", Tillinghast stated:

We regard the present tendency to stretch golf courses out to greater lengths than ever before, as an unfortunate and mistaken policy. It isn't how far, but how good. The fetish of distance is worshipped entirely too often and there should be a quick end to it.

In the big league with these three writers there was George Thomas. Unlike Tillinghast, Thomas wrote outside of golf. A man of means, his first interest was in rose breeding, concerning which he wrote two books. *The Practical Book of Outdoor Rose Growing* was published in 1914 and enjoyed many printings, even when Thomas had turned his attention to golf. His second rose volume, entitled *Roses for All American Climates* was published in 1924.

Thomas was a man who focused on the topic at hand, eventually moving on to another field when he grew bored. His forays into course design began in the early 1900s on the east coast, but his career truly blossomed when he moved to California in 1919. During the 1920s he produced the bulk of his design work and, as was his experience with roses, when he accumulated a body of knowledge, he organised it into a book. *Golf Architecture in America, Its Strategy and Construction* was published in 1927 and was viewed as a cornerstone volume. It may be surprising, considering his background in roses and landscaping, that Thomas wrote "Trees and shrubbery beautify the course and natural growth should never be cut down if it's possible to save it; but he who insists on preserving a tree where

The Raven at Three Peaks, Silverthorn, Colorado; Hurdzan/Fry Golf Course Design

Timeless golf course designs reflect the surrounding natural areas and are a good neighbour to them

it spoils a shot should have nothing to say about golf course construction". When golf no longer tickled his fancy, Thomas moved on to big game fishing producing his final book, *Game Fish of the Pacific* in 1930.

While these men are singled out because they truly were writers as well as architects, their contributions to golf literature could be no greater than the offerings of several others. Willie Park Jr., was the first professional to write a book about golf, *The Game of Golf*, making its debut in 1896. Park offered the perfunctory section on instruction, filling seven of the book's twelve chapters with how to play this shot and that. However, he gets down to business in "Laying Out and Keeping Golf Links", the first essay on design ever published by a practicing course architect.

The green should be laid out so as to test the capabilities of golfers without giving undue advantage either to the man who is a long driver, or to a man who excels at the short game. A golfer who can drive further than his neighbors is undoubtedly entitled to some advantage for being able to do this; but, as golf does not consist solely of long driving, the advantage should not be so great as to put out of court entirely the man who, driving a shorter ball, is more expert in approaching and putting.

Park's second book, *The Art of Putting*, was purely instructional in nature, with many photos and far less copy.

Although William Tucker Sr. never wrote a book, few others were as prolific during his era. Tucker, who hailed from England, was golf professional at Saint Andrew's in Hastings-on-Hudson, New York and an early authority on turfgrass, at a time when little scientific information was available. In different publications, including *Century Magazine, Golf Illustrated* and *Golfdom*, Tucker answered questions from superintendents, golf professionals and lay people about the design, grassing and maintenance of courses. Before the USGA Green Section became the authority on the subject, Tucker penned this introduction to an article for *Golfdom* titled "Green Subsoil: Structure and Fertilization for Good Permanent Turf".

In agrostology, the art of growing turf, the fundamentals come under 6 groupings: substructure, drainage, topsoil texture, internal respiration, percolation and sanitation. Grass will grow almost anywhere, but it takes intelligent construction to produce a desirable turf.

A Yale graduate, where he was influenced and coached by legendary Scot Robert Pryde, Max Behr was an accomplished player, winning the New Jersey Amateur in 1909 and 1910. In 1914, Behr became the first editor of *Golf Illustrated*, writing extensively on a range of topics, while compiling and editing the works of his pioneering contemporaries.

After the death of his wife in 1918, Behr resigned from the magazine and moved to the west coast, where he continued to write about golf and the design of courses. His writing career outlasted his design career, as he continued to put pen to paper for four decades. Indeed Behr's vocabulary exceeded most of his fellow writing architects and it brought an intellectual audience to the topic.

Thus, the golf course architect who knows the business of designing a hole will not stand on the projected tee and from there decide where bunkers should be placed. He will stand where the most propitious locations will be for the hole, so that he may become intelligent in composing hazards to defend it.

Also part of the California movement, but bringing a much different perspective to architecture than any of his associates, Wiles Robert Hunter was an active and much-published writer before turning his attention to golf. Hunter, the respected sociologist, wrote *Poverty* in 1904, *Labor in Politics* in 1915 and *Why We Fail as Christians* in 1919. Hunter was more of a consultant than an architect, feeding his ideas to Alister Mackenzie, and writing his only book on golf in 1926. *The Links* was considered a bible of course theory, illustrated with diagrams and photographs of the masterful work being done at the time. In the highly regarded volume, Hunter wrote:

I do not know how much will be spent this year in America on new construction, but, if past experience is any guide, much of that money will be wasted, and at least an equal amount will later be spent on these courses in altering, obliterating and rebuilding before work is satisfactorily finished.

Architectural activity on the west coast during the late 1920s centered around Dr. Alister Mackenzie, who had codified his architectural tenets in the 1920 volume *Golf Architecture*. It was not a writing project in the sense of sitting down to write a book, but rather a collection of transcribed lectures that he had delivered. Nevertheless, the small pocket-sized book probably had a greater influence on golf architecture than any other book written by an architect.

Mackenzie enumerated thirteen essential features of the ideal golf course, and though some were borrowed from other sources, all were repeated many times over by those who would follow.

"The course should be so interesting that even the plus man is constantly stimulated to improve his game in attempting shots he has hitherto been unable to play," wrote Mackenzie in one of his points. Another read "The course should have beautiful surroundings, and all the artificial features should have so natural an appearance that a stranger is unable to distinguish them from nature itself".

Mackenzie's writing outlived him. Starting a year after his death, excerpts of his work appeared in golf journals of the day. In February 1935, *Golfdom* published "Experts Needed: Neglecting to Employ Qualified Architects Has Cost Thousands in Muni Course Building" in which Mackenzie pointed out the opportunity municipal courses enjoyed when properly planned. Decades later, a long lost manuscript attributed to Mackenzie was brought to light, resulting in *The Spirit of St Andrews*. It was published in 1995.

Though he wrote little that was published during his lifetime, except for promotional brochures for his beloved Pinehurst, Donald Ross penned a book that also remained sequestered from the public's eye for half a century.

Finality in
Golf Course Architecture

FIFTEENTH HOLE—CYPRESS POINT
Note: This green was entirely artificial. The 17-mile drive ran across the site of the green

Dr. Alister Mackenzie
and Associates

CYPRESS POINT CLUB
PEBBLE BEACH, CALIFORNIA

OFFICES

Pasatiempo Country Club
Santa Cruz, California

Care of Agnew & Boekel
Federal Reserve Bank Building
San Francisco, California

Room 1609
105 West Munroe Street
Chicago, Illinois

Whitcomb House, Whitcomb Street
London, England

*Cypress Point Club in California by Alister Mackenzie features some of the world's
most striking bunkers*

Golf Has Never Failed Me is more a collection of observations than a narrative, though the lost commentaries have received considerable acclaim since appearing in book form in 1996. Ross discusses many of his courses in the book, as well as pontificating on such topics as trees, brush, drainage, pot bunkers, natural hazards, fairways on sandy soil and "The Game is Easier Today". Unlike many of the other architects mentioned, Ross had little influence on designers of his era through the written word. He wrote few articles that were published on a timely basis, and his one book debuted to an audience generations removed from his own. The influence that Ross has commanded results from the volume of first-class design work he did around the country, not his words. In the long lost manuscript Ross wrote:

Bunkers should be so placed as to be clearly in view, and in such locations as to make all classes of players think. Often, the very highest recommendation of a bunker is when it is criticized. That shows that it is accomplishing one thing for which it was built: It is making players think.

Harry S. Colt studied law at Cambridge University, where he was captain of the golf team. He practiced law briefly in the 1890s, before making inroads into golf as a player and administrator. By 1900, he was dabbling in course architecture, a hobby that would blossom into an influential career. With his partner of twenty years, C.H. Alison, he wrote *Golf Course Architecture* published in 1920, later also contributing to many works including Martin Sutton's 1919 volume *The Book of the Links* and its later edition.

In a section about the framework of courses, Colt wrote:

The architect may spend interesting hours in an attempt to use the natural features of the land to the greatest possible advantage. Experience will probably teach him that it is often impossible to get every ounce of value out of each individual feature on a good piece of ground, and also that it is bad policy to sacrifice several good holes on the altar of one that is of superlative merit. He will find it necessary to take an all-round view, to weigh the pros and cons of every possible scheme, which has brilliant points but is poor in the aggregate.

Many other architects have made contributions through their writing, though few produced the volume of material as the aforementioned composers. Alfred Tull, originally a construction superintendent for Walter Travis, wrote about construction and maintenance for *Golfdom*, including an article in September 1946 that reviewed a quarter of a century of course architecture. Tull summarized by saying:

We must however, be careful to so design our courses that the better players have to strive for accuracy and use judgment in their choice of direction, or we shall end up by breeding a race of golfers who can drive a mile and pitch over a barn, and nothing else.

A man of few words, William Flynn added to the dialogue about turfgrass in the 1920s and 1930s, writing an occasional article for the USGA Green Section. "Every course needs not be a Pine Valley or a National," said Flynn, "but every course should be so constructed as to afford incentive and to provide a reward for high-class play".

John Duncan Dunn contributed much to golf literature, though most of it was instructional in nature. Dunn authored eight books, including the 1920 volume *Intimate Golf Talks*. His brother Seymour Dunn wrote four books including *Standardized Golf Instruction*, which was reprinted many times. Both designed a number of courses, primarily in the north east.

James Braid began writing about course design as early as 1908, and included a chapter on the subject in his treatise, *Advanced Golf*. Averse to travel, Braid's influence would have been far greater had he crossed the ocean to America and promoted himself. Instead he offered advice on laying out courses and design style in his book.

Sir Guy Campbell, hereditary knight and prominent British course architect, who designed or redesigned a score or more courses before and after World War II, wrote *Golf for Beginners*, published in 1922, together with innumerable chapters in golf books. Like Max Behr, his eloquence equaled that of the great writers of English literature.

Thought of primarily as a player and winner of three British Open Championships, Henry Cotton was the author of ten books and contributed to a wealth of magazines and journals. He studied course architecture under Sir Guy Campbell; Cotton himself was knighted in 1987.

In the modern era, four men have done more for golf literature than all others combined. Foremost among them is Geoffrey Cornish, author of numerous reference volumes. Cornish began his writing career in the 1940s, while still an instructor at the University of Massachusetts, contributing turfgrass articles to *Golfdom* and other publications. After establishing an architectural firm in the 1950s, he produced informative articles on the design and construction side of the business, eventually authoring *Golf Course Design – An Introduction* in 1975, with partner Bill Robinson, for the National Golf Foundation. This was the first treatise on course design in many decades and opened the floodgates to the profusion of literature on the subject today.

In 1981, with celebrated co-author, Ron Whitten, Cornish completed *The Golf Course*, an amazingly detailed reference source that attempted to compile data on the world's golf courses and their designers, a task some thought impossible. The book enjoyed many printings and a worldwide appreciation, and gave birth to *The Architects of Golf*, a 1993 expansion and revision of the original.

In the decade since, Cornish has continued to add to golf's library. *Golf Course Design*, with Robert Muir Graves, is a text book widely used in landscape architecture classes; *Classic Golf Hole Design*, also with Graves, categorizes the prototypical holes and where the best examples are found; and *Eighteen Stakes on a Sunday Afternoon* is a compendium of and summarized writings on North American golf course architecture through history.

Making an equally important contribution to the golf industry, Dr. Michael Hurdzan has written a number of books and many articles in the past twenty years. His booklet, *Evolution of the Modern Green,* which was published in 1985, assembled historical and evolutionary data about the development of the putting green. A decade later, Hurdzan added similar treatment to every aspect of the golf course in his encyclopedic book, *Golf Course Architecture: Design, Construction & Restoration.* From the history of the hazard to the use of a computer in course design, this book provides the reader with an education grounded in history.

In 2003, Hurdzan offered *Building the Practical Golf Facility,* with case studies revealing how courses can be built without excessive budgets, sound advise that can be utilized by municipalities, individuals and organizations wishing to provide sporting value at palatable prices. In 2003, he also published *Selected Golf Courses by Hurdzan/Fry,* highlighting some of his firm's greatest projects and offering unusual insight into the design process and interactions with two dozen clients, and their resulting finished products.

On the other side of the Atlantic, two men have kept the literary banner aloft. Fred W. Hawtree, son of golf architect Frederick G. Hawtree, practiced course architecture first with his father and then on his own for five decades. As he turned the business over to his son, Hawtree pursued his writing, first writing *Elements of Golf Course Layout and Design* in the 1970s. He later added *The Golf Course: Planning, Design, Construction and Maintenance,* a jam-packed volume that enjoyed many printings after its initial release in 1983.

In 1991, Hawtree profiled H.S. Colt and his partners in *Colt and Co.,* and in 2003 he wrote a landmark book on the origin of golf-like games. *Triple Baugé* is a fascinating discussion on the heritage and development of golf, how the game evolved from other ball and stick games and where it was played before it was embraced and modernized by the Scots.

Donald Steel has been as prolific with the pen as he is at the drafting table. In the 1970s, Steel became the first golf correspondent for the London *Sunday Telegram,* a post he occupied until 1990. Starting in 1983, he added regular features for *Country Life* magazine and the first edition of *The Golf Course Guide to the British Isles.* Eight editions of that tome have been printed and Steel has gone on to pen many other books.

The Encyclopedia of Golf, with Peter Ryde and Herbert Warren Wind, is the best overall golf reference available and Steel also contributed a chapter to *The World Atlas of Golf.* In 1992, he added *The Classic Links* to his long list of successful titles.

Many others have written with insight and intellect. Foremost among them is Tom Doak, whose book, *The Anatomy of a Golf Course,* was an instant classic. He has written numerous articles for *Golf Magazine* and others, in addition to his cutting edge *Confidential Golf Guide.* That synopsis of some of America's finest courses was the first honest evaluation of the design characteristics of many great courses. Doak, together with co-authors Dr. James Scott and

Raymund Haddock, added *The Life and Work of Dr. Alister Mackenzie* in 2001, a scholarly dissertation that brings the architect to life.

Keeping a regular column in *Country Club* magazine for years, Desmond Muirhead had a rapt audience for his vanguard opinions about the golf industry. He wrote with flair and style, not unlike his golf designs.

Many others have written about their own experiences in the business, with design thoughts offered by Peter Alliss, Bill Amick, Pete Dye, Tom Fazio, Joe Lee, Rees Jones, Robert Trent Jones, Jr., and Sr., William Robert Love, Forrest Richardson and Jack Nicklaus, among others.

On The Other Hand some writers were involved in Design

Pioneer golf writer Horace Hutchinson planned Royal West Norfolk, the Isles of Scilly Golf Course, co-designed Royal Eastbourne and consulted on several other courses in the United Kingdom and United States. Hutchinson was a most prolific author, writing more than seventy books on a wide range of topics. Rudyard Kipling planned and built a course near Brattleboro, Vermont; Sir Arthur Conan Doyle prepared an early design of Jasper Park in the Canadian Rockies, it never became a reality; while President Franklin Roosevelt, something of a writer, planned and oversaw construction of a nine hole course on Campobello Island in Canada.

By the end of the twentieth century, several golf writers in North America were involved in course design. They included Ron Whitten who, with Stephen Kay, ASGCA, collaborated on one course and with Dr. Mike Hurdzan on another. Prolific writer Geoff Shackelford with some nine books to his credit planned and built a par 3 layout on his own and collaborated with Gil Hanse, ASGCA, on the design and construction of a full-length layout. Dr. Brad Klein, a convert from academia to golf editorship, played a major role, with ASGCA members Pete Dye and Tim Liddy, in developing Wintonbury Hills, one of Connecticut's new layouts. In Canada, newcomer Jeff Mingay, author of numerous essays and two books, assisted Rod Whitman in laying out a course and in redesigning others.

Transcending a wealth of persuasions, there is an undeniable link between course design and authorship, one that has flourished for more than a century.

Golf Course Architects Before 1960

With examples of their publications (not necessarily on design)

Alison, Charles Hugh, 1882-1995. *Some Essays on Golf Course Architecture*, 1920 with H.S. Colt. Contributed to *Golf Courses: Design, Construction and Upkeep*, 1933 and 1950 by Martin A.F. Sutton.

Bendelow, Tom, 1872-1936. Editor *Spalding's Golf Guide* and Author of *Golf Courses by the American Park Builders*, 1926.

Campbell, Sir Guy, 1885-1960. 1920 with Horace Hutchinson and S.V. Hotchkin *Golf for Beginners*, 1922, *Golf at Princes and Deal*, 1950. Contributed three chapters to *A History of Golf in Britain* by Darwin, et al.

Colt, Harry S., 1869-1951. *Some Essays on Golf Course Architecture*, 1920. Contributed to *The Book of Links* by Martin H.F. Sutton, 1912. Contributed to *Golf Courses: Design, Construction & Upkeep*, 1933 by Martin A.F. Sutton.

Conan Doyle, Sir Arthur, Laid out the original course in Jasper Park, Canada, pre-World War 1. Prolific author with no books on golf.

Cotton, Sir Henry, 1907-1987. *Golf*, 1931, *Hints on Play With Steel Shafts*, 1933, *This Game of Golf*, 1948, *Some Golfing Ifs*, 1948, *My Swing*, 1952, My *Golfing Album*, 1959.

Croome, Arthur Capel Molyneux, 1866-1930. *The Camberly Heath Golf Club*, 1913.

Demaret, James Newton, 1910-1983. *My Partner, Ben Hogan*, 1954.

Duncan, George, 1893-1964. *Golf for Women*, 1912, *Present Day Golf*, 1922, *Golf at a Gallop*, 1951.

Dunn, John Duncan, 1874-1951. *The ABC of Golf*, 1916, *Intimate Golf Talks*, 1920, *How to Drive; Approach; Putt*, 3 volumes, 1922, *Elements of the Golf Swing*, 1930, *Natural Golf*, 1931, *Golf*, 1941.

Dunn, Seymour, 1882-1959. *Golf Fundamentals: Orthodoxy of Style*, 1922, *Standardized Golf Instruction*, 1934, *The Complete Golf Joke Book*, 1953, *Golf Fundamentals*, 1922.

Dunning, Robert Charles, 1901-1979. *Green Construction*, 1960.

Evans Jr., Charles (Chick), 1890-1979. *Chick Evans Golf Book*, 1921, *Chick Evans' Guide to Better Golf*, 1924, *Caddy Manual*, 1928, *Ida Broke: Humor and Philosophy of Golf*, 1929, *Golf for Boys and Girls*, 1954.

Herd, Alexander (Sandy), 1868-1944. *My Golfing Life*, 1923.

Hunter, Robert W., 1874-1942. *The Links*, 1926.

Hutchinson, Horace Gordon, 1859-1932. *Golf: The Badminton Library*, 1890, *Hints on Golf*, 1886, *Bert Edward, The Golf Caddie*, 1903, *Golf Greens and Greenkeeping*, 1906, *The New Book of Golf*, 1912, *Fifty Years of Golf*, 1919, *The Lost Golfer*, 1930.

Jones, Robert Trent, 1906-2000. *Golf Course Architecture*, 1938.

Kipling, Rudyard, 1865-1936. One of the most prolific writers of English literature (none on golf) yet he dabbled in course design.

Langford, William B., 1887-1977. *Golf Course Architecture in Chicago District*, 1915.

Macdonald, Charles Blair, 1856-1939. *National Golf Links of America,* 1912, *Scotland's Gift: Golf,* 1928.

Mackenzie, Alister J, M.D., 1870-1934. *Golf Architecture,* 1920, *The Spirit of St Andrews,* early 1930s, not published until 1995.

Moone, Theodore, *Golf From a New Angle,* 1934.

Morrison, John S.F., 1892-1961. *Around Golf,* 1939.

Nelson Jr., John Byron, 1912- *Winning Golf,* 1946, *How to Score Better Than You Swing,* 1955.

Park Jr., Willie, 1864-1925. *The Game of Golf,* 1896, *The Art of Putting,* 1920.

Penninck, John Jacob Frank, 1913-1983. *Home of Sports – Golf,* 1952, *Golfer's Companion – Frank Penninck's Choice of Golf Courses.*

Pryde, Robert, 1870 – 1951. *The Early History of Golf in New Haven, Connecticut,* 1951.

Ross, Donald James, 1872-1948. *A Partial List of Prominent Golf Courses Designed by Donald J. Ross,* 1930, *Golf Has Never Failed Me,* written before 1914, published 1996 with editing by Ron Whitten.

Simpson, Thomas C., 1877-1964. *Modern Etchings and Their Collectors,* 1919, *The Architectural Side of Golf,* 1929, with W.H. Wethered, *The Game of Golf,* 1931. Contributed to *Golf Courses: Design, Construction and Upkeep,* 1933, by Sutton.

Stutt, John Hamilton, 1924- *Restoration of Derelict Land for Golf.*

Taylor, John Henry, 1871-1963. *Taylor on Golf: Impressions, Comments and Hints,* 1902, *Southampton Public Golf Courses (Handbook),* 1935, *Golf: My Life's Work,* 1943.

Thomas Jr., George Clifford, 1873-1932. *Golf Architecture in America: Its Strategy and Construction,* 1927, *Practical Book of Outdoor Rose Gardening,* 1914, *Game Fish of the Pacific,* 1930.

Thompson, Stanley, 1894-1952. *About Golf Courses, their Construction and Upkeep,* perhaps early 1930s.

Tillinghast, Albert W., 1874-1942. *Cobble Valley Golf Yarns and Other Sketches,* 1915, *Planning a Golf Course,* 1917, *The Mutt and Other Golf Yarns: A New Cobble Valley Series,* 1925.

Travis, Walter J., 1862-1927. *Practical Golf,* 1901, *The Art of Putting,* 1904.

Tucker, William Henry, 1871-1954. *A Golf Course for Your Community,* 1925, an essay.

Vardon, Harry, 1870-1937. *The Complete Golfer,* 1905, *How to Play Golf,* 1912, *Golf Club Selection,* 1916, *Progressive Golf,* 1920, *The Gist of Golf,* 1922, *My Golfing Life,* 1933. Contributed to *Success at Golf,* 1914.

Golf Course Architects After 1960

That were writers with examples of their publications (not necessarily on design).

Alliss, Peter, 1931- *Drive and Bunker Shot,* Flicker Book, 1955, *Alliss Through the Looking Glass,* 1963, *The Parkstone Golf Club,* Handbook, 1965, *Easier Golf,* 1969, *Play Golf with Peter Allis,* 1977, *Peter Allis' Bedside Golf,* 1980, *An Autobiography,* 1981, *More Bedside Golf,* 1982, *The Duke,* 1983, *The Who's Who of Golf,* 1983, *The Golfer's Logbook,* 1984, *The Open: The British Open Championship Since the War,* 1984.

Amick, William W., 1932- *The Executive Golf Course,* 1975.

Coles, Neil, 1934- *Neil Coles on Golf,* 1965.

Cornish, Geoffrey S., 1914- *Golf Course Design: An Introduction,* with William G. Robinson, 1975, *The Golf Course* with Ron Whitten, 1981, *The Architects of Golf* with Ron Whitten, 1993, *Golf Course Design* with Robert Muir Graves, 1998, *Eighteen Stakes on a Sunday Afternoon,* 2002, *Classic Golf Hole Design* with Robert Muir Graves, 2002.

Cotton, Sir Thomas Henry, 1907-1987. *Henry Cotton Says...,* 1962, *Study the Golf Game with Henry Cotton,* 1964, *The Picture Book of the Golf Game,* 1965, *Henry Cotton's Guide to Golf in the British Isles,* 1969, *Play Golf Better,* 1973, *Golf: A Pictorial History,* 1975, *A History of Golf Illustrated,* 1975, *Thanks for the Game: The Best of Golf with Henry Cotton,* 1980.

Devlin, Bruce, 1937- *Play Like the Devil,* 1967, *Australian Bruce Devlin Championship Golf,* Flip Book, 1970, *Bruce Devlin Flip Book Instructions, Drive and Wedge,* 1971.

Doak, Tom, 1961- *The Confidential Guide to Golf Courses,* 1988, *The Anatomy of a Golf Course,* 1992, *The Life and Work of Dr. Alister Mackenzie* with Dr. J.R. Scott and R.M. Haddock.

Dye, Alice, 1917- with Mark Shaw. *From Birdies to Bunkers,*

Dye, Pete, 1925- *Bury Me In A Pot Bunker,* 1995.

Faldo, Nick, 1959- *The Rough with the Smooth: Breaking Into Professional Golf,* 1980, *Enjoying Golf with Nick Faldo: A Personal Guide to the Game,* 1985, *A Swing for Life, Nick Faldo, the Autobigraphy,* 1997, *Life Swings,* 2004.

Fazio, Tom, 1945- with Cal Brown. *Golf Course Designs by Fazio,* 1990, *Golf Course Designs,* 2000.

Finger, Joe, 1918-2003. *The Business End of Building or Rebuilding a Golf Course,* 1972.

Graham, David, *Your Way to Winning Golf,* 1985.

Graves, Robert Muir, 1930-2003. *A Practical Golf Facility for Athletic Fields,* 1961, *Golf Course Design,* 1998 with G. Cornish, *Classic Golf Hole Design,* 2002 with G. Cornish.

Hawtree, Frederick W., 1916-2000. *Elements of Golf Course Layout and Design, The Golf Course: Planning, Designing, Construction and Maintenance,* 1983, *Colt and Company,* 1991, *Aspects of Golf Course Architecture 1889-1924,* published 1998, *Triple Baugé,* 1996.

Hurdzan, Michael John, Ph.D., 1943- *Evolution of the Modern Green,* 1985, *Golf Course Architecture: Design, Construction and Restoration,* 1996, *Building the Practical Golf Facility,* 2003, *Golf Greens: History, Theory, Design and Construction,* 2004.

Jones, Rees Lee, 1941- *Golf Course Developments,* 1974.

Jones, Robert Trent, 1906-2000. *Golf Course Architecture*, 1938, *Description of the Golden Horseshoe Golf Course at Williamsburgh Inn*, 1965, *Great Golf Stories*, 1982, *Golf's Magnificent Challenge*, 1989 with Larry Dennis.

Jones Jr., Robert Trent, 1939- *Golf by Design*, 1993, *Golf Courses of Robert Trent Jones, Jr.* 1997.

Lee, Joe L., *Gentleman Joe Lee* with Ron Whitten, 2002.

Love, William Robert, 1952- *The Environmental Approach to Golf Course Development*, 1992, revised 1999.

Miller, John Lawrence, 1947- *Pure Golf*, 1976.

Muirhead, Gordon Desmond, 1924-2001. *St Andrews: How to Play the Old Course*, 2000. This eloquent architect and writer also authored books on horticulture and a design column in *Executive Golfer*.

Nelson, John Byron, Jr., 1912- *Shape Your Swing the Modern Way*, 1976, *The Byron Nelson Story*, 1980.

Nicklaus, Jack William, 1940- *My 55 Ways to Lower Your Golf Score*, 1964, *Practice Tips*, 1965, *Reading and Controlling Putts*, 1965, *All About the Grip*, 1965, *Power Plus*, 1966, *The Best Way in Better Golf*, 1966, *The Best Way to Better Golf, Number 2*, 1968, *Take a Tip From Me*, 1968, *Jack Nicklaus, Profile of a Champion*, 1968, *The Best Way to Better Golf, Number 3*, 1969, *Winning Golf*, 1969, *The Greatest Game of All: My Life in Golf*, 1969, *18 Holes: The Master Professional Described His Tee to Green Technique To You*, 1970, *Jack Nicklaus Golf Handbook: 25 Self Contained Lessons by The World's Greatest Golfer*, 1973, *Golf My Way*, 1974, *Jack Nicklaus' Lesson Tee: Back to Basics*, 1977, *Total Golf Techniques*, 1977, *On and Off the Fairway: A Pictorial Autobiography*, 1978, *Play Better Golf, the Swing from A-Z*, 1980, *Jack Nicklaus Playing Lessons*, 1981, *Better Golf, Volume II*, 1981, *Better Golf, Volume III*, 1983, *The Full Swing*, 1984, *Nicklaus by Design*, 2002.

Norman, Greg, 1955- *Greg Norman, My Story*, 1983.

Palmer, Arnold Daniel, 1929- *Arnold Palmer's Golf Book: Hit It Hard*, 1961, *Graph-Check System for Golf*, 1963, *Portrait of a Professional Golfer*, 1964, *My Game and Yours*, 1965, *Arnold Palmer the Man and the Golfer*, 1966, *The Arnold Palmer Method*, 1968, *Situation Golf*, 1970, *Arnold Palmer Plays Merion*, 1970, *Go For Broke: My Philosophy of Winning Golf*, 1973, *495 Golf Lessons*, 1973, *The Rolex Book of Golf*, 1975, *Arnold Palmer's Best 54 Golf Holes*, 1977.

Player, Gary, 1935- *Play Golf with Player*, 1962, *Gary Player's Golf Secrets*, 1962, *Improve Your Golf*, 1962, *Gary Player Tells You All About the Shakespeare Fiberglass Wondershaft and What it Can Do For You*, 1964, *Grand Slam Golf*, 1966, *Positive Golf: Understanding and Applying the Fundamentals of the Game*, 1967, *Gary Player's Golf Class (Book 1) 100 Lessons*, 1967, *124 Golf Lessons*, 1968, *Gary Player's Golf Class*, 1968, *Gary Player's Golf Class (Book II) 100 Lessons*, 1969, *More Tips From Gary Player*, 1968, *Play Better Golf with Player Edutext*, 1970, *Good Test for the 1970 US Open, Hazeltine National Golf Club*, 1970, *The Medium Iron to the Green (8 Iron)*, 1971, *The Tee Shot (A Flipbook)*, 1971, *Weathering Sand and Storm*, 1971 *395 Golf Lessons*, 1972, *Gary Player World Golfer*, 1974, *Gary Player's Golf Guide*, 1974, *Gary Player's Golf Class (Book III), 162 Lessons for the Weekender*, 1975, *Gary Player on Fitness and Success*, 1979, *Gary Player's Golf Book for Young People*, 1980, *Gary Player's Golf Class (Book IV), 170 Lessons for the Weekender*, 1980, *Golfing S.A.*, 1980, *Gary Player's Golf Clinic*, 1981.

Photograph: courtesy of Gary Panks, ASGCA

Troon North, Arizona, by Jay Morrish, ASGCA, and Weiskopf, features small mounds that emulate larger ones behind them

Robinson, William Grieve, 1941- *Golf Course Design – an Introduction*, 1971 with Geoffrey Cornish.

Shackelford, Geoffrey, With eight books published which relate to course design, he has been the most prolific of writers on that subject in the contemporary era. He has designed a par 3 course and been an assistant to Gil Hanse, ASGCA on one layout.

Steel, Donald M., 1937- *The Golf Course Guide to the British Isles, The Golfer's Bedside Book,* 1971, *Guiness Book of Golf Facts and Feats*, 1980, *The Encyclopedia of Golf* with Peter Ryde and H.W. Wind, 1975, *The Classic Golf Links of England, Wales and Ireland,* 1992.

Thomson, Peter William, 1929- *This Wonderful World of Golf,* 1969, *The World Atlas of Golf,* 1976 with Pat Ward-Thomas, H.W. Wind and Charles Price.

Witteveen, Gordon C., *Practical Golf Course Maintenance: The Magic of Greenkeeping* with Michael Bavier, 1998, *A Century of Greenkeeping*, 2001, *Keepers of the Green: A History of Golf Course Management* with Bob Labbance, 2002, *Handbook of Practical Golf Course Maintenance*, 2003.

Weiskopf, Thomas Daniel, 1942- *Go for the Flag: The Fundamentals of Golf,* 1960.

Whitten, Ronald E., 1950- This author of many essays, who some say is the most knowledgeable writer on course architecture, has collaborated on design with Hurdzan and Fry, together with Stephen Kay. *The Golf Course*, 1981 with G. Cornish, *The Architects of Golf*, 1993 with G. Cornish, *Golf Has Never Failed Me* by Donald J. Ross, before 1914, edited 1996, *Gentleman Joe Lee*, with Joe Lee, 2002.

Lahinch Golf Club, Ireland. Alister Mackenzie nestled his bunkers into linksland

Photograph: courtesy of Ron Whitten

Robert Trent Jones, ASGCA, added a new course at Ballybunion, Ireland

Part III

The Bibliography

Make no mistake,
here is greatness and mystery …

A Round of Golf Courses – Patric Dickinson
as reported by Robert McCord in *The Quotable Golfer*

Woodland Golf Club, Allburndale, Massachusetts. Concentric mowing patterns around their greens, as developed by superintendents, are examples of one principle of art

Desert Mountain, Carefree, Arizona. The horizontal lines of this bunker, by Nicklaus, reflect the vertical lines of mountains behind them

Photograph: courtesy of Gary Panks, ASGCA

The Bibliography

IN THE EARLY years of the Republic, the literature depicting its emergence was intended to chronicle that critical period. It has made fascinating reading ever since. Likewise, the earliest literature of golf that first saw the light of day in the mother country was intended to chronicle and instruct. It continues to make fascinating reading.

In America, two of the earliest works contained the word "practical" in their titles. *Golf in America: A Practical Guide* by James L. Lee (1895) and *Practical Golf* by Walter Travis (1901). This tradition has lived on and in 2003, Dr. Michael Hurdzan's *Building a Practical Golf Facility* included that key word.

The three authors may have thought they were writing "how-to" books. Possibly, they were. Yet the writings of the first two have shaped golf and its courses ever since and have contributed to their magic. We suspect the Hurdzan book will do the same.

Understandably much of course design literature, on both sides of the Atlantic and worldwide, was conceived as a work of art and with a "reach for the stars" philosophy. Preparing this bibliography, we conclude that the literature of course design is both practical and visionary regardless of the intentions of the author. Whatever, it is fascinating.

Donovan's and Murdoch's *Game of Golf and the Printed Word (1566-1985)* is the most complete of all golf bibliographies. Covering golf literature in its entirety, they arranged their comprehensive work to correspond to the four eras of the golf ball:

> The Featherie (1620-1850)
> The Gutta Percha (1851-1900)
> The Rubber Core (1901-1960)
> The Hard Core (1961-)

This bibliography, on course design and related subjects however is arranged alphabetically by author.

51

Many of these literary efforts were authored by practicing course architects. On the other hand, many are written by authors with little or no experience in the profession, but still with boundless enthusiasm and superb literary ability. This mix of authors has added variety and brought forth new concepts. Without doubt the literature of golf, no matter its vintage, has inspired and instructed those who practice this art form.

Another wonderful bibliography has been published by H.R.J. Grant. The latter includes an essay by golf architect Fred W. Hawtree, describing the collecting of books on course architecture.

With so many publications included in our admittedly incomplete bibliography, we sought a way for readers to determine if a book or publication was worth seeking and, if found, what was a fair price. Accordingly we devised our own, subjective measure of content and its relative importance.

To that end, we established a Cornish/Hurdzan (C/H) rating scheme for subjects related to course architecture, that indicate to the researcher the importance of the book. Categories follow in a sequence somewhat similar to the manner in which a golf course project develops:

Letter	Category
F	*Feasibility* – the nuts and bolts of how and why someone determines to build a golf course, and where.
D	*Design* – the actual design process and related topics.
C	*Construction* – how the golf course is built.
M	*Maintenance* – turf grow-in and upkeep, together with a historical look at outdated methods.
H	*History* – insights into the past that impacted on course design, including events and people involved.
P	*Personalities* – in-depth, up-close and personal information concerning people important to golf and course architecture.
T	*Travel* – information for guiding the golf traveller to golf experiences.

Then we have a C/H ranking on a scale of one to five as below:

Number
1 Of some value
2 Good information, but not profound
3 Valuable information
4 Very important reference
5 A definitive source

With the increasing role golf courses play environmentally and societally, together with their beauty and the immense space they occupy, extensive collections of books related to them are becoming common. If collections are not large, it seems that alphabetic arrangement by author is the most convenient. Still Dr. Hurdzan's library is probably the world's largest concerning course design literature. He puts forward a method for arranging extensive collections that follows the bibliography.

Some books cover many subjects lightly, while others are focused on one subject.

Therefore, each entry in our bibliography is followed by a c/h rating of the subject groupings, along with the numeric value for how important or in-depth that subject is treated. Admittedly the c/h evaluation is subjective. Yet who better to do it than us? We have access to nearly all the books. However, we soon discovered that a major effort was involved in finding each book, reviewing the content, and rating it. These are our opinions; we welcome corrections, alterations or disagreements. Although we did not rate several books they are nevertheless important.

We also researched the current value of each book taking into account condition from new to used and original to reprint. Abbreviations used include: Orig – original, rep – reprint, LTD – limited edition. Ranges in value are often wide. Yet we want to give our readers an idea of what to expect to pay for a particular book. We include a partial list of names and addresses of established booksellers commencing on page 174.

Selecting books for this bibliography was not an easy process. It was in fact difficult, because we were limited to books that we have read or scanned. When we did not have access to a book, it was not included or not rated. Someday we hope to put together an errata sheet of books missed. So dear reader, if you have access to such a work, please forward a copy or photocopy of the publication to be reviewed, to the publisher.

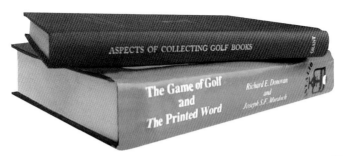

*These two comprehensive bibliographies of golf books have been joined by Daniel Wexler's
"The Golfer's Library"*

Golf Course Design and Construction

Adams, John. *The Parks of Musselburgh.* (Worcestershire, England: Grant Books, 1991, 154 pages, ISBN 0-907186-16-5. Willie Park Jr., has been called the doyen of golf course architects. This volume details the entire Park family and their role in golf, including their exploits as players, their business as club makers and the design careers of Willie, Junior and Senior, and Mungo.
C/H: D3, H5, P5, $100 – 150

Airey, Theres. Photographer, *see* Whitten, Ronald.

Akerman, Joseph Reid. Co-author, *see* Mead, Daniel W.

Allen, Sir Peter. *Famous Fairways: A Look at the World of Championship Golf.* (London, England: Stanley Paul & Co. Ltd., 1968, 164 pages). A travel book for golfers covering famous courses throughout the UK and the world.
C/H: D1, H2, P2, T4, $40 – 60

Allen, Sir Peter. *Play the Best Courses.* (London, England: Stanley Paul & Co Ltd., 1973, 264 pages). The book describes 104 courses in Great Britain, with personal insights into places and personalities associated with each. Allen is a wonderful writer whose books helped establish golf tourism in Europe.
C/H: D1, H2, P2, T4, $25 – 35

Allen, Sir Peter. *The Sunley Book of Royal Golf.* (London, England: Stanley Paul & Co., 1989, 160 pages, ISBN 0-091738-05-9). An account of clubs carrying the title "Royal". References are made to their designers.
C/H: D3, H4, P3, $30 – 85

Amick, William, ASGCA. "Cayman Golf". An Essay found in *Golf Course Design* by Robert Muir Graves and Geoffrey S. Cornish, discusses short courses on small parcels of land with a ball limited in flight distance.
C/H: D4, $N/A

Amick, William, ASGCA. "Golf on Derelict Land". An Essay found in *Golf Course Design.* by Robert Muir Graves and Geoffrey S. Cornish.
C/H: D3, F4, $N/A

Anderson, Tip. Co-author, *See* Muirhead, Desmond.

Arterburn, Todd A. *Public-Private Partnerships in Golf Courses.* (Columbia, MD: Rainmaker Golf Development, 2000, 24 pages, booklet). A step-by-step guide on how to structure a public-private partnership in a course.
C/H: F4, D1, C1, M1, $15 – 25

Bahto, George. *The Evangelist of Golf: The Story of Charles Blair Macdonald.* (Chelsea, MI: Sleeping Bear Press, 2002, 279 pages, ISBN 1-886947-20-1). Known as the father of American course architecture, Charles Blair Macdonald revolutionized course design. This book details his personal and professional life, complete with hole diagrams, course layouts and historic and modern photos of his crowning achievement, the National Golf Links of America. A fascinating and abundantly illustrated book that not only collates the information on Macdonald but also his two associates, Seth Raynor and Charles Banks, who continued his philosophy and

style. Their adaptations (sometimes exaggerated) of classic holes showcasing steep drop-offs and massive features still catch attention and helped focus attention on course design during the long dismal years of Depression and war (1929-1953).
C/H: D3, H5, P5, $50 – 85

Balfour, James. *Reminiscences of Golf on St Andrews Links.* (Edinburgh, Scotland, 1887, 68 pages). An account of the Old Course at St Andrews and how the links changed during the almost fifty-year playing career of Balfour. Anecdotes, advice on clubs, balls, caddies and merits of the game are included.
C/H: D2, H5, P2, $50 (rep) – 4,500

Bamberger, Michael. *To the Linksland.* (New York, NY: Viking Press, 1992, 196 pages, ISBN 0-670-84142-X). Not involving course design, this eloquent work provides the reader with a taste for the brand of golf played on links land, and why the links are of paramount importance to course design.
C/H: D2, T5, $15 – 35

Barclay, James A. *Golf in Canada: A History.* (Toronto, Canada: McLelland and Stewart, Inc., 1992). The definitive and superb history of golf in Canada. Achievements of Canadian course designers, including Stanley Thompson, a giant in the profession, are detailed by Barclay, a "north of the border" authority.
C/H: D3, H4, P3, T3, $15 – 50

Barclay, James A. *The Toronto Terror.* (Chelsea, MI: Sleeping Bear Press, 2000, 207 pages, ISBN 1-886947-93-7) with Foreword by Geoffrey S. Cornish. The first detailed compilation of the life and work of an architect who influenced many other designers. Stanley Thompson created masterpieces from coast to coast in Canada and the United States, as well as designs in the Caribbean and South America. His creations, including Highland Links in Nova Scotia; St George's near Toronto; Banff Springs and Jasper Park in the Canadian Rockies; and Capilano in Vancouver, rank among the world's greatest courses. If you combine the work of Robert Trent Jones and other Thompson protégés, you have an idea of how his concepts have affected golf architecture. One protégé, Cornish, in the Foreword, borrows from Thoreau to say Thompson "marched to a different drummer". Thompson was a character larger than life.
C/H: D3, H5, P5, $15 – 35

Barkow, J., with L. Cosmides and J. Tooby, Editors. *Adapted Mind.* (England: Oxford University Press, 1992, 656 pages). Includes on pages 555-579 a paper by G.H. Orians and J.H. Heerwagen concerning evolved responses to landscapes. No mention is made of golf in the paper. Yet conclusions suggest that golf courses are miniature savannahs. If true, it provides reasons why a hole can provide a player with a sense of well-being regardless of score. Probably we respond to features in the landscape because our ancestors survived on the savannahs of East Africa over tens of thousands of years by adapting themselves accordingly.
C/H: D3, $15 – 50

Bartlett, Michael, Editor. *The Golf Book.* (New York, NY: Arbor House, 1980, 282 pages, ISBN 0-87795-297-3), with photographs by Tony Roberts. This compendium of information includes several articles about course architecture including "Pine

Valley: Golf's American Shrine" by Joe Schwendman; "Monterey: How I Was Seduced by a Peninsula" by Cal Brown; and "Pinehurst Thirty Years Later" by Charles Price.
C/H: D3, H4, P2, $15 – 25

Barton, John et al. *Golf Digest's Places to Play.* (New York, NY: Fodor's Travel Publications, Inc., many volumes.) Important to course design, this work has been published regularly in recent years. Architecture editor Ron Whitten and the *Golf Digest* staff compiled it. Course architects' names are included.
C/H: D2, P2, T4, $10 each

Bauer, Aleck. *Hazards, Those Essential Elements in a Golf Course Without Which the Game Would be Tame and Uninteresting.* (Chicago, IL: Toby Rubovits, 1913, 61 pages). Essays by Colt, Purves, Ray, Mackenzie and others begin the volume. Analysis of outstanding hazards on famous holes follow. (Worcestershire, England: Grant Books, 1993, 88 pages, ISBN 0-907186-30-0, facsimile edition). Some say this is the first book length publication devoted entirely to course design.
C/H: D5, H3, $100 (rep) – 2,500

Bendelow, Stuart W., Sr. *Tom Bendelow 1868-1936: The Johnny Appleseed of American Golf.* (Self-published essay, 1999, 14 pages). Tom Bendelow's grandson attempts to pull together the rich contributions made to the game and growth of golf in the early 1900s. Tom is credited with over 700 courses. This is the most detailed account of him. Stuart Bendelow is working on a complete illustrated text concerning his grandfather.
C/H: D2, H3, P4, $15 – 25

Bendelow, Tom. *Golf Courses by the American Park Builders.* A rare, self-published advertising piece produced in the late 1910s or 1920s concerning the design and build services of a renowned but long gone firm. It is similar to the small booklet listing courses designed by Donald Ross.
C/H: D1, C2, H4, P1, $250 – 350

Bennett, Roger. *Golf Facility Planning.* $15 – 25

Benson, M.E. Co-author, *see* Gimmy, A.E.

Braid, James. *Advanced Golf or, Hints and Instruction for Progressive Players.* (Philadelphia, PA: George W. Jacobs & Co., 1908, 322 pages). The Open champion covers topics from playing in the wind to systems of practice, championship experiences and personal matters. Two chapters are specifically directed toward planning courses, including detailed descriptions on the character and placement of teeing grounds, bunkers and putting greens. Braid adds diagrams to illustrate principles and admonishes amateur designers to adhere to natural features whenever possible.
C/H: D4, H4, P4, $150 – 350

Brown, Cal. Co-author, *see* Fazio, Tom.

Brown, Cal. Co-author, *see* Machat, Udo.

Brown, J. Lewis. *Golf at Glens Falls.* (Glens Falls, NY: Glens Falls Country Club, 1923, 63 pages). An early and unique club history with a golfing fable as text and interesting hole diagrams that show not only the overhead view, but also a longitudinal section of each Donald Ross link.
C/H: D5, H3, $75 – 125

Brown, John Arthur. *A Short History of Pine Valley.* (Pine Valley, NJ: Pine Valley Golf Club, 1963, 38 pages). The first club history of Pine Valley, it was written by its long time president. Early construction photographs of the course and entries describe its design.

Browning, Robert. *A History of Golf.* (London, England: Dent, 1955, 236 pages). Chapter 26 is devoted to the development of course architecture while Chapter 9 explains why eighteen holes constitute a round. (Stamford, CT: Classics of Golf, 1985, facsimile edition).

C/H: D3, H5, P3, $50 – 75

Brummer, Andy. *TechTV's Guide to the Golf Revolution: How Technology is Driving the Game.* (Indianapolis, IN: Tech TV Press, 2003, 168 pages, ISBN 0735714061). This 8"x10" paperback is well done except that it treats each topic in a page or two. That makes for a quick, fun read, but not much substance. It addresses nearly every form of technological advance from "The Golf Gear", through course design and construction, swing instruction, training aids and golf fashions. Any concept marketed as "new" is probably highlighted in this book. Yet it serves to outline many subjects important to course design.

C/H: D2, C2, M1, $15 – 20

Butler, William. *The Golfer's Guide.* (Philadelphia: PA: J.B. Lippincott Co., 1907, 171 pages). The chapter "Links in the Making" advises "In the laying out of a course, the two main considerations should be variety in the holes, which is the essence of golf, and regard for the medium player, who generally constitutes the chief factor in the membership of a club".

C/H: F1, D3, P3, T4, $75 – 150

Campbell, Sir Guy. *Golf for Beginners.* (London, England: C. Arthur Pearson Ltd., 1922, 124 pages). Unusual chapters include "Clothes and the Man", "Selecting a Golf Ball" and "Course Construction and Green-Keeping". Full page diagrams detail the proper and improper placing of hazards, together with natural and artificially placed bunkers. Campbell concludes that "Too often expert advice is solicited, given, but only partially followed. Result failure, and a grossly unfair statement that it is the expert's fault".

C/H: D4, C3, M3, I-5, $25 – 75

Campbell, Sir Guy. Wrote three chapters on course design, *see* Darwin, Bernard et al.

Campbell, Malcolm. *The New Encyclopedia of Golf.* (New York, NY: Dorling Kindersley, 2001, 384 pages, ISBN 0-7894-8036-0). An excellent reference book on all facets of golf. Chapter Two, "The Modern Game", has a few pages on course architects and designers. Although general, it is very interesting as are the descriptions and maps of various courses around the world. Earlier editions were printed in 1991 and 1994.

C/H: D1, C1, M1, H3, P2, T4, $15 – 30

Caner, George C., Jr. *History of the Essex County Club 1893-1993.* (Manchester-by-the-Sea, MA: Essex County Club, 1995, 374 pages, ISBN 0-9641777-0-6). A wealth of historic photos accompany comprehensive text on the long history of this gorgeous Donald Ross course. The architect lived beside the 15th tee for four years. His role, as well as that of long-time professional "Skip" Wogan, and his son Phil, ASGCA, who followed in his father's footsteps, is clearly documented.

C/H: D3, H3, P2, $25 – 75

Cappers, Elmer Osgood. *Centennial History of The Country Club 1882-1982.* (Brookline, MA: The Country Club, 1982, 155 pages, Library of Congress Catalog # 81-69855). A complete account of this venerable property including the hiring of the first designer and professional Willie Campbell, plus the evolution of the course and the national events conducted on the site.
C/H: F1, D2, H5, P4, $50 – 100

Carroll, Michael, Photographer, *see* Shechan, Lawrence.

Clark, Robert. *Golf, A Royal and Ancient Game.* (First published by R. & R. Clark of Edinburgh for private distribution in 1875, it was republished in London by Macmillan in 1893 and 1899). According to Browning (see above) Clark included "extracts from an immense variety of ancient documents". It was a "collection of documentary odds and ends. Yet every writer on this phase of golf must acknowledge his indebtedness". Clark's book is one of the most coveted in golf literature. Copies are found in libraries such as the USGA.
C/H: H5, P4, $200 (3rd Edition) – 2,400 (1st Edition)

Colt, H.S. and C.H. Alison. *Some Essays on Golf Course Architecture.* (New York, NY: Charles Scribner's Sons, 1920). This is one of the earliest books on contemporary course design. Colt, his layouts and his philosophy, have exerted a pervasive and enduring influence on course design. The book includes contributions from Mackenzie, Hutchinson, Low and others, with chapters on placing bunkers, construction, labor saving, and financial considerations. (Worcestershire, England: Grant Books, 1990, 78 pages, ISBN 0-907186-10-6, facsimile edition). With Forewords by F.W. Hawtree and G.S. Cornish.
C/H: D5, C4, H3, M3, P2, $150 (rep) – 1,000

Colville, George M. *Five Open Champions and the Musselburgh Golf Story.* (Musselburgh, Scotland: Colville Books, 1980, 115 pages, ISBN 0-950717-90-8). An account of famous professionals who hailed from Musselburgh or were closely connected to its golf course. This book outlines their contributions to course design and their high stakes matches, club-making skills and influence on golf.
C/H: D1, H5, P4, $100 – 150

Connery, Sean, *see* Hamilton, David.

Cory, Gregory, et al. *Golf Course Development in Residential Communities.* (Washington, DC: Urban Land Institute, 2001, 303 pages, ISBN 0-87420-843-3). A textbook concerning aspects of course development in residential settings. Chapters include writings by several authors on course design, golf and real estate market economics, land planning and design, course management and the legal structure of golf course communities. Numerous case studies are presented.
C/H: F4, D4, C1, H2, $50 – 71

Cornish, Geoffrey S. *Eighteen Stakes on a Sunday Afternoon.* (Worcestershire, England: Grant Books, 2002, 218 pages, ISBN 0-907186-43-2). This is a chronicle of the literature that has accompanied the remarkable evolution of course design in North America, with numerous footnotes, asides and clarifications. Published in part for the American Society of Golf Course Architects, it emphasizes the evolution of North American course design from the period when Scottish professionals and designers dubbed the process derogatively as "18 stakes on a

Sunday afternoon" to the contemporary age of multimillion dollar layouts by highly skilled and intensely dedicated young designers.
C/H: D4, H5, P4, $60 – 100

Cornish, Geoffrey S. and Ronald E. Whitten. *The Architects of Golf.* (New York: NY: HarperCollins Publishers, 1993, 648 pages, ISBN 0-06270082-0). An update of *The Golf Course* with additional text, new architects, updated course lists and biographies, professionally organised master course list and useful appendices. The best single reference source for the industry, with an accumulation of information not available elsewhere. A cornerstone of the golf course architecture library.
C/H: D3, H5, P5, $35 – 150

Cornish, Geoffrey S. and Ronald E. Whitten. *The Golf Course.* (New York, NY: Rutledge Press, 1981, 320 pages, ISBN 0-8317-3947-9, Reprinted 1982, 1984 and 1987). A seminal work that includes data on all then known golf course architects and their work. It features architect bios, a textural history of the profession, as well as a listing of courses worldwide. Its popularity was in part due to a golfer's yearning to know who had designed a course he or she had played. Co-author Whitten went on to become the celebrated architecture Editor of *Golf Digest.*
C/H: D3, H5, P5, $35 – 150

Cornish, Geoffrey S. and William G. Robinson. *Golf Course Design…An Introduction.* (Lawrence, KS: GCSAA, 20 pages, no ISBN or date). An illustrated primer on course design and how it influences play, eye appeal and maintenance.
C/H: D5, $25 – 50

Cornish, **Geoffrey S.** Co-author, *see* Graves, Robert Muir.

Cornwell, David. Co-author, *see* Labbance, Bob.

Cosmides, L. Co-editor, *see* Barrow, J.

Cotton, Sir Henry. *Golf in the British Isles.* (Manchester, England: Cliveden Press, 1969, 125 pages, ISBN 7235 0534 9). Sir Henry chooses fifty-six golf courses on which he gives his personal view. Each has a crude map of the layout and a color picture or two.
C/H: D2, C1, M1, H3, P3, $35 – 50

Cousins, Geoffrey and Paul Kegan. *Golf in Britain.* (London, England: Routledge, 1975). A historical, societal and economic background of golf in Britain. It is hoped that someday a comparable work will be published for North America.
C/H: F3, H5, $25 – 35

Cousins, Geoffrey and Don Pottinger. *An Atlas of Golf.* (London, England: Butler & Tanner, Ltd., 1974, 96 pages, ISBN 0 17 152009 2). Written for the layman golfer and traveler, the book includes surprising detail that makes it worthy of being part of any book collection.
C/H: D1, M1, H4, P2, T3, $15 – 30

Crawford, MacGregor & Camby. *Stepping Stones to a Golf Course.* (Dayton, OH: Crawford, MacGregor & Camby, 1921, 18 pages, self-published booklet). A golf club manufacturer's contribution to stimulate the growth and development of golf courses after World War I. It is generalized but very interesting.
C/H: F1, D2, C1, M2, H3, $350 – 500

Crenshaw, Ben. *Chicago Golf Club 1892-1992.* Co-author, *see* Goodner, Ross.

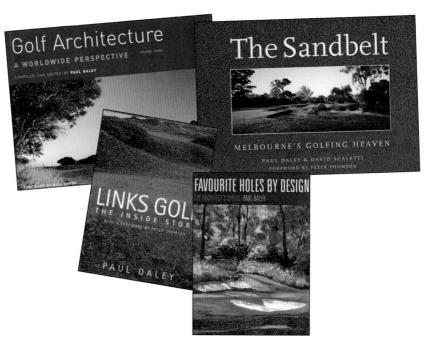

"Down Under" Daley wrote creative works that have contributed to the art form of course architecture and its comprehension

Crockford, Claude. *The Complete Golf Course, Turf and Design.* (Australia, 1993. Thomson, Wolveridge and Associates, limited edition of 1,000 copies, 150 pages). Part one: Design and construction of golf course features. Part two: Turf production and maintenance. Part three: Special problems in turf maintenance. Part four: Fundamental course maintenance.
C/H: C2, D2, M3, $100 – 150

Cronin, Tim. *The Spirit of Medinah: 75 Years of Fellowship and Championships.* (Medinah, IL: Medinah Country Club, 2001, 325 pages, ISBN 0-9709808-0-9). Few books are filled with more information and imagery than this encyclopedia of Medinah's existence. Many pages on architect Tom Bendelow clarify his role as one of America's finest pioneer designers.
C/H: F1, D3, C1, H4, P3, $50 – 75

Curtiss, Frederic H. and John Heard. *The Country Club 1882 – 1932.* (Brookline, MA: The Country Club, 1932, 213 pages). An elegant and thorough treatise includes maps of the original six, nine, eighteen and twenty-seven hole courses with early facts and anecdotes. It is an important American history book.
C/H: F1, D2, H5, P4, $250 – 500

Daley, Paul. *Favorite Golf Holes by Design: The Architects Choice.* (Melbourne, Australia: Full Swing Golf Publishing 2004.) Fifty Essays written by leading golf course architects from the major golf playing nations. Several of the most celebrated holes are featured. Beautifully illustrated including architects drawings.
C/H: F2, D5, C2, M2, H4, P3. $70

Daley, Paul. *Links Golf: The Inside Story.* (Melbourne, Australia: Hardie-Grant, 2000). Australian author Paul Daley discusses the ancient links of the United Kingdom, including lesser known ones, with eloquent prose and beautiful illustrations. Subjects include links villages, the coastal zone, rising sea levels, dune management, differences between inland and links golf, links styles and the over-watering, over-feeding and over-crowding of the ancient links.
C/H: D5, C3, M3, H4, $35 – 50

Daley, Paul. *Golf Architecture: A Worldwide Perspective, Volume One.* (Victoria, Australia: Full Swing Golf Publishing, 2002, 239 pages, ISBN 0-9581363-0-0; and Gretna, LA: Pelican Publishing Co.). An attractive horizontal format book filled with valuable thought-provoking essays on every facet of course design from designers around the world, illustrated with stunning color photography and characterized by elegant design and high quality workmanship. *Volume Two,* published in 2003, is equally comprehensive and enlightening. G.S. Cornish and D.W. Steel provide Forewords for Volumes I and II, respectively. Volume III published in 2005 with Foreword by Bill Coore, concludes this impressive trilogy.
C/H: F2, D5, C2, M2, H4, P3, $35 – 50

Daley, Paul. *The Sandbelt: Melbourne's Golfing Heaven.* (Melbourne, Australia: Plus Four Publishing, 2000, 140 pages). An illustrated celebration of Melbourne's thirteen golf courses in the "Sandbelt". It emphasizes the impact of Dr. Alister Mackenzie's 1926 visit and the distinctive bunkers and greens prominent in the region.
C/H: D5, C3, M2, H5, P4, $35 – 50

Darwin, Bernard. *A Round of Golf on the L(ondon) & N(orth) E(astern) R(ailway).* (London, England: London & North Eastern Railway, 1st Ed., 1925, 127 pages, paper). An excellent treatise on courses in England and Scotland with terrific pictures and locator maps. A peek into British courses in the middle of the Roaring Twenties. A cloth or hardcover edition, without maps and much smaller photographs, was also published. The paper cover edition is the better one. Author Darwin was a grandson of famed Charles Darwin, the naturalist.
C/H: D2, C1, H3, T4, $350 – 450

Darwin, Bernard. *Golf.* (London, England: Burke, 1954, 222 pages, Pleasures of Life Series). Darwin has two chapters, "The Links", and "Architectural". Related to course design, they are wonderful sources of information in the Darwin style.
C/H: D1, C1, M1, P1, $125 – 175

Darwin, Bernard. *Golf Between Two Wars.* (London, England: Chatto & Windus, 1944, 228 pages). Providing profound insights into how golf changed in the twenty years between 1919, end of World War I and 1939, beginning of World War II in Europe, Darwin has a chapter on "Architecture". He discusses how World War I has affected courses and their subsequent reconstruction.
C/H: D3, C2, M2, H4, P2, $25 – 100

Darwin, Bernard. *James Braid.* (London, England: Hodder and Stoughton, 1952, 196 pages). A biography of one of the world's greatest golfers who also designed many renowned layouts.
C/H: D1, H3, P5, $50 – 100

Darwin, Bernard. *The Golf Courses of the British Isles.* (London, England: Duckworth & Co., 1910, 253 pages, and Stamford, CT: Classics of Golf, 1988). Illustrated by New Zealander Harry Rountree with evocative watercolors, this is said to be golf's first "coffee table book". A finer tour of the great courses of the United Kingdom has yet to be written.
C/H: D1, H3, P3, T5, $45 (rep) – 1,400

Darwin, Bernard. *The Golf Links of France.* (Paris, France: J. Barreau & Co. and the French Railways, 1937, 19 pages). Darwin wrote the foreword to this advertising and map book that shows the location of courses along the French railways, prior to the German invasion. Pictures abound that provide insights into golf during that period.
C/H: D1, C1, M1, H3, T4, $350 – 450

Darwin, Bernard et al. *A History of Golf in Britain.* (London, England: Cassell & Co. Ltd., 1952, 312 pages). Includes three chapters by golf architect Sir Guy Campbell who writes that it is "pertinent to inquire what was the origin of these links or "green fields," ribands of turf so particularly and aptly fashioned for this particular pastime, and so generously pin-pointed the length of our shore. Nature was their architect, and beast and man her contractors". Campbell's passage on the origin of links land ranks among the most descriptive in the literature of design.
C/H: D2, C1, M1, H5, T2, $35 – 250

Darwin, Bernard. Co-author, *see* Wethered, Joyce.

Davis, Martin, Colin Montgomerie and Donald Steel. *How to Play Links Golf.* (Greenwich, CT: The American Golfer, 2001, 105 pages, ISBN 1-888531-09-6). The first chapter, "In Praise of Links", was penned by British writer and course architect Donald Steel. It provides an overview of links golf in Europe, with some philosophy. Most of the book is a picture clinic by Colin Montgomerie on how to play shots to score well on links holes. The final chapter, written by Steel, is on "A Brief History of Turnberry". It covers the inception of the courses, the impact of subsequent world wars, and the rebuilding of it by Mackenzie Ross after World War II.
C/H: D2, C2, H3, P2, $30 – 40

Davis, William H. *The World's Best Golf.* (Trumbull, CT: Golf Digest, 1991, and Pocket Books, a division of Simon and Schuster, 312 pages, ISBN 0-671-72555-6). This illustrated work followed a series by Davis and the editors of *Golf Digest* that began in 1974. Great golf courses worldwide are described. Judging from their choices, Bill Davis and his research editor Topsy Siderowf, wife of accomplished amateur champion Dick Siderowf, did not believe that a course had to be an extravaganza to make a contribution, although they always admired outstanding layouts. Photography is by Brian Morgan.
C/H: D2, H2, P1, T5. 4 = 15 – 30

Davis, William H. and the Editors of Golf Digest. *Great Golf Courses of the World.* (Norwalk, CT: Golf Digest, 1974, 280 pages, ISBN 0-914178-06-7). Includes a chapter titled "The Architect makes A Golf Course Great" by Herbert Warren Wind. It alone is worth the price of admission.
C/H: D1, H3, P3, T5, $15 – 30

Davis, William H. and the Editors of Golf Digest. *One Hundred Greatest Golf Courses and Then Some.* (Norwalk, CT: Golf Digest/Tennis, 1982, 279 pages, ISBN 0-914178-57-1). A revision of the 1974 work.
C/H: D1, H3, P3, T5, $15 – 30

de St. Jorre, John and Anthony Edgeworth. *Legendary Golf Clubs of the American East.* (Wellington, FL: Edgeworth Editions, 2003, 335 pages, ISBN 0-9658904-4-9). A beautifully produced book covering twelve of the finest golf clubs on the American East Coast. All clubs featured have strong architectural credentials. Chapters on each course discuss their architects and design. Clubs included are Seminole Golf Club, The Country Club, Merion Golf Club, Yeamans Hall Club, Pine Valley Golf Club, Newport Country Club, Myopia Hunt Club, Somerset Hills Country Club, Shinnecock Hills Golf Club, Oakmont Country Club, Ekwanok Country Club and The National Golf Links of America.
C/H: H4, P2, T4, $90

de St. Jorre, John and Anthony Edgeworth. *Legendary Golf Clubs of Scotland, England, Wales and Ireland.* (Wellington, FL: Edgeworth Editions, 1995, 311 pages in a similar style to the above, ISBN 0-9658904-1-4). This book covers: The Royal and Ancient Golf Club of St Andrews; Prestwick Golf Club; Royal Liverpool Golf Club; The Royal St George's Golf Club; Rye Golf Club; Sunningdale Golf Club; Swinley Forest Golf Club; Royal Worlington and Newmarket Golf Club; Royal West Norfolk Golf Club; Royal Porthcawl Golf Club; The Royal County Down Golf Club and Portmarnock Golf Club.
C/H: H4, P2, T4, $75 – 90

DeMay, Kenneth, F.A.I.A. "Planning the Adjacent Real Estate" an essay found in *Golf Course Design* by Robert Muir Graves and Geoffrey S. Cornish.
C/H: F2, D4, $90

Dennis, Larry. Co-author, *see* Jones, Robert Trent Sr.

Dickinson, Patrick. *A Round of Golf Courses.* (London, England: Evans Brothers Limited, 1951, 156 pages). A travel log of eighteen famous courses in Great Britain, this book provides information about their soils and vegetation and how these influenced their routing – information that you do not often find in a travel book. Charming drawings are provided to diagram the most famous holes as well as simple routing plans. This is an excellent work for those visiting these old courses and for architects attempting to copy classic golf holes. A Foreword by Bernard Darwin makes a major contribution.
C/H = D=2, H2, T3, $50 – 75

Diperna, Paula and Vikki Keller. *Oakhurst: The Birth and Rebirth of America's First Golf Course.* (New York, NY: Walker Publishing, 2002, 194 pages, ISBN 0-8027-1371-8). An account of a course born in the 1880s when none other existed in America, abandoned by 1910 when interest waned, and recovered in the 1980s by owner Lewis Keller and course architect Bob Cupp, ASGCA. The recovery was an archeological dig, and today the course is played with implements of the original era and mowed by a flock of sheep.
C/H: D2, H5, P2, $15 – 23

63

Doak, Tom. *The Anatomy of a Golf Course.* (New York, NY: Lyons and Burford, 1992, 242 pages, ISBN 1-55821-146-2). Authored by a youthful golf architect, belonging to a generation of immensely talented newcomers to the profession, this book should be read by all involved in master planning. With diagrams by Gil Hanse, another of the new generation who provided peer review for this bibliography, this is one of the first books to explain course design and strategy in lay terms, with insights, opinions and detailed explanations of how course features are planned, develop and influence play. An important addition to any collection of the genre.
C/H: D4, C1, M1, $15 – 25

Doak, Tom. *The Confidential Guide to Golf Courses.* (Chelsea, MI: Sleeping Bear Press, 1996, 361 pages, ISBN 1-886947-09-0). Opinions on the merits of courses around the globe, in the eyes of a course architect who also served for a few years as architecture editor for *Golf Magazine*. Doak visited nearly a thousand courses. His opinions are fascinating to designers who yearn to know what others think about their work, for better or worse, and to others.
C/H: D2, H2, P1, T5, $25 – 45

Doak, Tom and Dr. James S. Scott and Raymund M. Haddock. *The Life and Work of Dr. Alister Mackenzie.* (Chelsea, MI: Sleeping Bear Press, 2001, 231 pages, ISBN 1-58536-018-X). A detailed volume of one of golf's greatest architects but an enigma, from his days as a doctor to his retirement at Pasatiempo in Santa Cruz, California. It is the most candid and complete account of the renowned architect and reveals his character and mysteries that abound surrounding his life and career.
C/H: D2, H4, P5, $35 – 65

Doak, Tom. Author of an influential essay, *see* United States Golf Association.

Dobby, David L. *Royal Cinque Ports Golf Club, Deal.* (Worcestershire, England: Grant Books, 1992, 28 pages). A record of this links in its centenary year. Author Dobby, who is also the artist, has presented a study of this golfing ground. Royal Cinque Ports Golf Club is important in the annals of course architecture and so is the format of this book to club histories.
C/H: D2, M1, H3, $150 – 180

Dobereiner, Peter. *The Glorious World of Golf.* (New York, NY: McGraw Hill, 1973, 250 pages, ISBN 07-017150-5). Chapter 5, entitled "Secrets of the Great Courses", provides an interesting overview of widely known layouts, their architecture and history.
C/H: D3, H4, P2, T4, $20 – 40

Dobereiner, Peter. *The World of Golf: The Best of Peter Dobereiner.* (New York, NY: Atheneum, 1981, 287 pages). A collection of essays from various publications by a prolific golf writer. It includes several pertinent to course design, including one outlining Jack Nicklaus' early design philosophy.
C/H: D2, H3, P3, T2, $25 – 35

Donovan, Ken. Historian Donovan of Fortress, Louisbourg, Nova Scotia, has produced two important design essays. First is *Thinking Down the Road: Stanley Thompson, Canada's Golf Architect, Artist and Visionary, 1893-1953*. The second is *An Interview With Geoffrey S. Cornish: Stanley Thompson and the Construction of Cape Breton Highlands Links, Ingonish, Cape Breton, 1938-1939*. Both appeared in *The Nashwaak Review*, Fall 2004/Winter 2005 Edition. (St Thomas University, Fredericton, NB, Canada E3B 5G3). Each is important to course design.

The literature of course design includes outstanding biographies of architects

The first outlines the magnificent achievements of Stanley Thompson, the Canadian course architect, who provided standards worldwide with his Jasper, Banff, St George's, Capilano and Highlands Links layouts.

The second outlines construction of Highland Links, a "make-work" project on Cape Breton Island, Nova Scotia during the Great Depression. Built by over 100 men, to Thompson's design, with limitations on use of earthmoving equipment, Highland Links emerged under his direction as one of the world's greatest layouts. Frequently ranked number one in Canada, it has also been referred to as the Sistine Chapel of Golf. Frank Lloyd Wright emphasised that a "structure be *of* the hill", not *on* the hill. Thompson preceded him with layouts that emphasised "golf holes of the land". Historian Donovan does not mention this. Yet it is embodied in all Thompson holes at Cape Breton.

$25.00 (for this double issue)

Donovan, Richard E. and Joseph S.F. Murdoch. *The Game of Golf and the Printed Word 1566-1985.* (Endicott, NY: Castalio Press, 1988, 658 pages, ISBN 0-943895-00-6). The most comprehensive bibliography of books about golf, divided by golf ball eras and organised by author, with additional groupings of short titles and club histories.

C/H: H3, $100–800 (LTD)

Dunn, John Duncan. *Natural Golf.* (New York, NY: G.P. Putnam's Sons, 1931, 199 pages). Only a two-page chapter describes course design. Yet it includes "Where a club has a hard eighteen hole course and an easy one, everybody wants to play the hard one. Even ladies now-a-days scoff at ladies tees". Alice Dye might have convinced Mr. Dunn otherwise.

C/H: D1, H3, P3, $150 – 200

The Dye links style at the Tournament Players Course, Sawgrass, Ponte Vedra Beach, Florida

Harbour Town Golf Links, Hilton Head Island, South Carolina. Pete and Alice Dye, ASGCA, ushered in a return to links style in North America while creating scores of glorious golf courses

Dunn, Paul and B.J. *Great Donald Ross Golf Courses You Can Play.* (Lanham, MD: Derrydale Press, 2001, 279 pages, ISBN 1-58667-060-3). Descriptions and lore regarding the Donald Ross designed courses open to the public throughout the country, written by two avid golfing residents of Pinehurst.
C/H: D1, H4, P3, T5, $35 – 50

Dye, Alice, with Mark Shaw. *From Birdies to Bunkers: Discover How Golf Can Bring Love, Humor and Success Into Your Life.* Foreword by Nancy Lopez. (New York, NY: Harper Resource, an Imprint of HarperCollins, 175 pages, ISBN 0-06-052821-4, $29.95). Scanning this book, one may conclude that it is a love story concerning course architects Alice and Pete Dye, a husband and wife team, in a field where that is not unusual. Each of the Dyes is a member of the ASGCA and a past president of that prestigious organization. Studying the book, one concludes that it is a remarkable autobiography by a remarkable person in a remarkable profession. Not incidentally, Alice and Pete's two sons, Perry and P.B., are members of the ASGCA and creative designers. Paul Crichton, senior publicist of HarperCollins says "Dye has written the perfect gift book." We agree and add that it is an extra special contribution to the profession of course architecture.
C/H: D2, C2, H4, P4, $15 – 20

Dye, Pete with Mark Shaw. *Bury Me in a Pot Bunker.* (Reading, MA: Addison-Wesley Publishing, 1995, 241 pages, ISBN 0-201 40769-8). "While there are critics who believe my courses are too difficult," writes Pete Dye, ASGCA, "the ardent golfer would play Mt. Everest if somebody put a flagstick on top of it. Unless a few golf professionals are bellyaching about my course design, I wonder whether I have done enough to challenge them". Dye is regarded as either a creative genius or a demonic tormentor and he mentored some forty protégés. This memoir provides insight into how he revolutionized the game by designing courses that both delight and bedevil golfers. Together with his talented wife Alice, a great amateur golfer and Pete's alter ego, the Dyes have fashioned some of America's finest courses integrating deep pot bunkers, railroad ties and tiny target golf greens into modern design. Along the way they have impacted on course design and ushered in a new era, already referred to as the "Age of the Dyes". In this volume, Dye discusses eighteen of his projects in great detail, with insight and humor.
C/H: D3, C1, H4, P5, $15 – 30

Edgeworth, Anthony. Co-author, *see* de St. Jorre.

Edmund, Nick. *Classic Golf Courses of Great Britain and Ireland.* (New York, NY: A Bullfinch Press Book; Little, Brown and Co., 1997, 207 pages, ISBN 0-8212-2472-7). Basically a compilation of Strokesaver information on twenty-five famous UK golf courses that has been supplemented by some excellent text and pictures. A great reference to get exact yardages of features on individual golf holes.
C/H: D2, H1, T5, $10 – 20

Elliott, Mal. *Perry Maxwell's Prairie Dunes.* (Chelsea, MI: Sleeping Bear Press, 2002, 144 pages, ISBN 1-58536-073-2). Not much has been written about Maxwell, but here we get a little more of his personality, including a snapshot of the architect in a cowboy hat sitting on the beach in Florida. Since Prairie Dunes is one of the least visited top twenty-five courses in the country, this is a welcome tour of the terrific layout.
C/H: F1, D3, C2, M3, H5, P3, $35 – 45

Fall, R.G., Editor. *Golfing in South Africa.* (Cape Town, South Africa: South African Golf Ltd., 1958, 324 pages). A compendium of golf in South Africa that includes profiles of prominent players, descriptions of courses, greenkeeping hints, tournament results and a chapter on course architecture in South Africa by Robert Grimsdell, one of that country's own course architects.
C/H: D2, M2, H3, P2, T4, $25 – 50

Fay, Michael. *Golf, As It Was In the Beginning: The Legendary British Open Courses.* (New York, NY: Universal Publishing, 2002, 224 pages, Library of Congress Control Number: 2002058593). A well researched and beautifully illustrated book in the same style and panache as his Ross book. The pictures are indeed worth a thousand words.
C/H: D2, M2, H4, P2, T3, $30 – 40

Fay, Michael. *Golf, As It Was Meant To Be Played.* (New York, NY: Universe Publishing, 2000, 224 pages, ISBN 0-7893-0395-7). The Ross Society leader selects eighteen Ross holes and celebrates the vision of the architect and the joys of attempting to negotiate those holes.
C/H: D3, M2, H4, P4, T3, $25 – 35

Fazio, Tom with Cal Brown. *Golf Course Designs.* (New York: Harry Abrams, Inc., 2000, 203 pages, ISBN 0-8109-6717-0). Famous designer Tom Fazio writes on topics from "Using Terrain vs. Creating It" to "The Importance of Being Different", with many of his design ideas sprinkled throughout the text. Gorgeous photographs by Jean and John Henebry enhance the extensive tour of Fazio's highly-regarded work.
C/H: D4, C1, H2, P3, T3, $35 – 45

Fazio, Tom with Cal Brown. *Golf Course Designs by Fazio.* (Salt Lake City, UT: Paragon Press, 1984, 48 pages, no ISBN). A forerunner to his larger book published in 2000, this small volume features many photos and some text about individual projects.
C/H: D2, P2, T2, $20 – 40

Ferrier, Bob. *The World Atlas of Golf Courses.* (New York, NY: Mallard Press, 1990, 208 pages, ISBN 0-792-45284-4). Write-ups, course maps, scorecards, lore and history of the sixty-six best courses in the world, according to the author, with profiles of architects.
C/H: D2, M2, H4, P3, T5, $15 – 35

Finegan, James W. *A Centennial Tribute to Golf in Philadelphia* with Foreword by Arnold Palmer. (Philadelphia, PA: The Golf Association of Philadelphia, 1996, 497 pages). This story, covering all facets of Philadelphia golf, is a splendid book with abundant material on the outstanding courses of that metropolitan area and the architects that created them.
C/H: D2, C2, P4, H4, T2, $50 – 100

Finegan, James W. *All Courses Great and Small: A Golfer's Pilgrimage to England and Wales.* (New York, NY: Simon and Schuster, 2003, ISBN 0-7432-2388-8). Written by the author of *Blasted Heaths and Blessed Greens, A Golfer's Pilgrimage To The Courses Of Scotland* and *Emerald Fairways and Foam Flecked Seas, A Golfer's Pilgrimage To The Courses Of Ireland*; both published by Simon and Schuster, this work, by a favorite author of course architects, delves into the magic of the courses of England and Wales. It is conscientious in naming their designers, often providing biographical information.
C/H: D1, M1, P2, H4, T5, $15 – 22

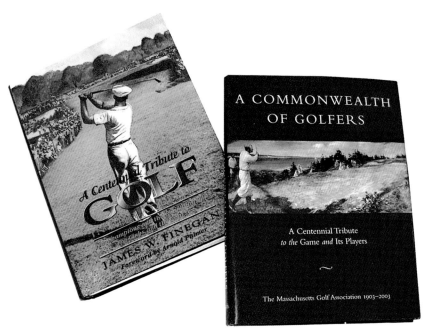

A Commonwealth of Golfers *by Lawrence Sheehan, with photographs by Michael Carroll, is a striking book covering a century of golf in Massachusetts.* Jim Finegan's A Centennial Tribute to Golf in Philadelphia *does the same for Philadelphia. Many regional histories including these provide generous coverage to course architects*

Finegan, James W. *Pine Valley Golf Club.* (State College, PA: Jostens Printing, 2000, 234 pages), Foreword by William C. Campbell. A scholarly work portraying the special camaraderie of Pine Valley, it is extensively and magnificently illustrated and documented.
C/H: D2, M2, P2, H4, $15 – 35

Finegan, James W. *The Outstanding Courses of Scotland and Ireland* (working title only). Golf course photography by Larence C. Lambrecht. (Publication date, May 2006. New York: Workman Publishing Co.).
C/H: D2, M2, P2, H4, TF, $60 (est.)

The editorial content is divided into Golf Courses; Places to Stay and Sightseeing. Description and analysis of courses and clubs, with emphasis on courses, comprise roughly seventy per cent of the book. Ninety Scottish and sixty-five Irish courses are presented. Forty of the Scottish courses are major and are accorded detailed treatment, including extensive pictorial coverage. Thirty-five of the Irish courses receive similar treatment.

The original architect is named, as are those architects who have done remodelling or added holes. The great majority of courses in the book were built many years ago, yet there is no skimping on contemprary layouts. thus, Craighead at Crail (Gil Hanse, ASGCA), Kingsbarns (Kyle Phillips, ASGCA). The European Club (Pat Ruddy), both K Club eighteens (Palmer and Seay, ASGCA), and Doonbeg (Greg Norman) are all covered in depth.

According to the author, this volume will look like a traditional golf course picture book, but will function as a serious golf traveller's best friend while it reveals the contributions of architects of these Scottish and Irish layouts.
C/H: T5, H2, $ 60

Forbes, Ross. *The Most Influential Golf Course Architects in the History of the Game.* (Self-published, 1987, 102 pages, 8½" x 11" format, soft cover, coil bound). This is an extraordinary effort made to fulfill a university degree requirement. It is both entertaining and informative. Mr. Forbes obviously has a passion for course architecture. Although one could debate some of his assertions, he does a great job in researching and presenting them. He devotes one chapter each to Mackenzie, Tillinghast, Ross, Wilson, Jones and Dye.
C/H: D2, P4, H3, $ =75 – 125

Forse, Ronald. *Classic Golf Courses and the Master Architects.* (Kansas: Golf Course Superintendents Association of America, 1995, 46 pages). Written as support material for a half-day seminar, this booklet features biographical information and examples of these architects' works. Mr. Forse provides additional interesting detail and color in his class.
C/H: D1, C1, P4, $10 – 15

Fox, G.D. *see* Two of His Kind.

Fry, Dana. Co-author, *see* Hurdzan, Michael.

Fullmer, Paul. *Presidents I Have Known.* (Brookfield WI. ASGCA publication pending May 2006.) Paul Fullmer, dynamic executive secretary (emeritus) of the ASGCA, penned this series of eloquent essays concerning each of the Society presidents. Intrinsically it is a history of the Society whose members have been remarkably active around the globe in designing and redesigning the world's golf courses.

Gallagher, Donald. *Woodland Golf Club.* (Auburndale, MA, 2002). Woodland, founded in 1896, was elected to the USGA in 1897 and incorporated in 1902. This superb history was published on the Club's 100th anniversary. Included is a tribute to forty year veteran superintendent Norman Mucciarone and incumbent David Mucciarone, his son. Architects of record include Wayne Stiles, Donald Ross, the present routing, Geoffrey Cornish, vast changes in the early 1960s, and Steven Kay, revisions in the 1990s.
C/H: D2, H4, P2

Garrity, John. *America's Worst Golf Courses.* (New York, NY: Macmillan Publishing, 1994, 148 pages, ISBN 0-02-043235-6). Many contemporary architects are mentioned in this often tongue-in-cheek tour of odd golf holes and courses throughout the country. Some designers are mentioned in a less than favorable light, and occasionally it is deserved. A hole at Wentworth-by-the-Sea in New Hampshire, by one of the authors of this bibliography, is featured. A combination of a Cape and Redan and an undulating fairway, the hole was immensely controversial.
C/H: D1, M1, T3, $10 – 20

German Railway System. *Golf in Germany.* (Berlin, Germany: Reichsbahnzentrale fur den Deutschen Reiseverkehr, 1930s, large foldout map). This is a rare work describing forty-seven pay-for-play courses of Hitler's Germany and what was being done to promote golf tourism. Courses pictured are simple in design and construction, but the settings are diverse and beautiful. *Golf in Germany* is more novel than substantive.
C/H: D1, C1, M1, H5, T2, $75 – 125

Gerrish, Timothy. "The Contours of Trash" excerpted from *Eighteen Stakes on a Sunday Afternoon*. Edited by Geoffrey S. Cornish (Worcestershire, England: Grant Books, 2002). The Gerrish essay emphasizes the use of capped landfills for golf and states that the Environmental Protection Agency says that thousands of landfills in the US will be closed and capped in coming years.
C/H: D1, C2, $N/A

Gilliland, Robert J. and Peter Macdonald. *Prairie Dunes: The First Fifty Years.* (Hutchinson, KS: Mennonite Press, 1987). An absorbing history of a famous club with a links type course, a thousand miles from an ocean but located on an ancient seabed. The original nine by Perry Maxwell and a nine hole addition by his son, Press, have become increasingly renowned. Text and illustrations include a vivid account of its design and construction, with photographs of horses and Fresno scrapers, the "bulldozers" of that day. Another section describes books and articles in periodicals that have included the history and architecture of this renowned layout.
C/H: D3, C3, M2, P4, $50 – 80

Gimmy, A.E. and M.E. Benson. *Golf Courses and Country Clubs: A Guide to Appraisal, Market Analysis, Development and Financing.* (Chicago, IL: Appraisal Institute, 1992, ISBN 0-922154-05-8). Data, presented as text, graphs and tables, are important for all involved in course development and management.
C/H: F4, D1, C1, M2, $20 – 30

Goodner, Ross. *Shinnecock Hills Golf Club.* (Southampton, NY: Shinnecock Hills Golf Club, 1966). A club history of this early and great American golf course, it chronicles the development of the course and many changes made to it over decades.
C/H: D2, H4, P2, $500 – 800

Goodner, Ross and Ben Crenshaw. *Chicago Golf Club 1892-1992.* (Wheaton, IL: Chicago Golf Club, 153 pages). Substantial portions of this club history are dedicated to the founder of the club, Charles Blair Macdonald. Biographical portions tell of his struggles to bring golf to America and the work that went into the construction of this course. As a founding member of the USGA, Chicago Golf Club has a special place in the history of the game, while its course, originally designed by Macdonald and later altered by Seth Raynor, has a special place in course architecture. A chapter is written by Club member Ben Crenshaw and illustrated with beautiful photographs.
C/H: D2, H4, P2, $75 – 100

Gordon, John. *The Great Golf Courses of America.* (Willowdale, Ontario, Canada: Firefly Books Ltd., 1999, ISBN 1-55209-149-X) with photography by Michael French. A Canadian's viewpoint of courses in the United States.
C/H: D1, M1, P2, T4, $35 – 50

Gordon, John. *The Great Golf Courses of Canada, Third Edition, Revised and Updated.* (Willowdale, Ontario, Canada: Firefly Books Ltd., 1999, 239 pages, ISBN 1-55209-341-7). John Gordon is one of Canada's leading golf writers and architectural critics, not that John criticizes much. However photographs taken by Michael French, along with the course descriptions and maps, provide a wonderful overview of Canada's magnificent courses.
C/H: D2, C1, M2, T5, $20 – 30

71

Govedarica, Tom. *Chicago Golf: The First 100 Years.* (Chicago, IL: Eagle Communications Group, 1991, 286 pages, ISBN 0-9630761-0-8). A detailed description of the origins of golf in Chicago with numerous course maps and mentions of architects, as well as the headquarters of the ASGCA, located in Chicago.
C/H: D2, C1, P3, H5, T3, $10 – 15

Graffis, Herb. *The PGA.* (New York, NY: Thomas Y. Crowell, 1975, 559 pages). A comprehensive history of the PGA of America, including references to courses designed by its members.
C/H: D1, P5, H5, $10 – 20

Grant, Donald. *Donald Ross of Pinehurst and Royal Dornoch.* (Scotland, Sutherland Press, 1973, 40 pages, booklet). A short treatise on the roots of Ross and how the geography and topography of Dornoch probably affected his design style.
C/H: D1, P4, H5, $25 – 50

Grant, H.R.J. and J.F. Moreton. *Aspects of Collecting Golf Books.* (Droitwich, Worcestershire, England: Grant Books, 1996, ISBN 0-9071-86653). This bibliography of books on golf includes a chapter by Fred W. Hawtree, titled "The Lore of the Layout: Collecting the Literature of Golf Course Architecture". Each chapter, written by an authority, provides a mini bibliography of books covering that subject. One chapter, by Robert C. Swanson, surveys golf bibliographies. This is a valuable bibliography that should be in the library of all collectors of books on golf.
C/H: D1, H5, P1, $400 – 500 (LTD)

Graves, Robert Muir and Geoffrey S. Cornish. *Classic Golf Hole Design: Using the Greatest Holes as Inspiration for Modern Courses.* (Hoboken, NJ: John Wiley & Sons, 2002, 323 pages, ISBN 0-471-41372-0). Tracing the roots of the prototypical holes in the United Kingdom and their spread in the United States, from the Redan to the Alps, this is a fascinating directory with a wealth of illustrative diagrams, maps, drawings and photographs.
C/H: D5, C3, H3, P2, $55 – 65

Graves, Robert Muir and Geoffrey S. Cornish. *Golf Course Design.* (New York: John Wiley & Sons, 1998, 446 pages, ISBN 0-471-13784-7). These prolific architects have designed hundreds of courses and taught thousands of people what they have learned. Each had fifty years or more of work in the field. Used as a textbook by Harvard University's Continuing Education Program, this widely distributed treatise has been embraced by other college-level programs as a textbook.
C/H: F5, D5, C5, M3, $50 – 65

Grimsley, Will. *Golf: Its History, People and Events.* (Englewood Cliffs, NJ: Prentice-Hall, 1966, 331 pages). Part IV, authored by Robert Trent Jones, includes descriptions of well-known courses with colored plate maps of each.
C/H: D2, H5, P3, T1, $ 35 – 50

Haddock, **Raymund M.** Co-author, *see* Doak, Tom.

Hamilton, David with Foreword by Sean Connery. *The Scottish Golf Guide.* (Edinburgh, Scotland, Canongate Publishing Ltd., 1982, Reprinted 1995, 1999).
C/H: D1, C1, H3, P3, T5, $25 – 35

Harber, Paul. *The Complete Guide to Golf on Cape Cod, Nantucket and Martha's Vineyard.* (Cape Cod, MA: The Peninsula Press, 1994, 159 pages, ISBN 1-883684-02-1). A superb guide that gives considerable space to course architects. The Guide helped Cape Cod to become an ever widely known golf destination.
C/H: D1, C1, H3, P1, T5, $10 – 20

Harrison, Mike. *The Official Guide to Jack Nicklaus Computer Golf.* (Greensboro, NC: Compute Publications International, 1990, 200 pages, ISBN 0-87455-236-2, paperback). Until the recently published *Nicklaus By Design*, this manual had the only treatise by Nicklaus on his design theories.
C/H: D3, P1, $10 – 15

Haultain, Arnold. *The Mystery of Golf.* (Boston, MA: Houghton, Mifflin, 1908, 151 pages). The book itself is something of a mystery. Reprinted in part in a leading periodical before World War I, it was dismissed as fanciful. One wonders if the reaction would be the same today in view of the thousands of glorious courses that have emerged worldwide. (Reprinted numerous times, including the Classics of Golf: Stamford, CT, 1986, with a Foreword by H.W. Wind and Afterword by John Updike.)
C/H: 1-4 (Instruction book for the brain), $35 (rep) – 1,000 (Orig)

Hawtree, Fred. *Aspects of Golf Course Architecture I (1889-1924).* (Worcestershire, England: Grant Books, 1998, 172 pages, ISBN 0-907186-27-0). Edited by H.R.J. Grant. Hawtree has compiled and annotated the best short writings on the subject by early British golf professionals, designers and writers starting with Horace Hutchinson's treatise in the *1889 Golfing Annual* concerning establishment and maintenance of courses. Photographs and sketches of early maintenance equipment are shown. Hawtree's work provides a ready reference, in essay form, of many important British authors and course architects.
C/H: D4, C2, M1, H5, P3, $50 – 60

Hawtree, Fred. *Colt & Co. Golf Course Architects.* (Oxford, England: Cambuc Archive, 191 pages, ISBN 0-9517793-0-3). The life of Harry Shapland Colt is detailed, including a wealth of letters between Colt and his business partner C.H. Alison. A small pamphlet is included with a complete listing of their design and remodeling work.
C/H: D3, C1, M1, H5, P5, $50 – 60

Hawtree, Fred W. *Elements of Golf Course Layout and Design.* (Surrey, England: Golf Development Council, 1980 (2nd ed), 26 pages). A small paperback booklet intended to guide potential developers of golf courses. It is still another example of high quality writing by Hawtree.
C/H: F2, D4, C2, H3, P1, $35 – 50

Hawtree, Fred. *The Golf Course: Planning, Design, Construction & Maintenance.* (London, England: E. & F.N. Spon, 1983, 212 pages, ISBN 0-419-12250-8). Directions, gradients, orientations, historical influences, cuts and fills, locations of hazards, contrasts, harmony, landscaping, specifications, billing, schedules, drawings, visibility and much more, this book covers every aspect of course development. Reprinted several times, it also provides useful information on the interchange between architect, committees and the owner's staff.
C/H: D5, C3, M2, $50 – 75

Hawtree, Fred. *Triple Baugé.* (Woodstock, Oxford: Cambuc Archive, 1996, 164 pages, ISBN 0-9517793-1-1). Fred W. Hawtree, son of course architect Fred G., practiced course architecture for fifty years before handing his design work over to his son, Dr. Martin Hawtree. Fred W. has delved into the historical facts regarding the early games with ball and stick played throughout Europe, and then tried to explore the minds and habits of players and course designers of the distant past. Hawtree postulates that Jeu de Mail is the medieval game most likely to have evolved into golf, offering some proof and illustrations to indicate it was an indoor game in Scotland that gravitated outdoors to the links, that provided the large spaces needed for the game.
C/H: D1, H5, P2, $30 – 40

Hayes, P. and Evans, R.D.C. *The Care of the Golf Course* (Bingley, 1992. Sports Turf Research Institute, p. 202 plus bibliography). Topics include: Golf Greens; Golf Tees; Golf Fairways; Semi Rough and Rough; Bunkers; Construction and Drainage; Pests and Diseases; Weeds; Pesticides and Legislation.

Heard, John. Co-author, *see* Curtiss, Frederic.

Hecker, Genevieve. *Golf for Women.* (New York, NY: The Baker & Taylor Co., 1902, 217 pages). This attractive and early American book features a wonderfully decorated cover and a wealth of advice inside on instruction and other topics by a two-time US Women's Amateur champion. In a nine page chapter on courses for women, Hecker discusses ideal soils, hole distances, placement of hazards and her favorite courses.
C/H: D3, M1, H1, T1, $20 (rep) – 250 (Orig)

Heerwagen, J.H. Co-author, *see* Orians, H.G.

Henderson, I.T. and D.I. Stirk. *Golf in the Making.* (London, England: Henderson and Stirk Ltd., 1979, ISBN 0-947758-02-X). A comprehensive illustrated history of playing equipment and ball technology. This work details the history of clubs and balls with passing references only to course architecture. Yet it is important in describing golf's evolution.
C/H: H5, P2, $50 – 100

Heuer, Karla L. with Cecil McKay Jr. *Golf Courses: A Guide to Analysis and Valuation.* (Chicago, IL: American Institute of Real Estate Appraisers, 1980, 128 pages, ISBN 0-911780-47-5). Although written from the perspective of appraising golf courses to establish their value, this book also details development, improvement and operation from a construction standpoint.
C/H: F3, D2, C2, M1, $25 – 50

Hill, David and Nick Seitz. *Teed Off.* (Englewood Cliffs, NJ: Prentice-Hall, Inc., 1977, 217 pages, ISBN 0-13-902247-3). Dave Hill was at his prime on the Pro tour in 1970 when the venue for the US Open was the Robert Trent Jones designed Hazeltine Golf Club in Chaska, Minnesota. Mr. Hill did not like the course and in the chapter of his book on "Architecture" he recounts how he said publicly that he "…thought Mr. Jones ruined a beautiful piece of farmland". The press then had a field day (no pun intended) with Hill's remarks; Mr. Jones was not impressed. Dave also recounted how after the Sunday round a charming and pleasant lady approached him and said "…'congratulations, I am Mrs. Robert Trent Jones.' I said, "It is nice to meet you, ma'am," and kept going because I figured she might be tempted to kill me if I gave in to the urge to chuckle". Later Rees Jones remodeled the course.

The chapter makes many basic design and philosophical points, most of which are quite sound. It is definitely a fun read. Although not mentioned, the wide publicity attending Hill's remarks may have been a plus for Trent in that his side of the story was put forward in major publications and on prime time, although the issue of American troops entering Cambodia without Congressional approval was raging at the same time.

C/H: D2, M2, H3, P4, $10 – 20

Hitch, Thomas K. and Mary I. Kuramoto. *Waialae Country Club, The First Half-Century.* (Honolulu, HI: The Waialae Country Club, 1981). Appendix A of this wonderful club history describes courses in the islands as of 1980 and their architects. Their roots, as in all states, can be traced to Scots.

C/H: D1, C1, M1, H4, P3, $30 – 50

Hopkins, Frank. *Golf Holes They Talk About.* (New York, NY: Redfield-Kendrick-Odell Co., 1927, 62 pages). A collection of sixty drawings of distinctive golf holes at metropolitan New York area courses, produced as a sports feature for the *New York Telegram* in the summer of 1927. Some architects are noted, along with famous members, events and features of the noteworthy holes.

C/H: D2, H3, P2, $300 – 400

Hopkinson, C.B. *Collecting Golf Books 1743-1938.* (London, England: Constable; Revised 1980 by Grant Books, Droitwich, Worcestershire, United Kingdom), with commentary by J.S.F. Murdoch.

H1, Original $1000 – 1200. Revised $500 - 650

Hotchkin, S.V. Col., M.C. *The Principles of Golf Architecture.* (Self-published in England: 1935, 26 pages). Although not well known, Colonel Hotchkin had mastered his craft, and he makes many interesting points. He even offers advise on buying a tractor.

C/H: D2, C1, M1, H4, $250 – 350

Hoteling, Neal. *Pebble Beach Golf Links: The Official History.* (Chelsea, MI: Sleeping Bear Press, 1999, 224 pages, ISBN 1-886947-04-X), with photography by Joann Dost. This history of one of America's most important courses is an interesting work of integrity. Space is given to the course architects involved in the development of Pebble Beach Golf Links and many of the grounds staff. That staff was then headed by the renowned Edward C. Horton, a graduate of the Stockbridge School of the University of Massachusetts and former superintendent of Winged Foot Golf Club and Westchester Country Club in Westchester, New York.

C/H: D3, C2, M1, H5, P3, $50 – 65

Huck, Barbara and Doug Whiteway. *One Hundred Years at St Charles Country Club: A Centennial History.* (Winnipeg, Canada: Heartland Publications, 2004). This is a grand and eloquent history of a club that has played an important role in the development of golf and the emerging society of Winnipeg, Manitoba and the Canadian west. With three courses by three architects of the Golden Age, namely, Tom Bendelow, Donald Ross and Alister Mackenzie, the Club is unique in Canada.

C/H: F1, D2, C2, H4, P3, $50 – 75

Hunter, Robert. *The Links.* (London, England: Charles Scribner's Sons, 1926, 163 pages). Hunter became interested in course architecture after visiting the classic courses of Great Britain in 1912. His treatise, said to be the first known American book on course design, is detailed and well illustrated with historic photographs of the classic courses while still in their original states. Hunter authored many essays on course design in periodicals starting his career as a champion of the underprivileged. He later ran for governor of Connecticut on the Socialist ticket. Still later he became involved with several of the nation's leading country clubs and became an opponent of President Franklin Roosevelt and the New Deal, although he had started his career as a champion of the poor. (Chelsea, MI: Sleeping Bear Press, 1999, 163 pages, ISBN 1-886947-51-1, facsimile edition edited by John Strawn).
C/H: D5, C3, M2, $55 (rep) – 800 (Orig)

Hurdzan, Michael, Ph.D. *Building a Practical Golf Facility.* (Chicago, IL: ASGCA, 2003, 120 pages) With financial assistance from the PGA and the USGA Foundation, this book is a step by step guide for those wishing to open modest and practical golf facilities. Dr. Hurdzan emphasizes three key words, "affordable," "accessible" and "sustainable" to describe the objective of his work, one that carries a mighty impact for golf. Available from the ASGCA for handling and mailing charges of $10.00, the objective is to promote affordable and welcoming venues for players. The National Recreation and Park Association also assists in its distribution. An updated edition is now available.
C/H: F3, D3, C2, $10

Hurdzan, Michael, Ph.D. *Evolution of the Modern Green.* (Chicago, IL: ASGCA, 1985, 24 pages, booklet). This well-illustrated pamphlet is the most lucid and complete account on the design and construction of golf greens. It includes a comprehensive discussion on the historical evolution, agronomic improvement, changing methodology and maintenance of the putting green. Hurdzan, a former president of the ASGCA, has extensive academic training in turfgrass management, as well as practical experience in course maintenance and design, and is eminently qualified to write on this topic. He begins in the late 1880s, when courses in America were maintained by grazing farm animals and sickle-bar mowing; incorporates the rise and fall of grassless sand greens; and the slow advances in turfgrass, techniques and knowledge in the early 1900s. Hurdzan credits trailblazer Fred W. Taylor, "a forgotten pioneer in early greens research", who developed several methods of greens construction that successfully "absorbed water from the sub-surface to the upper soil layers where the turf plants were actively growing". This was a breakthrough achievement, and one that Donald Ross would build upon during his experiments with green construction at Scioto Country Club around 1916. The model that Ross produced, with the help of Professor Vivian at Ohio State University, suggested the layering of soils to conserve water and resist compaction. With improvements made by Dr. Marvin Ferguson during the 1950s, it still serves as the basis for the USGA Green Section's method of greens construction.

Hurdzan makes it clear that building and maintaining a top quality green requires more than a scientific formula. Each green is a distinct entity subject to the sun,

wind, air, drainage, shade, temperature, humidity and orientation. Hurdzan gives greens personality, yet cautions they are as fragile and changeable as life itself.
C/H: D2, C2, M1, H2, $25 – 50

Hurdzan, Michael, Ph.D. *Golf Course Architecture: Design, Construction & Restoration.* (Chelsea, MI: Sleeping Bear Press, 1996, 406 pages, ISBN 1-886947-0-5). One of the most important modern books about designing and building golf courses, including the most detailed exposition yet on computer aided design, with chapters on economics, seedbed preparation and turfgrass establishment, bidding, construction sequence and many other timely topics. Hurdzan found his inspiration for this book in George Thomas' 1927 classic, *Golf Architecture in America,* hoping to provide a similar insight into the design theorems of today. In the book Hurdzan attempts to put right the discussion of design philosophy. "By limiting myself to a bare minimum of elements, I tried to use those same exact elements in different ways to illustrate the philosophies of penal, heroic, strategic and freeway design. This is a very misunderstood area that writers and even designers have confused for years, making gross mistakes such as talking about strategic design of a clearly penal course". Other unique chapters include "The Beautiful and the Ugly" and "Golf and the Environment". Hurdzan suggests that the courses of 2020 may look like the courses of 1920 when simple, natural methods worked best. Every day there are seemingly more limitations placed on course developers that limit the options and artistic expression available to the designer, perhaps altering golf course architecture in ways we can not yet imagine.
C/H: D5, C4, M2, H1, $50 – 75

Hurdzan, Michael J., Ph.D. *Golf Course Architecture: Evolution in Design, Construction and Restoration Technology.* (Hoboken, NJ: John Wiley & Sons, 2005, 434 pages, ISBN 0-471-46531-3). Golf course architecture is evolving at a prodigious pace and enough that it justified an extensive rewrite of the 1996 edition of this book. This volume can be seen as a stand alone replacement for the original edition, or together they can help the reader understand where and how golf architecture is evolving. The 2005 edition has at least sixty per cent new material in both writing and photographs.
C/H: F3, D5, C5, M1, $75 – 90

Hurdzan, Michael, Ph.D., and Dana Fry. *Selected Golf Courses: Photos and Essays, Volume I.* (Columbus, OH: Hurdzan and Fry, 2003, 383 pages, ISBN 9-9728553-0-0). Edited by Ron Whitten with photography by John and Jeannine Henebry, this book must rank among the most impressive on golf courses. The authors and architects discuss individual projects in personal detail. Privately published, the work is available from Hurdzan/Fry Golf Course Designs, Inc., 1270 Old Henderson Road, Columbus, OH 43220. Fittingly, it is dedicated to the late Jack Kidwell, a past president of the ASGCA, and Dr. Hurdzan's mentor.
C/H: D3, C1, H1, P3, T2, $50 – 75

Hurdzan, Michael, Ph.D. *Golf Greens: History, Design and Construction* (Publisher: John Wiley and Sons, ISBN 0-471-45945-3). The most complete publication ever concerning golf greens, this is a literary landmark for course architects, superintendents and in fact for agronomists and all golfers. For the first time everything concerning greens is explored while Chapter 9 entitled *Postscripts: My Personal Experiences Building Greens* and *The Future of Greens* is an inspired blend of history and prophecy that is sure to have an impact on our art form far into the future.

Hutchinson, Horace. *British Golf Links* (London, England: J.S. Virtue & Co. Ltd, 1897, 331 pages). No reference source before it, and few in the 106 years since, have portrayed a more vivid picture of golf links in the United Kingdom. Using hundreds of illustrative photographs of the courses, Hutchinson describes each with a sensitivity to the design and how it was achieved. Individual holes are revealed in detail and greenkeeping hints, profiles of famous players and descriptions of annual events abound.
C/H: D2, H5, P3, T2, $1,000 – 1,200 Facsimile reprint 2005 – $85

Hutchinson, Horace. *Golf Greens and Green-keeping.* (London, England: George Newnes and Country Life, 1906). With contributions by experienced course architects Colt, Fowler, Braid, Lees, Hilton and others, Hutchinson covers design, construction and upkeep of greens in every soil and climate. Hilton's chapter, "Remarks on the Laying Out of Courses" includes, "Picnics are but things of a day, but a putting green on a golf links is a fixture for many years to come – at least it should be so". (Hoboken, NJ: John Wiley & Sons, 2002, 219 pages, ISBN 1-57504-158-8, facsimile edition.)
C/H: D3, C5, M5, H5, $65 (Facsimile) – 1,000 (Orig)

Hutchinson, Horace. *Golfing.* (London, England: George Routledge and Sons, Ltd., 1901 (6th ed.), 121 pages). A chapter on "Links" discusses why "…we look to St Andrews with pious veneration as the alma mater…" as a model for course design and development. Hutchinson touches on such topics as the link's soils, grasses, bunkers, variety of holes. He compares and contrasts St Andrews with other famous and established courses. He mentions modifying sandy soils with "clay road scrapings" and "pitch forking" them. Rolling greens are also discussed.
C/H: F1, D2, C2, M1, H4, $150 – 200

Jacobs, Timothy. *Golf Courses of Jack Nicklaus.* (New York, NY: Popular Culture Ink, 1990,, 192 pages, ISBN 0-8317-3920-7). A compilation of Nicklaus' best courses during the early phase of his design career.
C/H: D3, M1, H3, P2, $35 – 60

Jacobs, Timothy. *Great Golf Courses of the World.* (London, Grange Books, 1990, 192 pages, ISBN 0-85627-074-0). A study of productions of course architects on the eve of the profession's greatest decade.
C/H: D2, M1, P1, T5, $15 – 25

Jenkins, Dan. *Sports Illustrated's The Best 18 Golf Holes in America.* (New York, NY: Delacorte Press, 1966, 160 pages, Library of Congress Catalog # 66-20116). One of the most renowned of golf writers, Jenkins spins his tales about holes from Pebble Beach to Pine Valley, Seminole to Cherry Hills, throwing an occasional bone to the course architect.
C/H: D2, C1, M1, H4, P3, T1, $25 – 100

Johnson, Joseph. *The Royal Melbourne Golf Club: A Centenary History.* (Victoria, Australia: The Royal Melbourne Golf Club, 1991, 256 pages). A stunning and detailed history of one of the world's great clubs, including drawings by and biographical information on course architect Alister Mackenzie.
C/H: D3, C2, M1, H5, P4, $50 – 100

Johnston, Alastair J. and James F. Johnston. *The Chronicles of Golf: 1457-1857.* (Cleveland, OH: Alastair Johnston, 1993, 734 pages, ISBN 1-878843-07-9). This monumental work, tracing the earliest origins of golf, is a cornerstone for a golf library. Numerous references to the establishment of clubs, the laying out of links, the players of the day and greenkeeping methods are included.
C/H: F1, D2, C2, H5, P4, $1250 – 2000 (LTD)

Jones, Rees. *Bethpage Black Course: Field Notes.* (New York, NY: Travel and Leisure Golf, 2001, 100 pages). One of the most unique books in all of course architecture literature – ever! Travel and Leisure Golf published this booklet as a gift to special guests, advertisers and supporters. Accordingly it was never available for purchase. The number of copies printed was limited, and it was bound in soft leather, document cover, rather than a traditional front and back cover. Although this alone makes it unique, it is what's inside that sets it apart.

When Rees Jones, ASGCA, accepted the task to restore the classic Tillinghast course on Long Island, known as Bethpage Black, for the 2002 US Open, he made extensive field notes. On each hole he made a drawing and then annotated it with his private and professional thoughts about what needed to be done to develop the full potential of the hole as originally conceived by Tillinghast. These notes appear as an overlay, along with Rees' commentary about the hole. This is a special book, about a special project, authored by a special person in the world of course design who has contributed a special feeling to the art form ever since he revised The Country Club for the 1988 Open.
C/H: D4, C2, M2, H4, P3, $75 – 125

Jones, Rees and Guy L. Rando. *Golf Course Developments.* (Washington, DC: Urban Land Institute Technical Bulletin 70, 1974, 105 pages, Library of Congress Catalog # LC-73-86554). Options, alternatives and variations in site development, with construction methods, costs and analysis. When published in 1974, it was perhaps the first book devoted entirely to course design in nearly fifty years. A seminal and influential work, it was later updated by Philips,1986 and Muirhead and Rando, 1994.
C/H: D3, C1, H2, $25 – 50

Jones, Robert Trent. *Golf Course Architecture.* (New York, NY: Thompson & Jones, 37 pages). Written before he was Trent Jones Sr., this charming and informative booklet includes early photos of some of Stanley Thompson's, with whom Jones was still partnered at time of publication, greatest courses. In addition, Thompson's dynamic young protégé writes on construction, the value of sketches, his theories of course design and the evolution of a golf hole. A rare pamphlet that foretold the new direction of golf, it indicated the vision of a person who was to exert an immense impact, following the dismal years, on the field of course design and the playing fields of the game.
C/H: D3, C3, M1, H5, P2, $1,000

Jones, Robert Trent, ed. *Great Golf Stories.* (New York, NY: Garland Books, 1987). Essays by prominent writers and architects. One by Red Hoffman of the *Newark News* discusses penal architecture while another by Alistair Cooke outlines the introduction of a Russian Consulate in San Franscisco to Golf by Robert Trent Jones Jr. around the time the latter was about to build a golf course in Moscow. Essay after essay is fascinating and each is introduced by Robert Trent Jones Sr.

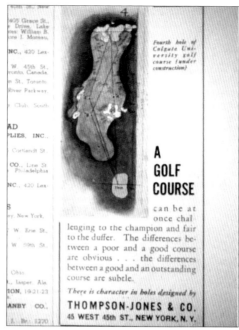

Trent Jones Sr. and Jr. together with Rees, have exerted an enormous impact on course design

Stan Thompson's protégé, Robert Trent Jones, became one of the most inflential course architects ever

Jones, Robert Trent Jr., *Golf by Design: How to Play Better Golf by Reading the Features of a Course.* (New York: NY: Little, Brown and Company, 1993, 276 pages, ISBN 0-316-47298-0). Renowned architect Trent Jones Jr., ASGCA, explains how to beat the challenges devised by course architects by successfully reading the features of the course. In doing so, he adds yet another dimension to a round of golf. In the Foreword, Tom Watson says "This book will help you see the course in a new, more confidant way ... Yet it will improve your game".
C/H: D3, C2, M2, H1, T3, $25 – 35

Jones, Robert Trent Sr. with Larry Dennis. *Golf's Magnificent Challenge.* (New York, NY: McGraw-Hill, 1989, 287 pages, ISBN 0-07-032816-1). Written in an autobiographic style, this lavishly illustrated coffee table book traces the career, thoughts and successes of Robert Trent Jones as he forever changed the profession of golf course architecture and influenced this art form more than any other person in history.
C/H: D4, C3, M2, H3, T3, $50 – 75

Jones, Robert Tyre (Bobby), Jr. *Golf is My Game.* (Garden City, NY: Doubleday, 1960, 255 pages, Library of Congress Catalog # 60-13386). Chapter 21 presents drawings by George W. Cobb, ASGCA, of each of the eighteen holes of Augusta National as they were in 1960. Chapter 17 outlines the improvements in golf courses and turf from the Golden Age to 1960. Throughout the text, Jones is revealing and refreshing.
C/H: D3, C1, H4, P3, $25 – 35

Jones, W. Pete. *A Directory of Golf Courses Designed by Donald Ross.* (Raleigh, NC: Martini Print Media, 1994, 32 pages). A list of design projects by state, with a brief history of Donald Ross Associates. At least ten editions were printed as information was compiled and updated.

C/H: D1, H4, $25 – 50

Joy, David. *Scrapbook of Old Tom Morris.* (Chelsea, MI: Sleeping Bear Press, 2001, 229 pages, ISBN 1-886947-45-7). A beautifully produced fictional scrapbook of the life of Old Tom. Many entries in the scrapbook are based on his works as are photographs and maps of courses that he worked on. Entries include his dual role of greenkeeper and professional at Prestwick and St Andrews.

C/H: D1, C1, M2, H5, P5, $45 – 65

Kains, Robert. *Golf Course Design and Construction.* (Guelph, ON: University of Guelph, 1993). This study, including abundant illustrations, is the text for a correspondence course on course design provided by the University of Guelph.

C/H: F1, D4, C2, M2, $25 – 35

Kato, Shunsuke. *What Makes a Good Golf Course Good* (Japan, 1991, 256 pages). Mr. Kato shares his great design insights on such subjects as the intellectual challenges of design, how nature and golf flow together, integrated planning and green maintenance and technology. The text is in Japanese and English.

C/H: D4, M3, H2, P2, $125 – 150

Kato, Shunsuke. *A Good Golf Course Merges into the Nature* (Japan, 1996, 144 pages, for private circulation). Mr. Kato continues to share his great design insights: "It is important to the architect to plan the coexistence with nature. If the designer returns the things given by the nature, the nature will watch over you warmly always."

C/H: D4, M3, H2, P2, $1 – 50

Kegan, Paul. Co-author, *see* Cousins, Geoffrey.

Keller, Vikki. Co-author, *see* Diperna, Paula.

Kendall, Brian. *Northern Links: A Duffer's Unforgettable Journey Through the World of Canadian Golf.* (Toronto, Canada: Penguin Books, 2001, ISBN 0-6708884-2). The work itself is unforgettable, with descriptions of courses by renowned Stanley Thompson and other great Canadian golf architects including Bob and David Moote, Doug Carrick, Tom McBroom, Graham Cooke, Les Furber and others.

C/H: F1, D2, C2, H3, P3, $35 – 50.

Kerr, John. *The Golf Book of East Lothian.* (Edinburgh, Scotland: T. and A. Constable, 1896, 516 pages plus appendices). Rich in history, full of pictures of the principle protagonists and ever conscious of the evolution of the golfing grounds, this masterwork acknowledges the seminal architects of golf and is a cornerstone book, by any standard.

C/H: D1, H5, P5, Large Paper Edn $3,000, 1st Trade edn $1000 – 1,500, reprint $400 – 500

Kirk, John. *The Golf Courses of Robert Trent Jones, Jr.* (New York, NY: Gallery Books, 1988, 192 pages, ISBN 0-8317-3921-5). A review of courses around the world designed by the firm of R.T.J., II. With excellent photography, it shows the full range of design skills of this architect.

C/H: D3, C1, M1, H2, P2, T4, $45 – 75

Kladstrup, Donald M. *The Evolution of a Legacy.* (Rochester, NY: Oak Hill, 1994, 43 pages). This booklet was painstakingly researched and written prior to the 1995 Ryder Cup, and traces the evolution of the golf holes at Oak Hill through four designers, Donald Ross' 1924 original creation, Robert Trent Jones' mid 1950s improvements, George and Tom Fazio's 1976 redesign of four holes, and finally Craig Schreiner's, ASGCA, restoration in the mid 1990s. It includes course maps from 1923 and 1995, as well as each hole as originally designed and subsequently modified over the years. This is a marvelous journey into the minds and through the time period from wood shaft to graphite and titanium clubs. One can spend hours with the booklet and still feel the design information it offers has not been exhausted.
C/H: D4, C2, M2, H5, P4, $75 – 100

Klein, Bradley S., Ph.D. *A Walk in the Park: GolfWeek's Guide to America's Best Classic and Modern Golf Courses.* Foreword by Tom Fazio. (Champaign, IL: Sports Publishing, LLC, 2004, 200 pages, ISBN 1-58261605-1, $39.95). This majestic volume includes architectural and historical profiles of the top fifty classic, pre-1960, and top fifty modern, 1960 and after, golf courses in the United States. It explains the process of golf course ratings, and presents diverse essays on architecture, construction, maintenance, playability and the character of golf course culture. Two-thirds of the book is by Klein; the rest is by *GolfWeek* senior writers who are veterans at covering tournament golf and the golf industry. The Foreword by Tom Fazio provides the rationale for rankings and looks at their importance to course architecture despite abundant controversy concerning them. One essay by Scott Kauffman provides updated cost figures by Hurdzan-Fry for low- and high-end layouts. Another puts forth Forrest Richardson's concept for the strategy of a 385 yards par 4. Still another provides a guideline for a green-fee, "at least $10.00 of green fee for every million in course construction and facility development costs…". *A Walk in the Park,* its valuable contents and the magnificence of the presentations make this work both an outstanding coffee table book and a useful reference. Dr. Klein has long been interested, indeed intensely so, in course architecture. He has written the definitive biography of Donald Ross, is the editor of *Golfweek's SuperNews* and directs the golf course ratings for *Golfweek* Magazine. This is a coffee table book providing visual and narrative descriptions of *Golfweek's* 2004 listing of the top fifty classic courses, 1959 or earlier, and the fifty top modern ones, post 1960. The insights and illustrations are immensely informative and very valuable to course architects, especially those who aspire to have their work make that list.
C/H: D2, M2, H2, P2, T5, $35 – 50

Klein, Bradley S., Ph.D. *Cultural Links: An International Political Economy of Golf Course Landscapes.* (University of Minnesota Press, 1999. *Sportcult,* pages 211-226). Written by the erudite Dr. Bradley Klein, author of four books on course design and one on political science, former tour caddie and Clark University professor, this essay explores "course design as one moment in the unfolding of modernity". Klein states that golf courses deserve to be taken seriously as works of art, culture, politics and economy. While several aspects of the paper are controversial, it deserves wide study as it explores the impact of the world's 25,000 golf courses on society.
C/H: F1, H3, P1, $25 – 50

Former tour caddie and college professor Dr. Bradley Klein, now editor of Golf Week's Super News *has written four books related to course design together with several essays and a book on government. His scholarly productions have made a huge contribution. As a caddie he was sought by VIPs including Pat Ward-Thomas. Bradley Klein has contributed to the* New York Times *together with several golf and professional journals*

Klein, Bradley S., Ph.D. *Discovering Donald Ross: The Architect and his Golf Courses.* (Chelsea, MI: Sleeping Bear Press, 2001, 367 pages, ISBN 1-886947-55-4). An account of the career of America's most revered designer, detailing his personal life, travel, business relationships, design projects and philosophies. Klein has produced a definitive and captivating book that sets a standard for biographical and professional portraits of course architects and those in other professions. Master of his art, Ross was a founder of the American Society of Golf Course Architects.
C/H: D3, C3, M1, H5, P4, $65 – 85

Klein, Bradley S., Ph.D. *Rough Meditations.* (Chelsea, MI: Sleeping Bear Press, 1997, 220 pages, ISBN 1-886947-17-1). Essays on course architecture and other topics from the architecture editor of *Golfweek*. As a respected student of the game, Klein does not hold back on judgments that are both sharp and entertaining.
C/H: D3, H3, P3, M2, $20 – 25

Klein, Bradley S., Ph.D. *Desert Forest Golf Club: the First Forty Years* (Carefree, AZ: Desert Forest Golf Club 2004, 162 pages, ISBN 0-9758976-08). Original photography by Tony Roberts. The book also comes with a DVD shot and edited by Grant McClintock. An unusual club history that explores the design and development of the pioneer Arizona desert course, Desert Forest Golf Club. The book details the growth of the

Phoenix area, the development of real estate and recreation in Scottsdale, and the founding ideals behind the visionary town that would become Carefree in the early 1960s. Two chapters focus on the virtually unknown course designer, Robert "Red" Lawrence, 1893-1976, a founding member and twice president of the ASGCA. The book also looks at the identity and culture of this unique, low-key club. Unlike most club histories, this one is not about the members and who won what club event. It is about the design and maintenance of this links-style golf course. The book includes a close look at the Club's distinguished super-intendents and its maintenance practices that keep it the only private club in the Phoenix area that does not overseed in winter. It also covers the restoration and desert reclamation project undertaken by designer and member Tom Weiskopf.
C/H: D2, C1, M1, H3, T4, P1, $40 – 50

Kroeger, Robert. *The Golf Courses of Old Tom Morris.* (Cincinnati, OH: Heritage Communications, 1995, 351 pages, ISBN 0-9618291-3-3, $39.95). Both a biography of Old Tom and a discussion of his design, the book provides details and incidents in his life about which little has been written. Old Tom has had a profound worldwide influence on course design and maintenance, probably more than anyone in the first 500 years of golf.
C/H: D3, C1, M1, H4, P4, $50 – 75

Kroeger, Robert. *To the 14th Tee: A Pilgrimage to the Links of Scotland.* (Cincinnati, OH: Heritage Communications, 2001, 194 pages, ISBN 0-961291-4-1). A wonderful story about a father taking his sons on a golf vacation to Scotland, and what they learned and experienced playing some of the "hidden gems". Kroeger is an experienced golf traveler who is passionate about researching people and places connected with golf. His insights into parenting, Scottish golf and its architecture make this an important addition to any library on course design.
C/H: D1, M1, H2, P2, T5, $25 – 145 (LTD)

Kuramoto, Mary I. Co-author, see Hitch, Thomas K.

Labbance, Bob. *The Old Man: The Biography of Walter J. Travis.* (Chelsea, MI: Sleeping Bear Press, 2000, 259 pages, ISBN 1-886947-91-0). This comprehensive book starts with the emigration of Travis' parents from England to Australia, his move to the United States at the age twenty-three, his exposure to golf, and subsequent winning of three US Amateur and one British Amateur Championships. Travis turned to course design during a long and successful competitive career. He designed two dozen courses while also writing extensively on the subject in two books and as editor of *The American Golfer* magazine. His influence in the early years of American golf cannot be discounted; and his courses featured superb routing, cleverly placed hazards and taxing tests of putting skill at the conclusion of each hole.
C/H: D3, C1, H4, P4, $20 – 30

Labbance, Bob and David Cornwell. *The Maine Golf Guide.* (Stockbridge, VT: New England Golf Specialists, 1991, 208 pages, ISBN 0-9622354-1-5), with Foreword by Geoffrey S. Cornish. By the authors of *Vermont Golf Courses: A Player's Guide* (1987) and *The Golf Courses of New Hampshire: From the Mountains to the Sea* (1989), this trilogy includes information on course architects that attracted wide attention and helped to prove the statement that "golfers yearn to know who designed courses they play".

No course in northern New England escaped their attention as they explored venues from St Croix, Maine to Stamford, Vermont and at several hundred stops in between.
C/H: D1, M1, H2, P1, T5, $15 – 25

Lafaurie, Andre-Jean. *Great Golf Courses of the World.* (Paris, France: Abbeville Press, 1990, 192 pages, ISBN 0-896660-016-5). A picture book with a continental perspective, including brief descriptions of layouts.
C/H – D1, H2, P1, T4, $20 – 30

Langford, William B. *Golf Course Architecture in the Chicago District.* (Chicago, IL: Self-published, 1915, 17 pages). Mr. Langford was a founding member of the American Society of Golf Course Architects in 1947. His career spanned two World Wars and Depression. In this publication, written early in his career, he is specific to the Chicago area and offers sound advice on working with heavy clay soils, building natural looking bunkers, design strategy and economy in construction and maintenance.
C/H: D3, C2, M2, H4, $1,500 – 2,000

Leach, Henry. *The Happy Golfer.* (London, England: Macmillan and Co., 1914, 414 pages). This is one of the most charming and best written books in the rich literature of golf. Leach tours the world, discoursing on the values of this layout and the challenge of that. Along the trail he encounters designers such as Charles Blair Macdonald, Harry Colt and others.
C/H: D2, M2, H3, P2, T3, $350 – 500

Lee, James P. *Golf in America: A Practical Manual.* (New York: Dodd, Mead & Co., 1895). This seminal work was written between the founding of the USGA in 1894 and the first National Championships the following year. The author's purpose, according to Frank Hannigan, was to "explain and recruit" at a time when there were only about fifty-five courses in the United States. By 1900, the number had grown to a thousand, so perhaps the recruiting was successful. According to respected Steve Melnyk "The author had a vision for the future of golf". Lee credited Willie Davis correctly, not Willie Dunn as later thought, as creator of the earliest Shinnecock Course. (Far Hills, NJ: USGA Rare Book Collection, 1986, with Preface by Frank Hannigan and Introduction by Steve Melnyk, facsimile edition).
C/H: D2, C2, M1, H4, P4, $100 (rep) – 3,000 (Orig)

Leigh-Bennett, E.P. *Some Friendly Fairways.* (London, England: Southern Railway, 1930, 57 pages). Written as a travel guide to stimulate golfers' use of railroads, this booklet gives insights into many courses in England, with small, but charming pictures. Not much design or construction information, but an interesting and delightful read.
C/H: H3, T4, $75 – 100

Love, William R., ASGCA. *An Environmental Approach to Golf Course Development.* (Chicago, IL: The American Society of Golf Course Architects, 1992, updated 1999). Aspects of course design and their significance to the environment are put forward in text and convenient checklist form by an accomplished architect. It is the definitive text on course development in relation to the environment and a valuable resource for those involved in developing golf courses. Love's academic training was in architecture as contrasted to landscape architecture. Still, his love and deep feeling for the environment arise throughout his text. (*See also* Love, William R., pages 120 and 133). A third edition is pending.
C/H: F3, D4, C1, M1, $20 – 25

Low, John L. *Concerning Golf.* (London, England: Hodder and Stoughton, 1903, 217 pages). This significant book provides a background for what was to come in the next century and it was the first to codify the principles of course design. A chapter titled "Concerning The Links" defines a "good test of golf," and explains why St Andrews "has the most perfect golfing hazards which the mind can imagine". (Far Hills, NJ: USGA Rare Book Collection, 1987, facsimile edition.).
C/H: D3, M1, H4, P3, $50 (rep) – 200 (Orig)

Lowe, Iain MacFarlane. *Scottish Golf Links: A Photographer's Journey,* with historical commentary by David Joy and architectural observations by Kyle Phillips, ASGCA. (Ann Arbor, MI: Clock Tower Press, 2004. ISBN 1-932202-12-9.) This book describes over fifty courses with magnificent photographs and text. The courses stretch along the coast of Scotland from St Andrews to Nairn and Dornoch.
C/H: T3, $40

Lyle, Sandy with Bob Ferrier. *The Championship Courses of Scotland.* Surrey, England; Kingswood, Tadworth; World Works Ltd., The Windmill Press, 1982. An extraordinary informative work with fine illustrations.
C/H: D2, C1, M1, H3, T4, P1, $25 – 35

Macdonald, Charles Blair. *Scotland's Gift—Golf.* (New York, NY: Charles Scribner's Sons, 1928, 341 pages). A book that is a must for inclusion in a golfer's library. Macdonald is considered to be the Father of American Golf Course Architecture, a title he may have coined himself, but fitting. This visionary formalizes many principles, including rules, competitions and administration of golf, and also offers his insight and expertise on the design and construction of golf courses. (Stamford, CT: The Classics of Golf. Ailsa, Inc. Facsimile edition with Foreword by Herbert Warren Wind and Afterword by Alistair Cooke).
C/H: D3, C1, M2, H3, P4, $35 (rep) – 3,500 (LTD)

Macdonald, Peter. Co-author, *see* Gilliland, Robert J.

Machat, Udo. *Poppy Hills, Pebble Beach, CA.* (Berkeley, CA: Sport Images, 1998, 144 pages, ISBN 0-9618712-4-S). Each hole at this Robert Trent Jones Jr. course is described. The photography is by Machat.
C/H: D3, C1, M1, P2, $35 – 45

Machat, Udo with text by Cal Brown. *The Golf Courses of the Monterey Peninsula.* (New York, NY: Simon and Schuster, 1989, ISBN 0-671-67849-3). A beautifully illustrated work with eloquent and informative text with photographs by Machat.
C/H: D2, C1, P2, $35 – 45

Mackenzie, Dr. Alister. *Golf Architecture: Economy in Course Construction and Greenkeeping.* (London, England: Simpkin, Marshall, Hamilton, Kent and Co., 1920, 135 pages). This little book has held a mighty message for golf architects since its publication in 1920. A cornerstone book on course architecture, it includes thirteen general principles and numerous anecdotes and illustrations that set the tone and direction of the profession for decades. (Worcestershire, England: Grant Books, 1982, 90 pages, Classics of Golf Facsimile Edition ISBN 0-9040889-16-1; reprint with additional material).
C/H: D4, C3, M1, H2, P2, Orig $1200, Grant Books 150 Classics of Golf $40

Three architects of the golden era wrote books that never saw the light of day until decades later. Writer Lee Tyler authored two works of fiction involving course architects and superintendents

Mackenzie, Dr. Alister. *The Spirit of St Andrews.* (Chelsea, MI: Sleeping Bear Press, 1995, 268 pages, ISBN 1-886947-007). Written in 1933 but not published, Mackenzie's step-grandson discovered the seven chapters in an old desk he inherited from his father who had served as Mackenzie's secretary. The architect reviews courses, shares design secrets, recounts anecdotes and explains the classic holes with rare insight.
C/H: D3, C3, M2, H3, P4, $20 – 25

Macpherson, Scott. *The Evolution of The Old Course.* (Edinburgh, Scotland: Hazard Press, 2005, 144 pages. Foreword by Peter Thomson). The authors have not yet read Macpherson's work. Nevertheless statements in advance publicity including one by eminent writer Ron Whitten stating that until now the evolution of the Old Course has not been thoroughly documented and another "…understanding the past enables us to comprehend the present and foresee the future" impresses us. The latter statement embraces one of the premier objectives of this Bibliography.

Mahoney, Jack. *The Golf History of New England.* (Weston, MA: New England Golf, 1995, 237 pages). Available in some pro shops, this hard cover work is an update of Mahoney's 1973 paperback on the same subject, but with additional information on course designers.
C/H: D1, H5, P4, $5 – 10

Mair, Norman. *Muirfield: Home of The Honourable Company.* (Edinburgh, Scotland: Mainstream Publishing Company, 1994, 167 pages, ISBN 1-85158-617-2). A club history prepared for The Honourable Company of Edinburgh Golfers and their home course at Muirfield. Chapters on the history of the course include pictures of various architectural plans used during alterations. One chapter covers maintenance of the course and its famous bunkering.
C/H: D2, C1, H4, P2, $35 – 55

Martin, H.B. *Fifty Years of American Golf.* (New York, NY: Dodd, Mead & Co., 1936, 423 pages). Martin's detailed examination of golf's first fifty years in America contains tales of triumph and travail, all part of the history of the game in the New World, and delivered with the author's whimsical yet authoritative style. Most notable for those interested in architectural history is Chapter 25, "Golf Architects and Famous Courses". It reviews the history of course design in America up to the mid 1930s. Martin begins this section by introducing Willie Dunn as creator of Shinnecock Hills on Long Island, a course later discovered to have been first designed by Willie Davis. But designs of those years were far from the norm, says Martin, who states that, "Almost anyone could improvise a golf course in the last decades of the 19th century because so few knew anything about the game, there was no standard of comparison".
C/H: D1, H5, P4, $50 (rep) – 600 (Orig)

Massy, Arnaud, Translated by A.R. Allinson. *Golf.* (London, England: Methuen & Co. Ltd., 1914, 128 pages). This volume by the French professional concerns instruction. However, the final chapter is titled "Laying Out a Golf Course". Massy's straightforward advice is intended for amateurs who inherit a piece of land suitable for the game. "I advise you to take your time before giving the order to begin," the champion writes. "Good golf links are not established in a moment; months are required to utilize all the resources of the ground".
C/H: D3, C2, M2, P2, $50 – 75

McCarthy, John Francis. *The Beauty of Golf in New York State.* (Auburn, NY: Summerfield House, 1989, 98 pages, ISBN 0-9623716-0-2). With beautiful photographs of golf holes from Long Island to the western counties, the book celebrates every strata of golf from municipals to the magnificent. Course architects are named for each layout. Daily fee layouts, including municipals, come across exceedingly well for beauty and playing interest.
C/H: D1, H3, T4, P3, $25 – 35

McCord, Robert R. *The Best Public Golf Courses in the United States, Canada, the Caribbean and Mexico: A Complete Guide to 617 Courses.* (New York, NY: Random House, 1996, 829 pages, ISBN 0-679-76903-X). As well as his course profiles, McCord provides abundant biographical and design information concerning the most prolific course architect in each region of North America.
C/H: D2, C1, M1, T5, $25 – 50

McCord, Robert R. *The Quotable Golfer.* (New York, The Lyons Press, 2000, 346 pages, ISBN 1-55821-998-6). With quotes concerning all aspects of golf, one chapter is devoted entirely to those by or concerning architects and architecture.
C/H: D1, P2, $10 – 20

McDonnell, Michael. Co-author, *see* Player, Gary.

McKay, Cecil, Jr. Co-author, *see* Heuer, Karla L.

McKinsey and Co. Co-author, *see* National Golf Foundation.

McMillan, Robin. *The Golfer's Home Companion.* (New York, NY: Simon & Schuster, 1993, 285 pages, ISBN 0-671-70054-5). The twenty page architecture section includes "Fifteen Steps to the Perfect Golf Course" by Rees Jones, essays on short par fours, greens and bunkers by Tom Doak, and "How to Build Your Own Golf Course" by David Earl. The section is a fun and informative one.
C/H: F2, D2, C2, M2, H2, T3, $15 – 25

Mead, Daniel W. and Joseph Reid Akerman. *Contract Specifications and Engineering Relations.* (New York: McGraw Hill, 1956). An engineering text used by one generation of course designers as a guide to engineering law, it became a standard for many design libraries, although it never mentioned golf architecture.
C/H: D2, C1, $25 – 35

Millard, Chris. Co-author, *see* Nicklaus, Jack.

Miller, Dick. *America's Greatest Golfing Resorts.* (New York, NY: Bobbs-Merrill Co., 1977, 239 pages, ISBN 0-672-52133-4). Includes information and photographs of architects such as Dev Emmet, Trent Jones, Joe Finger, Pete Dye, Donald Ross and others.
C/H: D1, H3, P3, T4, $10 – 20

Miller, Michael and Geoff Shackelford. *The Art of Golf Design, Landscapes by Michael G. Miller and Essays by Geoff Shackelford.* (Chelsea, MI: Sleeping Bear Press, 2001, 189 pages, ISBN 1-886947-30-9). Miller has produced dozens of paintings of famous golf holes using photographs from the actual era the courses were constructed. Writer Shackelford offers thoughtful essays to accompany the paintings.
C/H: D3, C1, T2, $35 – 65

Mingay, Jeff. *Classic Golf Course Restoration.* (Hoboken, NJ: John Wiley & Sons, Publication pending 2005, ISBN 0-471-47271-9, $75).

Montgomerie, Colin. Co-author, *see* Davis, Martin.

Moone, Theodore. *Golf From a New Angle.* (London, England: Herbert Jenkins Ltd., 1934, 248 pages, Foreword by J.H. Taylor). Written in the form of letters to his son, British writer Moone, who planned at least four courses in the British Isles, enthuses on many golfing topics. His discussions are in the form of "family conversations" avoiding "those tiresome circumlocutions which the eager writer is often compelled to insert as shock absorbers between himself and the 'gentle reader'". Using diagrams and references to other sources, Moone includes a chapter concerning soil and another on architecture, and still another on the geology of the golf course. It is a unique book with passages such as "The design of a good golf course can be likened to the construction of a musical symphony".
C/H: F1, D4, C1, M1, H2, P1, $60 – 80

Moreton, John F. *The Golf Courses of James Braid.* (Worcestershire, England: Grant Books, 1996, 126 pages, ISBN 0-907186-75-0). The book begins with a wonderful Foreword by J. Hamilton Stutt, a founding member of the British Institute of Golf Course Architects, whose father constructed many of Braid's courses. Braid worked with more than 150 clubs and a small write-up on his involvement with most of them is included. Also laid in are course maps of Gleneagles and Royal Blackheath.
C/H: D3, C1, H5, P4, T2, $35 – 45

Moreton, J.F. Co-author, *see* Grant, H.R.J.

Morgan, Brian. *A World Portrait of Golf.* (New York, NY: W.H. Smith Publishers, 1988, 224 pages, ISBN 0-8317-9625-1). A massive testament to the photographic skills of kilt-bedecked Morgan with introductions to the courses of their homeland by Gary Player, Peter Thomson, Tsuneyuki Nakajima, Roberto De Vicenzo, Jack Nicklaus and others.
C/H: D1, H1, P2, T4, $35 – 65

Morrison, J.S.F. *Around Golf.* (London, England: Arthur Barker Limited, 1939, 246 pages). C.H. Allison contributes a chapter on the Oxford and Cambridge Golfing Society; Sir Guy Campbell writes on St Andrews and Golf; and Dr. A. Diemer Kool, secretary of the Kennemer Golf and Country Club in Holland, discusses manures, "forking" greens, the need to alter mowing directions and keeping a diary of work performed.
C/H: M3, H4, $120 – 150

Moss, Richard J. *Golf and the American Country Club.* (Chicago, IL: Illinois University Press, 2000, ISBN 0-252-026422-X). This seminal and authoritative history of country clubs in America tells the story of the crucial relationship between golf and the private club, moving from the early history of golf clubs in the 1890s to a discussion of the status of the country club in contemporary society. It contends that the country club was an attempt to reconstruct the American village, a reality and an image that was being destroyed by the broad forces of modernization. Between 1890 and 1930, private golf clubs enjoyed rapid growth and during this period golf in the United States became linked, for good or ill, with the upper class and their private enclaves.

Depression and war clearly hurt the progress, although the 1950s brought a partial revival with a strong resumption of country club development in the 1960s. At that time it became a subject in a much larger debate about fairness and equality in American life. Perhaps more importantly, Americans began to find substitutes. For example, the private gated community proved to be an ideal replacement for the private club and it became an important new way of providing golf to affluent Americans with many choices as to how they spent their increased leisure time.

As a postscript to *Golf and the American Country Club*, one could argue that by the end of the twentieth century private golf clubs were making a comeback in the form of non-equity clubs developed with a profit motive. Membership in them was attractive to those who sought less crowded courses and more clubhouse amenities than public golf offered despite the magnificence of contemporary daily fee layouts.

Muirhead, Desmond with Tip Anderson. *St Andrews, How to Play the Old Course.* (Newport Beach, CA: Newport Press, 2000, ISBN 0-615-11220-X). Written by a leading and innovative course architect collaborating with a renowned St Andrews golf professional, this volume describes the architecture of each hole on the Old Course and how Anderson would play it.
C/H: D4, M1, H3, P3, $40 – 50

Mulvoy, Mark and Art Spander. *Golf: The Passion and the Challenge.* (New York, NY: Rutledge Books, 1977, 256 pages). Includes a chapter titled "Sculpting the Land: The Making of a Golf Course" that touches on many course designers through history and their influence on the game, with numerous illustrations of the world's great courses.
C/H: D2, H2, P2, T2, $15 – 25

Mungeam, Mark A., ASGCA Cornish, Silva and Mungeam, Inc. "Civil Engineering as the Academic Background for Golf Course Design" found in *Golf Course Design* by Robert Muir Graves and Geoffrey S. Cornish.
C/H: D1, P2, $N/A

Murdoch, J.S.F. *The Library of Golf 1743-1966.* (Detroit, MI: Gale Research, 1968, 314 pages). Perhaps the most complete bibliography of golf books until 1988, with insightful commentary by one of the world's greatest collectors of golf books. This book is more of an education than a reference source.
C/H: A Reference Source, $450 – 700 (LTD)

Murdoch, Joseph S. Co-author, *see* Donovan, Richard.

National Golf Foundation. *Golf Course Design and Construction.* (Jupiter, FL: National Golf Foundation, 1990). Basic sound advice.
C/H: F3, D3, C2, M2, $35 – 50

National Golf Foundation and McKinsey & Company. *A Strategic Perspective on the Future of Golf, An Executive Summary.* (Jupiter, FL: National Golf Foundation, 1999). Realistic view of what may lie ahead for golf.
C/H: F4, D1, H1, $35 – 50

Nicklaus, Jack with Chris Millard. *Nicklaus by Design: Golf Course Strategy and Architecture.* (New York, NY: Harry N. Abrams, Inc., Publishers, 2002, 288 pages, ISBN 0-8109-3249-0). Nicklaus provides insight into his work, with details about Muirfield Village and other favorite projects. Many beautiful pictures.
C/H: D4, C2, H2, P3, $35 – 50

Norton, Richard L., Vice President, National Golf Foundation. "Golf Course Financing" found in *Golf Course Design* by Robert Muir Graves and Geoffrey S. Cornish.
C/H: F4, D1, C1, $N/A

Orians, G.H. and J.H. Heerwagen In Barkow, J., with L. Cosmides and J. Tooby, Editors. *Adapted Mind (see Barkow, J.).* This publication includes a chapter on evolved responses to landscapes, something of intrinsic significance to course architects.

Ortiz-Patino, Jamie. *Valderrama The First Ten Years 1985 – 1995.* (London, England: Jamie Ortiz-Patino, 1995, 135 pages, ISBN 0-9526131-1-5). Everything that Mr. Ortiz-Patino does is first class and professional. This treatise is no exception. Valderrama Golf Club, a leader in Europe, demonstrates the positive impact a course can have on the environment. This book addresses that concept with great text and beautiful pictures. But for those who study course design, it is the chapter on "The Robert Trent Jones Design Philosophy" that may hold the greatest interest. Valderrama was one of Jones' favorite projects.
C/H: F2, D3, C2, M2, H5, P4, $35 – 50

Pace, Lee. *Pinehurst Stories: A Celebration of Great Golf and Good Times.* (Pinehurst, NC: Resorts of Pinehurst, Inc., 1991, 226 pages, ISBN 0-9630688-0-6). As one would expect, this history of Pinehurst features information on Donald Ross and his course architecture. That alone qualifies it for this bibliography, but the book also has an essay on how Pete and Alice Dye were influenced by Pinehurst, and Ross beginning when Pete was in the service at Fort Bragg. One chapter concerns the Maples family and the impact of Pinehurst on their own course design. This is a fascinating book.
C/H: D3, C3, M2, H5, P4, $40 – 60

Park, Willie Jr. *The Game of Golf.* (London, England: Longmans Green and Co., 1896, 277 pages). An influential chapter on course design was one of the first ever written, and served as a guideline for many who followed. Park was considered to be the doyen of contemporary golf architecture and many of his principles have been the basis for increasingly sophisticated design. In the architecture chapter Park made the legendary statement "The laying out of a golf course is by no means a simple task".
C/H: D3, C1, M1, H3, P2, $40 (rep) – 600 (Orig)

Pennink, Frank. *Homes of Sport: Golf.* (London, England: Peter Garnett Ltd., 1952, 209 pages). A tour of the finest golf links in the British Isles with notations on their designs.
C/H: D1, M1, P1, T4, $20 – 35

Peper, George. *Golf Courses of the PGA Tour.* (New York, NY: Harry N. Abrams, Inc., 1986, 303 pages, ISBN 0-8109-0994-4). A celebration of courses that professionals play, with references to the architects who designed them.
C/H: D1, H2, P2, T4, $20 – 35

Peper, George, Editor, with Tom Doak. *Golf in America: The First Hundred Years.* (New York, NY: Harry N. Abrams, Inc., 1988, 304 pages, ISBN 0-8109-1032-2). This historical review of golf in America contains an excellent chapter on the history of course architecture. The text is complemented by historical photographs, plans and current photographs of the greatest courses and designers in the country.
C/H: D2, C1, H4, P2, $50 – 75

Peper, George and the Editors of *Golf Magazine.* *The 500 World's Greatest Golf Holes.* (New York, NY: Artisan, 442 pages, ISBN 1-57965-162-3). This is one of the most beautiful and informative books on individual golf holes ever written. Mentions of course architects are abundant.
C/H: D2, H2, P2, T4, $20 – 40

Peter, H. Thomas. *Reminiscences of Golf and Golfers.* (Edinburgh, Scotland: James Thin, 1890, 55 pages). A discourse on play at St Andrews including discussions of the links and how they have changed over the years.
C/H: D1, M1, H4, P3, $150 (rep) – 1,500 (Orig)

Phillips, Patrick L. *Developing with Recreational Amenities: Golf, Tennis, Skiing, Marinas.* (Washington, DC: Urban Land Institute, 1986, 257 pages, ISBN 0-87420-664-2). Integrating golf into planned developments.
C/H: F1, D1, $20 – 35

Pilley, Phil. *Heather and Heaven: Walton Heath Golf Club 1903-2003.* (Surrey, England: Walton Heath Golf Club, 2003, 256 pages, ISBN 0-9544498-0-0). A club history that sets a new standard, with detailed information, quality graphics and a wealth of ephemera about the venerable club. Architects Herbert Fowler and James Braid are profiled.
C/H: D2, C1, M1, H5, P4, $35 – 50

Player, Gary with Michael McDonnell. *To Be The Best.* (London, England: Sidgwick & Jackson Limited, 1991, 165 pages, ISBN 0-283-06007-7). Player's reflections include a chapter on course architecture. In it he reveals his theories of design.
C/H: D2, H3, P3, $20 – 30

Pottinger, Don. Co-author, *see* Cousins, Geoffrey.

Price, Charles. *The American Golfer.* (New York, NY: Random House, 1964, 244 pages, Library of Congress Catalog # 64-20037). Several pages outline C.B. Macdonald's admonitions concerning course design that continue to influence architects on both sides of the pond.
C/H: D2, H4, P3, $25 – 45

Price, Charles. *The World of Golf: A Panorama of Six Centuries.* (New York, NY: Random House, 1962, 307 pages). Although this book includes little on design, it contains great background material for those interested in it.
C/H: H5, P4, $20 – 40

Price, Robert. *Scotland's Golf Courses.* (Aberdeen, Scotland: Aberdeen University Press, 1989, 235 pages, ISBN 008-037958-3). Focusing on the geology of the landforms on which courses have been built, this book describes those in the homeland of golf. With the playing fields of the game occupying increasing acreage, along with increasing ability to modify landforms by moving earth, this work is of importance to course developers and architects worldwide and is fascinating reading for anyone.
C/H: F2, D3, C1, M1, H3, P1, T3, $35 – 50

Quirin, Dr. William L. *America's Linksland: A Century of Long Island Golf.* (Chelsea, MI: Sleeping Bear Press, 202, 279 pages, ISBN 1-58536-087-2). A tour through the history of Long Island, New York's golf heritage, concentrating on the design of the classic courses, the men who built them and the environmental conditions that made them possible.
C/H: D3, C2, M1, H5, P4, $35 – 45

Quirin, Dr. William L. *Golf Clubs of the MGA: A Centennial History of Golf in the New York Metropolitan Area.* (Elmsford, NY: Metropolitan Golf Association, 1997, 317 pages, ISBN 0-89204-590-6). A bible for the region, featuring descriptions of prominent golf clubs in the Met section, it includes a chapter on architects and a section on courses that no longer exist.
C/H: D1, H4, P4, $35 – 50

Quirin, Dr. William L. *The Garden City Golf Club Centennial Anniversary.* (Garden City, NY: The Garden City Golf Club, 1999). With a course description by Tom Doak, an Epilogue by Ben Crenshaw, information on designer Devereux Emmet and considerable material regarding club member and re-designer Walter Travis, this book includes a wealth of architectural expertise.
C/H: D3, C1, H5, P4, $50 – 75

Rando, Guy L. Co-author, *see* Jones, Rees.

Rathbun, Mickey. *Double Doglegs and Other Hazards: The Life and Work of Larry Packard.* (Kernersville, NC: Airlie Hall Press, 2002, 220 pages, ISBN 188675214-1). An enjoyable and exceedingly well-written book, this look at the career of the ninety year old course architect reveals not only the breadth and quality of his work, but the personality and good nature of the man himself. It catalogs many great contributions to the game, environment and society by this person who remained almost unheralded, although he was an influential president and longtime member of the ASGCA.
C/H: D2, C1, H4, P5, $30 – 40

Rawson, Chris. *Where Stone Walls Meet the Sea: Sakonnet Golf Club, 1899-1999.* (Little Compton, RI: Sakonnet Golf Club, 1999, 614 pages). Very much a member's club history, this massive volume also features a surfeit of information about Alex Findlay, designer of the 1901 course; and Donald Ross, designer of the current course. Ross lived at nearby Quaker Hill Farm in summer, maintaining an office at the complex. Portions of many Ross letters are excerpted, in addition to details of construction and early maintenance.
C/H: D3, C3, M2, H4, P3, $75 – 100

Ray, Edward. *Inland Golf.* (London, England: T. Werner Laurie Ltd., 1914, 245 pages). The 1912 Open champion is one of the first to discuss inland courses versus links golf. One chapter of the book deals with "The Rise of Inland Golf" another with "The Negotiation of Inland Hazards" and yet another on "The Grass Bunker". Perhaps the most illuminating chapter is on "Some Famous Inland Courses". Nothing earthshaking, but a very interesting read.
C/H: D2, C1, M2, H3, T3, $150 – 200

Ray, Edward. *Driving, Approaching, Putting.* (London, England: Methuen & Co., Ltd., 1922, 48 pages). A small book but with a few chapters on "Hazards" "The Water Hazards" and "British Golf Courses". A charming glimpse into the mind of the 1912 Open champion.
C/H: D1, C1, M1, H4, T1, $75 – 175

Richardson, Forrest L., ASGCA. *Routing the Golf Course: The Art & Science that Forms the Golf Journey.* (Hoboken, NJ: John Wiley & Sons, Inc., 2002, 511 pages, ISBN 0471-43480-9). In his teens, Richardson published a leaflet on course design for distribution to friends. Carrying this intense interest in course design forward, the author later entered private practice in course architecture. In this extensive volume, he has brought together all the elements of routing and delivered them with textbook-like precision, yet in an entertaining fashion.
C/H: D5, C1, H4, P3, $50 – 75

Richardson, Forrest L. and Mark Fine. *Bunkers, Pits and Other Hazards: A Study of Golf's Defining Character.* (Hoboken, NJ: John Wiley & Sons, Inc., 2005, 320 pages, ISBN 0-471-68367-1). Richardson and Fine have taken a very focused look at golfing hazards and how they affect the play and psychology of golfers. A new book that could easily become a classic.
C/H: F1, D5, C3, H3, $80

Riddell, Gervase Carre. *Practical Golf Course Design and Construction.* (Victoria, Australia: Gervase Riddell, 45 pages, no date, ISBN or price, booklet). A member at Royal Melbourne and designer and remodeler of courses in Australia, Riddell explains how to design a golf course.

Robertson, James K. *St Andrews – Home of Golf.* (St Andrews, Fife, Scotland: J&G Innes Ltd., 1967, 171 pages). Each hole is illustrated in detail with how-to-play-it remarks. The worldwide impact of the Old Course is outlined.
C/H: D1, H4, P4, $20 – 25

Robertson, Kolin. *Some Yorkshire Golf Courses.* (Leeds, England: Apsley Press, 1935, 132 pages). Robertson anoints himself as one of the early critics of golf courses, green committees and golf architecture. Although he confines himself to thirty-one courses in and around Yorkshire, home to Alwoodley, Leeds, Moortown, etc., his remarks are quite interesting. The pictures, graphics and advertisements sprinkled throughout are low resolution but nonetheless interesting, too. This region was the early adult home of Dr. Alister Mackenzie. Accordingly he is referred to a fair amount throughout the book.
C/H: D2, C1, M2, H4, $400 – 600

Robinson, William G. Co-author, *see* Cornish, Geoffrey.

Ross, Donald J. *Golf Has Never Failed Me.* (Chelsea, MI: Sleeping Bear Press, 1996, 258 pages, ISBN 1-886947-10-4). Written long ago before Ross, who hailed from the Scottish links, assumed his pre-eminent status in the golf hierarchy, the manuscript was discovered by architect David Gordon who gave it to the ASGCA. Its publication was sponsored by the Society with Ron Whitten as editor. Ross was accessible, friendly, casual, off the cuff, and personable. You became his friend, confidant and compatriot soon after meeting him. He was funny, irreverent and never took himself too seriously – and it all comes through in this long lost manuscript. Yet one suspects that despite his patience, Ross "did not suffer fools gladly" and could be gruff on occasion.
C/H: D4, C3, M3, H4, P4, $20 – 35

Rubenstein, Lorne. *A Season in Dornoch: Golf and Life in the Scottish Highlands.* (New York, NY: Simon and Schuster, 2001, 242 pages, ISBN 0-7432-2336-5). Societal features of the village are described together with the history, playing characteristics and lore of Royal Dornoch golf course where Donald Ross was once the greenkeeper. This eloquent work, while not specific to course architecture, impacts on the profession and art form.
C/H: H2, P2, T2, $15 – 25

Sato, Akiro. *The History of Golf Course Development Worldwide.* (Tokyo, Japan: Interaction, Inc./Environment Green Newspaper, 2001). This impressive Japanese work, published in honor of the introduction of the game to Japan a century ago, has not as yet been translated into English. Highlighting Japanese design and designers, it also profiles course architects from around the world.
C/H: D3, H3, P3, $75 – 125

Scarth, John. *A Round Forever.* (Cottesloe, Australia: Golf Partners International, 2001, 101 pages). A description of Alister Mackenzie's work in Australia and New Zealand, but slanted to Mick and Vern Morcom, father and son who worked on their own and

with Mackenzie to design and build courses. Included are Morcom's 1938 forgotten chronicles that appeared in Melbourne's newspaper, *The Herald*. They include site selection, course design, course construction, turfing the course and remodeling.
C/H: D3, C3, M2, H5, P4, $ 50 – 75

Scarth, John and Neil Crafter. *The Treasury of Australian Golf Course Architects.* (Molly Mark, Australia: Publication Pending). A collection of biographic profiles of course architects based in Australia, who are responsible for the magic and mystery of the links and courses of the Southern Hemisphere.
C/H: D2, C1, H4, P5, $50 – 75

Scott, Dr. James S., Co-author, *see* Doak, Tom.

Seagram Distillers Company. *Seagram's Guide to Strategic Golf.* (New York, NY: GEMI Studios, 1960, 34 pages, paperback, 5"x 8" format). Written as an advertising piece for Seagram's Spirits, this small, full color, paperback covers a lot of subjects lightly. However, it is interesting and was a way to interest the casual golfer in course design and strategy. The bulk of the booklet is about golf instruction and was prepared by Phil Galvano, PGA.
C/H: D1, M1, H3, $25 – 35

Seitz, Nick. Co-author, *see* Hill, David.

Seelig, Pat. *Historic Golf Courses of America.* (Dallas, TX: Taylor Publishing, 1994, 192 pages, ISBN 0-87833-858-6). Nearly fifty of the top courses in America are profiled with notes included about course architects.
C/H: D1, C1, H4, P4, $25 – 35

Shackelford, Geoff. *Alister Mackenzie's Cypress Point Club.* (Chelsea, MI: Sleeping Bear Press, 2000, 189 ages, ISBN 1-886947-64-3). Having unearthed a priceless cache of large format photographs, taken by Julian Graham of Cypress Point, in the archives of the Bancroft Library at the University of California at Berkeley, Shackelford has organised them for a hole by hole tour of the revered course with fascinating commentary. A prolific writer, Shackelford appeared on the golf scene in the mid 1990s. Since then, his eloquence and research, as demonstrated in his books and a monthly column in *Golfdom* magazine, have made a contribution to the game and its playing fields. By no means its least contribution, it has aroused interest in the literature of design by laypersons.
C/H: D4, C2, H5, P5, $25 – 35

Shackelford, Geoff. *Grounds for Golf – The History and Fundamentals of Golf Course Design.* (New York, NY: Thomas Dunne Books, 2003, 300 pages, ISBN 0-312-27808-X). A primer covering all aspects of course design, the text is enhanced with wonderful sketches and drawings by Gil Hanse, ASGCA; revealing photography by the author; and a liberal dose of quotations by great designers of the past.
C/H: D5, C1, M2, H4, P3, $20 – 30

Shackelford, Geoff. *Masters of the Links: Essays on the Art of Golf and Course Design.* (Chelsea, MI: Sleeping Bear Press, 1997, 243 pages, ISBN 1-886947-27-9). Great architectural essays on golf, including the best material ever written on golf courses, old and new, by the greats of the game, including Mackenzie, Crenshaw, Dye, Doak and Tillinghast. A section on contemporary design brings new voices to the floor. A glossary, a list of golf architecture-related websites and a

bibliography of related publications are just what the golf architecture junkie ordered. Yet there is a lot more to this comprehensive work.
C/H: D4, C3, M2, H5, P3, $20 – 25

Shackelford, Geoff. *The Captain: George C. Thomas, Jr. and His Golf Architecture.* (Santa Monica, CA: Captain Fantastic Publishing, 1996, 207 pages, no ISBN). Following a very limited edition (25) in 1995 this definitive work includes a chapter on Thomas' passionate hobby, rose hybridizing, though most of the book involves his career in course architecture. The design is handsome, the golf architecture section extensive, the photographs stunning black and whites, the course descriptions filled with bits from unpublished manuscripts, private conversations, newspaper and magazine clips and walking tours. Text is also devoted to William P. Bell, Thomas' associate on his Southern California designs. Bell was an accomplished architect in his own right and a founding member of the ASGCA.
C/H: D4, C2, H5, P3, $25 – 35

Shackelford, Geoff. *The Future of Golf in America.* (Seattle, Sasquatch Books, 2005, 229 pages, ISBN 1-57061-456-3). Geoff Shackelford is one of today's most prolific, insightful and passionate writers on course architecture. Some say he is opinionated; that is apparent in this book. Yet it does not detract from the message that golf is evolving into something different from what it has been for the past 500 or more years. Our view is that this is an important non-illustrated book intended to make us better understand forces at work that may be selling out golf's tradition and history. Whatever, we believe this is essential reading for contemporary or would-be golf course architects and indeed for all dedicated to the royal and ancient game. Shackelford's book is surely a call to arms to restore traditions and to protect examples of classic golf architecture.
C/H: D2, C1, H5, P3, $22

Shackelford, Geoff. *The Golden Age of Golf Design.* (Chelsea, MI: Sleeping Bear Press, 1999, 212 pages, ISBN 1-886947-31-7). This handsome horizontal format treatise succeeds on three levels: it is a good read, a revealing picture book and a welcome reference source. Shackelford has delved into the lives of the architects who created all the tremendous courses in American golf's first heyday, and illustrates it with a collection of 186 historic photographs and thirty drawings. Personal data and background information on the architects helps us to understand their work; ten paintings by Mike Miller, former director of golf at Riviera Country Club, enlighten the text. Sidebars describe key figures of the period such as Marion Hollins and Samuel Morse.
C/H: D4, H5, P3, $50 – 65

Shackelford, Geoff. *The Good Doctor Returns.* (Chelsea, MI: Sleeping Bear Press, 1998, 162 pages, ISBN 1-886947-43-0). A work of fiction, it features a return to earth of renowned architect, Dr. Alister Mackenzie, using his philosophy as a basis for his feelings about contemporary design. Written in the first person by frustrated course architectural assistant John Grant, the two team up for one last design.
C/H: D1, H2, $10 – 20

Shackelford, Geoff. *The Riviera Country Club: A Definitive History.* (Pacific Palisades, CA: Riviera Country Club, 1995). A history of this important American club, with an extensive biographical section detailing the life and writings of George

Thomas. Understanding the evolution of the course is a major contribution of the book, while an introduction by Ben Crenshaw provides insight into the monumental task of constructing Riviera.
C/H: D3, C2, M1, H5, P4, $50 – 75

Shackelford, Geoff. *Lines of Charm.* (Ann Arbor., MI. Ann Arber Media Group, 2005, 144 pages, ISBN 1-58726-260-6). Stories, quotes and anecdotes from a diverse assortment of characters – those master architects from golf's golden age.
C/H: P1, H1, $20

Shackelford, Geoff. Co-author, *see* Miller, Michael.

Shaw, Mark. Co-author, *see* Dye, Alice.

Shaw, Mark. Co-author, *see* Dye, Pete.

Sheehan, Lawrence, with photographs by Michael Carroll. *A Commonwealth of Golfers: A Centennial Tribute to the Game and its Players.* (Norton, MA: The Massachusetts Golf Association, 2002, ISBN 0-971-99530-3). With eloquent text and superb photography, this magnificent book is a fitting tribute to golf in a state that has made large contributions to the game. Clubs and courses in all areas of the Commonwealth are described, with course architects given their due. One essay extols the vision of pioneer turfgrass educator Lawrence S. Dickinson of the University of Massachusetts, then Massachusetts Agricultural College, who established the first ever college level course on turfgrass science. Fifty years before environmental awareness became increasingly universal, visionary Dickinson speculated that golf courses and their open spaces worked together for the betterment of the environment and society.
C/H: D2, C2, M3, H5, P4, $20 – 35

Sheehan, Lawrence. *A Passion for Golf.* (New York: Clarkson Potter, 1994, 160 pages, ISBN 0-517-59363-7). Writing in 1994, Sheehan indicated with prescience that computers would soon become valuable tools in course design. One chapter describes the office of course architect Dr. Michael Hurdzan and his library, perhaps the world's largest on golf course design.
C/H: H2, P2, $20 – 35

Shelly, Warner. *Pine Valley Golf Club: A Chronicle.* (Pine Valley, NJ: Pine Valley Golf Club, 1982, 107 pages). Unlike some club histories that contain bits and pieces of information of architectural interest, this book devotes more than half its contents to the subject. Often it shows three pictures of a hole, from when first built to what it evolved to by 1982. Written descriptions of each hole also contain insights into its architecture and its creator, George Crump.
C/H: D4, C2, P2, $50 – 150

Simpson, Tom. Co-author, *see* Wethered, H.N. and Simpson, T.

Smith, Douglas LaRue. *Winged Foot Story: The Golf, the People, the Friendly Trees.* With sketches by Rachel M. Therrien. (Mamaroneck, NY: Winged Foot Golf Club, 1984, updated 1994). A treatise of eloquence by a member of the club, Winged Foot's West and East courses are considered by many in the world of golf to be America's best thirty-six holes. This history describes the courses colorfully and tells the stories of the champions who have played on them over the eight decades of Winged Foot's life. It also deals with the genius of the architect who designed them, A.W. Tillinghast, who described the two courses as "his model". Winged Foot is a parkland course, and the book is unique for the manner in which it tells the reader about its trees and Tillie's appreciation for them.

Steeped in legend and lore with its ten national championships, Jack Nicklaus calls Winged Foot "tradition rich" due to the memorable events in the great tournaments that have been played here. Scenes pictured from golf's Golden Age up to the present are also interesting, lending proof to the words of *The New York Times* columnist, Dave Anderson, to say that "Winged Foot is golf, and golf is Winged Foot". The book is a true collector's item.

C/H: D1, M3, H5, P2, $75 – 175

Smith, Garden G. *The World of Golf.* (London, England: The Isthmian Library by A.D. Innes & Co. Limited, 1898, 330 pages). Smith and contributors W.J. MacGeagh, W.G. Van Tassel Sutphen and Miss Amy Pascoe, cover the finest clubs of the era, etiquette, golfing style, golf in America and a chapter on "The Making and Keeping of Golf Courses". On the eve of the Heathland Era, Smith laments that "there are few suitable spots left on our coast" for golf and suggests how inland sites can be transformed. He also cites existing hazards and how planners can mimic them in differing environments. Finally, Smith cautions that:

Any man who dreams that the golf course which he has laid out will meet with universal approval, is doomed to disappointment. Let them rave. Look to your putting greens, your tees, and your hazards, and let the golf take care of itself.

C/H: D3, M3, H4, P3, $300 – 400

Sorensen, Gary L. *The Architecture of Golf.* (Self-published by Gary L. Sorensen, 1976, 106 pages, paperback, 8½"x11" format). We believe that this well done publication was a distillation of his Ph.D. thesis in landscape architecture from Texas A & M. It covers all aspects of the design process and was illustrated by the author. He also did a complete job researching and citing his references, so that it is eminently scholarly. Mr. Sorensen was briefly active as a course architect.

C/H: F3, D4, C3, M2, H3, $125 – 200

Soutar, Daniel G. *The Australian Golfer.* (Sydney, Australia: Angus & Robertson, 1906, 280 pages). Originally from Carnoustie, Scotland, Soutar spent much of his career in Australia compiling an impressive competitive record. This is believed to be the first book on golf published in Australia and includes a chapter on course architecture.

C/H: D1, $200 – 300

Spander, Art. Co-author, *see* Mulvoy, Mark.

Steel, Donald. *Classic Golf Links of Great Britain and Ireland* (USA Edition: *Classic Golf Courses of England, Scotland, Wales and Ireland*). (Gretna, LA: Pelican Publishing, 1992, 223 pages, ISBN 0-88289-965-1). Enchanting photographs, scorecards, maps of the links and write-ups on many of the United Kingdom's finest links layouts are included. Steel is a British author, editor and architect, with many fine courses on both sides of the Atlantic to his credit.

C/H: D1, H1, P1, T5, $20 – 35

Steel, Donald. *Golf Facts and Feats.* (London, England: Guinness Superlative Ltd., 1980, 256 pages, ISBN 0-85112-242-6). Skimpy on design, yet this book includes interesting background material.
C/H: H2, $20 – 25

Steel, Donald, Peter Ryde and H.W. Wind. *Encyclopedia of Golf.* (New York, NY: Viking Press, 1975). This is one of the finest reference sources in golf with a wide range of topics covered concisely. Many courses are included and their architects.
C/H: H4, P3, T3, $20 – 35

Steel, Donald. *see* Davis, Martin.

Steinbreder, John. *Golf Courses of the US Open.* (Dallas, TX: Taylor Publishing Company, 1996, 187 pages, ISBN 0-87833-940-X). What makes the book so interesting, in addition to famous courses it features, is the mix of old photographs with new, as well as occasional references to the designers or remodelers and their intent. This is a good reference with generalized architectural observations about each course and the Opens they hosted.
C/H: C2, M1, H4, P2, $15 – 25

Stimpson, Edward S. III. *Forty One Years From Invention to Convention.* (West Falmouth, MA: The Lighthouse Press, 1995). This pamphlet, by the son of the inventor, provides a history and description of the Stimpmeter, the device that measures speed of greens, and one that has contributed to the speed of putting surfaces to the approval of some and disapproval of others. For better or for worse, the Stimpmeter, updated in 1978, has forced designers to plan flatter greens.
C/H: D1, M2, H2, P2, $20 – 25

Strawn, John. *Driving the Green.* (New York, NY: HarperCollins, 1991, 344 pages, ISBN 0-06-016659-2, and Burford Books, 1997). A descriptive non-fiction work detailing the trials and tribulations of an owner and his architect, the celebrated Arthur Hills, in bringing the development of Ironhorse Golf and County Club in Florida to a successful conclusion. Having spent months at the site before and during construction, Strawn, a historian and former Reed College professor, produced a realistic, stranger-than-fiction account of what is involved in course planning, permit acquisition, and construction. It narrates the story of the design and construction of a residential community course in West Palm Beach, Florida. Author Strawn says he was a fly on the wall during the planning, design and construction process, events scheduled for twelve months that eventually would stretch over two and a half years, a not atypical trajectory in a process made steadily more complicated by regulatory requirements.

Strawn conducted extensive interviews with the course architects, Arthur Hills and Mike Dasher, the developers, Alan Sher and Josh Muss, the land planners, the lawyers, the bureaucrats in the permitting agencies, and the contractors. The heavy equipment operators and the laborers are also central to the story, which is told from the bottom up as well as the top down.

Strawn examines the history of course design in the United States, from the early, somewhat casual style of laying out a course employed by Scottish golf professionals to the university-trained design professionals of the present. *Driving the Green* also considers the history of turfgrass development. Bermudagrass turf made golf in the South practical, helping create the historic population shift to the Sunbelt, and the evolution of the profession of golf course superintendent.

Wadsworth Golf Construction built Ironhorse, which opened in 1990. Company founder Brent Wadsworth, profiled in *Driving the Green*, is the Henry Ford of the golf course construction industry. He was not the first course builder, but he did create the contemporary model for course construction, and his influence saturates the business he pioneered.

C/H: F2, D4, C3, H4, P2, $20 – 25

Strawn, John. Author of an influential essay. See USGA *Golf, the Greatest Game.*

Sutton, Martin A.F., Editor. *Golf Courses: Design, Construction and Upkeep, Second Edition.* (Reading, England: Sutton & Sons, 1950, 192 pages). With the Great Depression over and World War II ended, but with the Korean War about to erupt, this is a monumental work for a recovering economy. Not only does it update a 1933 edition, but adds important contributions by British golf architects Philip Mackenzie Ross, Tom Simpson, C.H. Alison and C.K. Cotton, together with English born American Robert Trent Jones. The latter was starting his career, one which would impact on his art form far into the future. In the introduction, Bernard Darwin provides insight into the world of golf and its playing fields during the recovery years before Korea erupted. Following the end of that war, in 1953, Sutton's book made a major contribution to golf courses, their architects and their turf as they regained their glory following almost a quarter century of Depression and war.

C/H: D4, C4, M5, H5, P2, $350 – 450

Sutton, Martin H.F., Editor. *Golf Courses: Design, Construction and Upkeep, First Edition.* (London, England: Sutton & Sons, 1933, 152 pages). A wealth of information on putting greens, with reminiscence by H.S. Colt and design articles by T. Simpson and C.H. Alison.

C/H: D4, C4, M4, H5, P2, $450 – 550

Sutton, Martin H.F., Editor. *The Book of the Links, A Symposium on Golf.* (London, England: W.H. Smith & Sons, 1912, 212 pages). Design, fertilization, vegetation, finance and organic methods are some of the topics covered in this classic.

C/H: D4, C3, M3, H5, P2, $300 – 400

Taylor, Dawson. *St Andrews, Cradle of Golf.* (New York: A.S. Barnes and Co., 1976). Information on the history and charm of the Old Course at St Andrews is put forward by text and illustrations, together with diagrams of each hole. Course architect Robert Trent Jones provides a chapter describing the Old Course from his unique perspective.

C/H: D3, C1, H3, P2, $20 – 45

Taylor, J.H. *Golf, My Life's Work.* (London, England: Jonathan Cape, 1943). Appearing in the middle of World War II, with civilization still in the balance, this work, by a great golfer and course architect, did not receive the accolades it deserved. Yet it is important to the history of the game and the architecture of its playing fields.

C/H: D1, H3, P4, $50 – 75

Taylor, J.H. *Taylor on Golf: Impressions, Comments and Hints.* (London, England: Hutchinson & Co., 1902, 338 pages). Taylor wrote this volume at the start of his successful career. Forty-one years later, he followed with an autobiography. Here he covers every topic possible, including lengthening the courses, the acceptance of risks and the upkeep of golf links.
C/H: D2, C2, M2, H5, P3, $300 – 400

Taylor, Joshua. *The Art of Golf.* (London, England: T. Werner Laurie, 1913, 161 pages). This compendium includes instruction, rules, etiquette, greenkeeping and a chapter by brother J.H. Taylor on "The Evolution of the Bunker". Accompanied by numerous excellent early photos of important bunkers, the authors pay tribute to Tom Dunn, a pioneer among golf architects.
C/H: D2, C1, H4, P2, $75 – 125

Thomas, George C., Jr. *Golf Architecture in America: Its Strategy and Construction.* (Los Angeles, CA: The Times-Mirror Press, 1927, 342 pages). Regarded as the American classic on course design, this book has inspired generations of designers and writers. It covers many of the greatest courses of the day and why they were important, together with most aspects of design. This work has also inspired generations of designers and writers, and as a reference book helped restore course architecture following a quarter of a century of neglect during the Depression and World War II, when the art form was almost lost (Chelsea, MI: Sleeping Bear Press, 1997, 342 pages, ISBN 1-886947-14-7, facsimile edition; USGA Rare Book Collection, 1990).
C/H: D5, C4, M2, H4, P2, $50 (rep) – 900 (Orig)

Thompson, Stanley. *About Golf Courses, Their Construction and Upkeep.* Published in the 1930s, this booklet disappeared until a copy was found by one of his protégés, Geoff Cornish. Authored by Thompson, a course architect of vision who "reached for the stars" and created masterpieces such as Capilano in Vancouver, Banff and Jasper in the Canadian Rockies, St George's near Toronto and Highland Links on Cape Breton, Nova Scotia. (Revised Publication 2003 by The Stanley Thompson Society, 42 Hernshaw Crescent, Etobicoke, Ontario M9C 3M4).
C/H: D4, C2, M3, H2, $35 (rep) – 1,000 (Orig)

Tillinghast, A.W. *The Course Beautiful.* (Basking Ridge, NJ: TreeWolf Productions, 1995, 120 pages, ISBN 0-9651818-0-4). Foreword by Rees Jones. Edited and compiled by Rick and Stuart Wolffe and Bob Trebus. The first collection of essays from the architect's long writing career. In the Foreword, Rees Jones states that Tillinghast was a genius. This, and the two works that followed to complete the trilogy, prove that statement.
C/H: D4, C2, M2, H4, P3, $25 – 35

Tillinghast, A.W. *Reminiscences of the Links.* (Basking Ridge, NJ: TreeWolf Productions, 1998, 160 pages, ISBN 0-9651818-1-2). Foreword by Frank Hannigan. Edited and compiled by Wolffe, Wolffe and Trebus, the book is even richer than the first with terrific photographs, revolutionary writing and astonishing admissions. Consider the fact that Tillie took a 17 on the closing hole at Garden City, or his suggestion that some day Bethpage will rank as one of the great golfing Meccas of the world.
C/H: D4, C2, M2, H4, P3, $25 – 35

Photograph: courtesy of Superintendent Casper McCullogh

Stanley Thompson, Canadian course architect, pioneered elaborate bunker shapes at Banff Springs in the Canadian Rockies. Banff's bunkers mirror mountains in the background.

Stanley Thompson claimed that the links of Scotland are the bible of course design

Tillinghast, A.W. *Gleanings From the Wayside.* (Short Hills, NJ: TreeWolf Productions, 2001, 160 pages, ISBN 0-9651818-2-0). Foreword by G.S. Cornish. Tillinghast offers his impressions of golf in Mexico, California, San Antonio, Tulsa, Puget Sound, the Adirondacks, Michigan and many locales in between. He lets his opinions fly on trees, lengthy par 3's, winter greens, teeing grounds, sand pits, green committees and blind holes. This is the final volume of a trilogy of the writings of this truly great architect. Edited by Wolffe, Wolffe and Trebus, the trilogy is immensely significant to course design.
C/H: D4, C2, M2, H4, P3, $25 – 35

Tillinghast, A.W. *Planning a Golf Course.* (Philadelphia, PA: A.W. Tillinghast, Ca 1917 privately printed, 28 pages, small format (3½" x 8") paperback). Tillinghast wrote this as an advertising piece for his course design business as well as his "Lilliput Links"™, which was "an accurate working model in Plasticine … for any space, and varying in size from the large, putting green … to the more ambitious tracts of several acres". The booklet features many sketches and explanations of strategic design of various golf holes designed by Tillinghast, in the same simple style as he used in his articles on design when he wrote the column "Our Green Committee Page" for *Golf Illustrated.*
C/H: D2, C1, H4, P3, $1,000 – 1,500

Tolhurst, Desmond. *Golf at Merion.* (Ardmore, PA: Merion Golf Club, 1989, 176 pages, ISBN 0-9623346-0-X). The intrinsic value of this club history to course architects and others is that it describes each hole and illustrates how the existing hole has changed from its original design. It is intensely interesting to see how this historic course has evolved. Truly this work is a history lesson and shows why Merion is a classic. Early chapters focus on the design by Hugh Wilson. The book has been expanded and republished in 2005.
C/H: F1, D2, C1, H3, $50 – 150

Tolhurst, Desmond. *St Andrew's Golf Club: The Birthplace of American Golf.* (Rye Brook, NY: Karjan Publishing, 1989, 175 pages, ISBN 0-96237). Part one is a reprint of the 1938 history, written by H.B. Martin, which places the actions taken by John Reid and his friends, to establish the first golf club in America, into historical context. Part two includes the redesign of the course by Jack Nicklaus.
C/H: D3, C2, H5, P2, $25 – 45

Tooby, J. Co-editor, *see* Barkow, J.

Travis, Walter J. *Practical Golf.* (New York & London: Harper & Brothers Publishers, 1901, 225 pages). This comprehensive book examines all aspects of the game of golf, but the information most relevant to the field of golf architecture is found in Chapter XII, "The Construction and Upkeep of Courses". Travis provides a broad critique of the scores of new layouts appearing around the United States at the turn of the century. "There are comparatively few golf-links in this country, in the true sense of the term, while there are hundreds of courses. Most links are situated close to the sea, and the nearer they are to the level of the sea, the better they are," he says. In Travis' opinion, the sandy soil of a true links produces "finer and less luxuriant" grasses than those grown on inland soils, and therefore leads to better

greens. Many of Travis' tenets hold true today, and his influence on golf and design is profound. Three subsequent editions were published with additional material.
C/H: D3, C2, M2, H4, P3, $75 – 125

Tufts, Richard S. *The Scottish Invasion.* (Pinehurst, NC: Pinehurst Publishers, 1962, 121 pages). Tufts provides a brief review of golf in America, particularly as it relates to Pinehurst, the early Scottish greenkeepers, professionals and Donald Ross.
C/H: D1, H4, P2, $100 – 150

Tull, A.H. *The Relationship of the Design of Golf Courses to Low Maintenance Cost.* (Self-published, 1934, 7 pages). Alfred Tull was a partner in Emmet, Emmet and Tull, Golf Course Architects in New York, when he authored the 5" square booklet. His particular focus is on greens, especially large ones, as well as advocating use of hard fescue mixtures for banks and fairways. Nothing profound in this booklet, but it is only one of a few pieces of insight from this productive designer.
C/H: D1, C1, M1, H4, $400 – 500

Tulloch, W.W. *The Life of Old Tom Morris.* (London, England: Werner, Laurie, 1908). Little was written about Old Tom's design philosophy or greenkeeping practices for this 1908 tribute, though there is a wealth of information about matches, club and ball making and his home life. (Reprints from London, England: Ellesborough Press for the Golf Course Superintendents Association of America, 1982; and Far Hills, NJ: USGA Rare Book Collection, 1992).
C/H: D1, C1, M1, H5, P5, $200 (rep) – 1,500 (Orig)

Two of His Kind. (G.D. Fox). *The Six Handicap Golfer's Companion.* (London, England: Mills and Boon, Ltd., 1909, 148 pages). This oddly titled book has a chapter written by a course architect, who wrote a chapter "On Handicapping and Other Points". Colt, who was that architect, was an excellent player and it is interesting to read his views on a golf related subject other than course design.
C/H: H2, $50 – 75

Tyler, Lee. *The Case of the Missing Links – A Golf Mystery.* (Santa Barbara, CA: Fithian Press, 1999, 190 pages, ISBN 1-56474-302-0). The setting for this work of fiction is Pebble Beach, California, home and business headquarters of Sheldon R. Moore III, the most famous (and most reviled) course architect in the world. Someone has stolen the only set of plans for his best yet course design. The fact that he, himself, did not design it, nor any of his other courses, although he put his name on all, becomes apparent in this tale of golf, greed, and tongue in cheek skullduggery. Author Tyler wins points for a realistic description of a mysterious profession.
C/H: Recreational, not educational, $10 – 25

Tyler, Lee. *The Teed Off Ghost.* (Santa Barbara, CA: Fithian Press, 2002, 205 pages, ISBN 1-56474-389-6). The Kohala Coast of the big island of Hawaii is widely regarded as a "hotbed" of golf. But will the newest and most innovative of the resort area's courses be able to open for play? It would seem to be haunted by malicious and spooky spirits. Part local lore, part Hawaiian history, and all golf, this fiction story has a course superintendent as a principal character.
C/H: Recreational, not educational, $10 – 25

United States Golf Association. *Golf: The Greatest Game.* (New York: NY: Harper Collins, 1992, 271 pages, ISBN 0-06-017135-9). An anthology by persons widely known in the world of golf, this book celebrates the first 100 years of the game in the United States. "The Architect's Vision" by Tom Doak is insightful, detailed, comprehensive, thought provoking and enjoyable reading. Another chapter, by John Strawn, provides a concise history of the USGA.
C/H: D2, H5, P1, $15 – 30

Uzzell, Thomas. *Golf in the World's Oldest Mountains.* (Montreal, Canada: The Manoir Richelieu, 46 pages). Written as a hard cover advertising piece in book form, it is a hole by hole account of the Herbert Strong designed Manoir Richelieu Golf Course on Murray Bay in Quebec. Each hole has two drawings, one plan view and the other as a tee to green cross section, along with a picture of it. Mr. Strong is often credited for his design genius. This book provides a glimpse into the work of a skilled, but not well-known designer.
C/H: D3, C1, M1, H4, P3, $800 – 1,000

Vardon, Harry. *How to Play Golf.* (Philadelphia, PA: George W. Jacobs & Co., 1912, 187 pages). One of six books Vardon authored during his career, this volume offered the chapter "Golf Course Architecture". Vardon lobbies for a strategic or heroic philosophy, rather than the common penal style of his day. "It is a good thing to tempt a player to go boldly for the pin, and he is apt to become frightened (and reasonably so) when he knows that the slightest excess of courage may bring irretrievable disaster upon his head".
C/H: D2, C1, H3, $200 – 300

Vardon, Harry. *The Complete Golfer.* (New York, NY: Doubleday, Page & Co., 1905, 340 pages). Over twenty editions of this book were later published until a final printing in 1928. Instruction, competition, impressions of courses and personal matters were contained, as well as a chapter on "The Construction of Courses". It is interesting to note that Vardon cautioned, "A good course is not made in a day or a week. Perhaps the cleverest and most ingenious constructor could not in a whole year make one which was in all respects the best that the land could give".
C/H: D2, C1, H3, $200 – 300

Ward-Thomas, Pat, Herbert Warren Wind, Charles Price and Peter Thomson. *The World Atlas of Golf.* (New York, NY: Random House, 1976). With a Foreword by Alistair Cooke, written by a team of acclaimed golf writers, and superbly illustrated, this book ranks among the most beautiful and informative writings related to course design. It describes the spread of golf around the world from Scotland. Summations of famous courses worldwide invariably include mention of their architects. Peter Thomson, one of the authors and five times winner of the Open, is an acclaimed Australian course architect with many courses "down under" to his credit.
C/H: D3, C2, M2, H4, P4, T5, $25 – 50

Weeks, Edward. *Myopia, A Centennial Chronicle, 1875-1975.* (Hamilton, MA: Myopia Hunt Club, 1975, 151 pages, Library of Congress Catalog # 75-34768). Though Myopia's membership has always been equally divided between equestrian and golfing interests, the golf course was so highly regarded that the Club hosted four

US Opens in its early years. Herbert Leeds, captain of Myopia and designer of the course, was a legendary character, and this book pays homage to him as well as his golf courses and the Club itself. Author Weeks, a Myopia member, was at one time the controversial but famous editor of *The Atlantic Monthly*.
C/H: H4, P2, $75 – 100

Wethered, H.N. *The Perfect Golfer.* (London, England: Methuen & Co., 1931, 246 pages). A lengthy chapter titled "The Perfect Architecture" starts out theoretically, speaks of artistry in the landscape and gets down to specifics of bunkering and "simplicity and restraint of design".
C/H: D2, H3, P2, $175 – 250

Wethered, H.N. and T.C. Simpson. *The Architectural Side of Golf.* (London, England: Longmans, Green & Co., 1929). Regarded by some as the British classic on the subject, this comprehensive discussion of course design features fascinating insights and examples, punctuated with Simpson's ink sketches with color washes, so detailed that a golfer might say "I can read that green". (Worcestershire, England: Grant Books, 1995, 211 pages, ISBN 0-907186-55-6, with a Foreword by Arthur Hills, ASGCA, facsimile edition).
C/H: D5, C4, M3, H5, P3, $150 (rep) – 2,400 (LTD)

Wethered, H.N. and T.C. Simpson. *Design for Golf.* (Norwich, England: Sportsman Book Club, 1952, 203 pages). Less expensive and subsequent printing of the first edition.
C/H: D5, C4, M3, H5, P3, $40 (rep) – 125 (Orig)

Wethered, Joyce and Roger with Bernard Darwin, Horace Hutchinson and T.C. Simpson. *The Game of Golf, The Lonsdale Library Volume IX.* (London, England: Seeley, Service & Co., Ltd., 1931, 251 pages). Simpson contributes four chapters on architecture and upkeep to this classic compilation. Photographs and drawings are used to enlighten the works of the classic designers of the day, with many examples cited.
C/H: D4, C4, M4, H5, P1, $60 – 100

Wethered, Roger. Co-author of *The Game of Golf, The Lonsdale Library*, Volume X.

Wexler, Daniel. *Lost Links: Forgotten Treasures of Golf's Golden Age.* (Chelsea, MI: Clock Tower Press, 2003, 240 pages, ISBN 1-932202-03-X). This is a companion volume to his first. It details a dozen courses described in *The Missing Links*, but is now fully fleshed out with more complete information, as well as chapters on lost nines and lost individual holes at famous clubs. There is also a section of maps of prominent golfing cities with locales noted where there used to be courses.
C/H: D1, C1, H3, P2, $20 – 35

Wexler, Daniel. *The Missing Links.* (Chelsea, MI: Sleeping Bear Press, 2000, 222 pages, ISBN 1-886947-60-0). A handsomely produced book, detailing the sad stories of some of the most important American golf courses ever built, now gone forever. From George Thomas' El Caballero in Tarzana, California to Charles Blair Macdonald's Lido Golf Club on Long Island, dozens of terrific courses have been lost to development, neglect, bad business practices failed to attract audience, but most of all the dismal state of course development from 1929 to the end of the Korean War in 1953.
C/H: D2, C1, H4, P4, $20 – 35

Wexler, Daniel. *The Golfer's Library: A Reader's Guide to Three Centuries of Golf Literature.* (Sports Media Group, 2500 South State Street, Ann Arbor, M148104, 2004, 477 pages. ISBN 1-58726-107-3). A wonderful bibliography of golf literature and a book that includes an equally wonderful section concerning books on course design. Along the way there is a gratifying sentence by Wexler: "...I am one who believes strongly that golf's greatest feature is the uniqueness of its playing fields...".
$25

Whigham, H.J. *How to Play Golf.* (Chicago, IL: Herbert S. Stone & Co., 1897, 335 pages). This remarkable book included early American instruction, the first use of action photography, advice for staging tournaments, with the 1898 national results, and a chapter "The Making of a New Course". Whigham's thirty page discourse covers soils, turf, bunkers, trees, lay of the land, clubhouse location, routing, distances, rolling, watering and putting greens. Son-in-law of C.B. Macdonald, and a US Amateur champion in his own right, in a section titled "Benefit of Better Courses" Whigham writes "I am confident that the gradual improvement in the various courses all over the country will make golf more and more desirable for its own sake, and not for the glory or rewards which at present give it a spurious value".
C/H: D2, C1, M2, H3, P3, $250 (rep) – 450 (Orig)

Whiteway, Doug. Co-author, *see* Huck, Barbara

Whitten, Ronald, with photography by Theres Airey. *Gentleman Joe Lee, Fifty Years of Golf Design.* (Boynton Beach, FL: Joe Lee Scholarship Foundation, Inc., 2002). Intrinsically this is course architect Joe Lee's autobiography with celebrated author Ronald Whitten's touch. Lee's courses are widely admired for their beauty, strategy, and beneficial impact on the environment. His colleagues invariably described Joe Lee as a "true gentleman".
C/H: D2, C2, H3, P5, $35 – 50

Whitten, Ronald E. Co-author, *see* Cornish, Geoffrey.

Wind, Herbert Warren. *Following Through.* (New York, NY: Tickner & Fields, 1985, 414 pages, ISBN 0-89919-398-6). A compilation of Wind's eloquent pieces that appeared in *The New Yorker* over a period of some twenty years. Wind is a champion of architects; he elevated their status through his widely respected writing and a stirring address to the ASGCA in 1977.
C/H: D1, H3, P3, T1, $10 – 20

Wind, Herbert Warren. *The Story of American Golf.* (New York, NY: Simon and Schuster, 1956). Although sketchy, important information on course design is included.
C/H: D1, H4, P3, $300 – 400 (Orig)

Wind, Herbert Warren. *The Story of American Golf.* (New York, NY: Alfred A. Knopf, 1975, 592 pages, ISBN 0-394-49020-7). This third edition has a section devoted to contemporary architecture in the 1970s.
C/H: D1, H4, P4, $50 – 75

Wind, Herbert Warren (Editor). *The Complete Golfer.* (New York, NY: Simon and Schuster, 1954). Authored in the recovery years following World War II, this cornerstone compilation of mid-century includes a chapter by Robert Trent Jones with routing plans of eight famous courses. Some say the book started Wind on his road to fame while Jones' chapter added to his.
C/H: D1, H3, P3, T1, $35 – 45

Wind, H.W. Co-author, *see* Steel, Donald.

Wind, H.W. Co-author, *see* Ward-Thomas, Pat.

Windeler, Robert. *Links With a Past: The First 100 Years of the Los Angeles Country Club, 1897-1997.* (Los Angeles, CA: The Los Angeles Country Club, 1997, 311 pages, ISBN 0-9660424-0-9). This is said to be the finest club history ever produced with detailed information on architects Herbert Fowler and George Thomas and their role in the design of the two courses at the Los Angeles Country Club. Elegant design, stunning photography and premium materials in the book and slipcase make this a highly desirable volume with valuable information.
C/H: D2, C2, M1, H5, P4, $60 – 80

Wright, Harry. *A Short History of Golf in Mexico and the Mexico City Country Club.* (New York, privately printed, 1938). Golf was introduced to Mexico in 1900. By December of that year, the San Pedro Golf Club had been organised, playing on clay greens. New courses followed, and the first big tournament was held in 1905 at the San Pedro Club with seven US golfers participating, including professionals Willie Anderson, Bernard Nicholls, and Alex and Willie Smith. Willie, then engaged as professional at the San Pedro Club, soon laid out the Mexico City Country Club and went on to win the Open Championship of Mexico in a field that included many American and British professionals. In 1907 Willie moved the San Pedro Club to Churubusco, where he laid out another course. Following tranquil years, the revolutionary period from 1912 to 1920 threatened golf in that nation, with Mexico's only course designer Willie Smith losing his life. His course, its bunkers and mounds were the scene of several battles. But by 1926, golf was again on the rise with a dozen clubs organised throughout the country. The Mexico Golf Association was formed that year and founder Harry Wright, author of this classic work, was elected president of the organization. Wright was also president of the Mexico City Country Club.
C/H: D2, C2, H4, P2, T1, $300 – 400

Young, Philip. *Tillinghast: Creator of Golf Courses.* (Pearl River, NY: Classics of Golf 2005). The definitive biography of one of the truly great course architects, often called "Tillie the Terror".
Special limited edition $79.00; hard cover trade edition $45.00

Young, Philip. *Golf's Finest Hour: The Open at Bethpage Black.* (Pearl River, NY: Classics of Golf 2004). The chronicle of the 2002 US Open Championship, this book provides an in depth look at the course set up and modified by Rees Jones.
ASGCA Special limited edition $45.00; hard cover trade edition $27.00

Young, Philip. *Golf For The People: Bethpage and the Black.* (Bloomington, IN: Author House). A detailed history of Bethpage, one of the largest ever golf projects.
Hard cover $19.50; Paper $10.50; Electronic $3.95

Golf is at its best when played in natural environments. North American golf courses are returning to traditional settings. (Devil's Pulpit, near Toronto, Canada: Hurdzan/Fry Golf Course Design)

Changes in color, texture, and elevation enhance visual interest with such spectacular settings
Course features can be quite simple, functional and easy to maintain
(The River Course, Keystone, Colorado: Hurdzan/Fry Golf Course Design)

Hole 12, Blackrock Country Club, Hingham, Massachusetts, course architect Brian Silva, ASGCA

Hole 15, Shaker Hills Golf Club, Harvard, Massachusetts, course architect Brian Silva, ASGCA

Annuals and Yearbooks

Literature of course design has included many golfing yearbooks and annuals since they first appeared in the 1880s. Some have contained brief manifestos from course designers that would otherwise go unpublished; and have provided a timely snapshot of the profession in specific eras. Course architects, including Tom Bendelow and W.N. Follet, have served as editors. This is a partial list of annuals, arranged alphabetically by the most important word in the title.

American Annual Golf Guide and Yearbook. (New York, NY: Angus Press, 1916-1931); Editors P.C. Pulver, W.H. Follet, a course architect who edited editions from 1920 to 1923, John G. Anderson and J. Lewis Brown.

D.B. Golf Annual. Auckland, New Zealand, 1974-1980; James Wallace, Editor.

DeWitt's Golf Year Book. Miami, FL: DeWitt's Golf Year Book, 1953, with editions in 1958 and 1960; William O. DeWitt, Editor and publisher.

Fraser's Golf Directory and Yearbook. Montreal, Canada and New York, NY: Fraser Publishing, 1923-1937; Robert Ness Balsillie, Editor. Name changed to Fraser's International Golf Year Book in 1924, thereafter encompassing golfing events worldwide.

Golf Almanac. Lincolnwood, IL: Publications International, 1993; David Aretha, Editor.

Golf Clubs of the Empire. London, England: The Golfing Annual, 1925-1932; T.R. Clougher, Editor.

Golf Digest Almanac. Norwalk, CT: Golf/Tennis Digest, 1984-2003; William Davis, Editor. This publication includes "100 Greatest Courses," "Best Public Courses" and "Directory of Courses You Can Play" each list citing architectural credit.

Golf Digest Places to Play. New York, NY: Fodor Travel Publications, several editions. A listing of courses in the US, Canada, Mexico and the Caribbean as rated by public players who visit them. Course architects are named.

Golf in Europe. Zurich, Switzerland, 1961-1972; H.T. Osterman, Editor.

The Golfer's Handbook. Cupar, Scotland: John Innes Publishing, followed by John Menzies and later Simpkin Marshall, 1899-2003; Robert Forgan (and many others) Editors.

The Golfer's Year. London, England: Nicholas Kaye Ltd., 1950-1953; Tom Scott and Webster Evans, Editors. The 1951 edition included a memorable essay by course architect Sir Guy Campbell on "How Golf Courses Evolved".

The Golfer's Year Book 1930. (New York, NY: The Golfer's Year Book, Inc., 1930, 690 pages). This year book contains an essay by golf architect Charles Banks entitled "Golf Course Design and Construction" and one by scientist Dr. John Monteith on "USGA Green Section Audits its Work". Articles are short but full of interesting detail.
C/H: F2, D3, C3, M1, H4, $35 – 50

Golfer's Yearbook. New York: NY: National Golf Review, 1931-1939; William Richardson and Lincoln Werden, Editors. The 1932 Edition featured an article by Robert Tyre Jones Jr., regarding Augusta National and titled "The Ideal Golf Course". The 1938 Edition also featured an essay by a then little known but dynamic young architect of that day, namely Robert Trent Jones, and one by an established designer, Alfred Tull of the firm of Emmet, Emmet and Tull. Both architects later became prominent in the American Society of Golf Course Architects. "Principles of Good Architecture" by Jones was an influential piece while "Modern Golf Course Construction" by A.H. Tull included prescient information on soil mixes for greens and other areas of a course.

Golfing Annual. London, England: Horace Cox Publishers, 1888-1910; C.R. Bauchope, Editor, followed by David Scott Duncan. The 1889-1890 Edition had one of the first written pieces on course design, twelve pages penned by Horace Hutchinson and titled "How to Lay Out Links and How to Preserve Them".

Harpers Official Golf Guide. New York, NY: Harper & Brothers, 1900–1902, William G. Sutphen, Editor. This is a continuation of the course listings from Newman's Official Golf Guide.

Heineken World of Golf. London, England: Stanley Paul Publishers, 1993— ; Nick Edmund, Editor.

Nisbett's Golf Yearbook. London, England: James Nisbett Publisher, 1905-1914; James L. Low, Editor.

The Official Golf Guide. New York, NY: Century Engraving Co., 1899; Josiah Newman, publisher and Editor. This is one of the first publications in the US to mention course designers.

Pelham Golf Year. London, England: Pelham Books; 1981, Louis Stanley, Editor.

John Player's Yearbook. London, England: Queen Anne Press, 1973-1977; George Simms, Editor. Later the name was changed to World of Golf, published by Macdonald and James of London, 1978-1980, with an American edition published by Two Continents, 1977.

Playfair Golf Annual. London, Playfair Books Ltd., 1950-1953; Leonard Crawley, Editor. The four volumes included a column on course architecture; the 1950 Edition featured a piece by Henry Cotton with five design principles of "cardinal importance". In 1951, the architecture entry was penned by Sir Guy Campbell and titled "The Best Ever? The Links Anthology of a Golf Course Artificer" in which he selected the best holes in the United Kingdom.

Reference Yearbook of Golf. Canoga Park, CA: International Golfer, 1971-1973; John C. Alicoate, Editor.

Shell's Wonderful World of Golf. Houston, TX: Shell Oil, 1964-1970; Herbert Warren Wind and Charles Price, Editors. A series of matches conducted annually between leading professional golfers at some of the world's best golf courses are described. Detailed descriptions of the venues with architectural references abound.

Spalding's Athletic Library. New York, NY: American Sports Publishers, 1893-1895; Stewart Balfour, Editor. The title was then changed to Spalding's Golf Guide, 1896-1931. Prolific course architect, Tom Bendelow, served as editor from 1907-1916.

Spalding's Golfers Yearbook. London, England: Stanley Paul Publisher, 1960; Fred Pignon, Editor.

World of Professional Golf. Cleveland, OH: IMG Publishing, 1968-2003; Mark McCormack, Editor. The modern day source on golf events throughout the world, with mentions of architects in course descriptions.

Turfgrass Science and Management

"Ever since the first golf courses were constructed in the United States in the late 1800s, significant amounts of time and money have been spent on the selection evaluation and propagation of grasses for use as playing surfaces."

James T. Snow, National Director, USGA Green Section in *Golf Course Design* by Graves and Cornish.

"Grass is the forgiveness of nature. Her constant benediction."

John J. Ingals, Senator from Kansas, 1873-1891

Adams, W.A. and R.J. Gibbs. *Natural Turf for Sport and Amenity: Science and Practice.* (Wallingford, England: CAB International, 1994, 404 pages, ISBN 0-85198-720-6). A science based information source that groups "golf courses and bowling greens", into one long chapter, and does a nice job of integrating. The comparison between bowls and greens helps to understand how to design for maintenance.
C/H: D1, C3, $35 – 55

Agnew, Michael, Ph.D. Co-author, *see* Christians, Nick.

Arthur, Jim. *Practical Greenkeeping.* (St Andrews, Scotland: The Royal and Ancient Golf Club, 1997, 271 pages, ISBN 0-907583-04-0). Consulting agronomist to The Royal and Ancient Golf Club and 500 other clubs in the United Kingdom, Arthur believes in a natural, mean-and-lean, hard-and-fast style of course preparation and maintenance as he details and illustrates personal experiences in his book.
C/H: D2, C3, M5, P2, $40 – 50

Baker, S.W., Ph.D. *Sands for Sports Turf Construction and Maintenance.* (United Kingdom: The Sports Turf Institute, 1990, 67 pages, ISBN 0-9503647-8-9). Dr. Baker is a leading European authority on sand based rootzone construction. This booklet is a brief summary of his research and experience, especially with golf greens in various European climates. It is similar to the USGA booklet on green construction, except Baker appears to be more open to alternative methods to fit certain situations. It is not very technical but highly informative.
C/H: D1, C3, M2, $15 – 30

Barron, Leonard. *Lawns and How to Make Them, Together With the Proper Keeping of Putting Greens.* (New York, NY: Doubleday, Page and Company, 1910, 174 pages). The section on putting greens was written by course architect Walter Travis. Subsequent editions were published by the National Garden Association as part of the Garden Library series.
C/H: C1, M3, H3, $30 – 40

Bavier, Michael. Co-author, *see* Witteveen, Gordon.

Beale, Reginald. *Lawns for Sports: Their Construction and Upkeep.* (London, England: Simpkin, Marshall, Hamilton, Kent & Co., 1924, 276 pages). Manager at the James Carter Company, Beale writes on golf courses and sports fields, with costs of construction, descriptions of mowing equipment, maintenance budgets, use of charcoal and other topics – accompanied by beautiful illustrations.
C/H: D3, C2, M4, H5, $150 – 300

Beale, Reginald. *The Practical Greenkeeper.* (London, England: James Carter & Co., 1907, 68 pages). Articles by Horace Hutchinson on "Manures and Compost" and Peter Lees on "Worms in Putting Greens" are included. (Note: This paperback was published for many years until at least 1936. All editions are valuable additions to a library).
C/H: D2, C3, M4, H4, $125 – 175

Beard, James B., Ph.D. *Turfgrass: Science and Culture.* (Englewood Cliffs, NJ: Prentice-Hall, 1973, 658 pages, ISBN 0-13-933002-X). Sections on turfgrass, their environments and cultural practices are included.
C/H: D2, C2, M5, H3, $35 – 50

Beard, James B., Ph.D. *Turf Management for Golf Courses.* (Minneapolis, MN: Burgess Publishing, 1982, 642 pages, ISBN 0-02-307660-7). The bible of turfgrass management for many years, it provided information on every facet of course maintenance and administration.
C/H: F1, D4, C3, M5, H3, $60 – 100

Beard, James B., Ph.D. *Turf Management for Golf Courses, Second Edition.* (Hoboken, NJ: John Wiley & Sons, 2002, 793 pages, ISBN 1-57504-092-1). In the works for sixteen years, it was published with the assistance of dozens of scientists, researchers, superintendents, administrators and golfers, with numerous updates and graphic improvements to the First Edition. This is the most comprehensive turfgrass work ever published and a tribute to its author who has made massive contributions to turfgrass science and management.
C/H: F1, D5, C4, M5, H3, $100 – 125

Beard, James B., Ph.D., Harriet J. Beard and David P. Martin. *Turfgrass Bibliography 1672-1972.* (Lansing, MI: Michigan State University Press, 1977). This is the most complete bibliography concerning turfgrass, with 16,000 entries arranged by author and 40,000 by subject. Dr. Beard, a recognized giant in this field, compiled the bibliography over a ten year period as supporting literature for "Turfgrass Science and Culture". According to the *USGA Green Section Record*, January-February, 2004, "The Beard Turfgrass Library is the finest personal collection of turf-related material in existence."

Beard, Harriet J. Co-author, *see above.*

Beard, James B., Ph.D. Co-author, *see* Tani, Toshikazu.

Brede, Doug, Ph.D. *Turfgrass Maintenance Reduction Handbook.* (Chelsea, MI: Ann Arbor Press, 2000, 374 pages, ISBN 1-57504-106-5). Brede is a Penn State graduate, with experience as an assistant superintendent at Valley Brook Country Club in Pennsylvania. He obtained advanced degrees under renowned Dr. Joe Duich. Brede writes "Reduced turf maintenance translates directly into money savings and more leisure time – not to mention less reliance on valuable natural resources". Soils, fertilizers, pesticides, mowing, renovation and "Grasses That Demand Less Maintenance" are all described.
C/H: D1, C3, M5, H3, $75 – 95

Bunnell, Todd B. Co-author, *see* McCarty, L.B.

Campbell, John. *Greenkeeping.* (Essex, England: A. Quick & Co., Ltd., 1982, 88 pages). Campbell was links supervisor at St Andrews from 1960 to 1974 and shares his theory and practice of course maintenance.
C/H: D1, C1, M3, H1, $25 – 50

Carrow, R.N., Ph.D. and R.R. Duncan, Ph.D. *Salt-Affected Turfgrass Sites.* (Hoboken, NJ: John Wiley & Sons, 1998, 301 pages, ISBN 1-57504-091-3). Salt-affected sites are on the rise due to wastewater irrigation, coastal locations of golf courses and their building in environmentally sensitive areas. This scientific discourse covers all ramifications concerning the increasing salt problem.
C/H: C1, M5, H1, $50 – 75

Carrow, R.N., Ph.D., D.V. Waddington, Ph.D., and P.E. Rieke, Ph.D. *Turfgrass Soil Fertility and Chemical Problems.* (Hoboken, NJ: John Wiley & Sons, 2001, ISBN 1-57504153-7).
C/H: C1, M5, $75 – 95

Carrow, Robert, Ph.D. and R.R. Duncan, Ph.D. *Salt-Affected Turfgrass Sites, Second Edition.* (Publication pending 2005, Hoboken, NJ: John Wiley & Sons, ISBN 0-471-47266-2).
C/H: C1, M5, H1, $70 – 80

Carrow, R.N., Ph.D. Co-author, *see* Duncan, R.R.

Casler, M.D., Ph.D. and R.R. Duncan, Ph.D. *Turfgrass Biology, Genetics, and Breeding.* (Hoboken, NJ: John Wiley & Sons, 2003, ISBN 0-471-44410-3). This work deals specifically with the science behind the major types of turfgrass.
C/H: M5, $80 – 95

Christians, Nick, Ph.D. *Fundamentals of Turfgrass Management.* (Chelsea, MI: Ann Arbor Press, 1998, 301 pages, ISBN 1-57504-051-4). Describes grasses, soils, fertilization, mowing, irrigation, insects, diseases, professional care and standards for athletic fields, lawn care and golf courses.
C/H: C1, M5, $70

Christians, Nick, Ph.D. *Fundamentals of Turfgrass Management, Second Edition.* (Hoboken, NJ: John Wiley & Sons, 2003, ISBN 0-471-45478-8).
C/H: C1, M5, $ 40 – 50

Christians, Nick, Ph.D. and Michael L. Agnew, Ph.D. *The Mathematics of Turfgrass Maintenance.* (Hoboken, NJ: John Wiley & Sons, 2000, 176 pages, ISBN 1-57504-147-2) Popular aid to calculating fertilizers, areas, pesticides, irrigation and seeding amounts together with numerous other calibrations.
C/H: M5, $35 – 50

Cobb, Patricia P., Ph.D. Co-author, *see* Schumann, Gail.

Crockford, Claude. *The Complete Golf Course: Turf and Design.* (Victoria, Australia: Thomson Wolveridge & Associates, 1993, 150 pages, ISBN 0-646-13031-5). Crockford, course manager at Royal Melbourne for forty years, shares his secrets of course maintenance.
C/H: D3, C3, M4, H2, $125 – 175

Cubbon, M.H., Ph.D., and M.J. Markuson. *Soil Management for Greenkeepers.* (Amherst, MA: Self-published, 1933, 152 pages). Cubbon was an assistant professor of agronomy and Markuson was an assistant professor of Agriculture engineering at Massachusetts State College. This was probably the first textbook specifically on soils, written for greenkeepers. It was the definitive text of its day and covered not only the science of soils, including chapters on "Fertilization of Golf Greens",

"Fertilization of Fairways" and "Watering Greens". The final chapters were devoted to teaching basic Agricultural engineering skills.
C/H: C2, M3, H4, $200 – 300

Daniel, W.H., Ph.D. and R.P. Freeborg, Ph.D. *Turf Manager's Handbook.* (Cleveland, OH: Harcourt Brace Jovanovitch, 1979, Library of Congress Catalog # 78-71794). Authored by two of the nation's leading turfgrass scientists, this is a convenient and reliable work covering every aspect of turf culture and maintenance.
C/H: D1, C3, M4, H3, $25 – 35

Davis, Fanny Fern. Contributed an essay, *see* United States Department of Agriculture.

DeFrance, J.A. Contributed an essay, *see* United States Department of Agriculture.

Dernoeden, Peter H., Ph.D. *Creeping Bentgrass Management: Summer Stresses, Weeds and Selected Maladies.* (Hoboken, NJ: John Wiley & Sons, 2000, 133 pages, ISBN 1-57504-143-X). Comprehensive discussions of stresses on creeping bentgrass with sections on biological approaches, new generation fungicides and plant growth regulators.
C/H: C1, M5, $35 – 45

Diesburb, Kenneth. Co-author, *see* Dunn and Diesburb.

Duncan, R.R., Ph.D. and R.N. Carrow, Ph.D. *Seashore Paspalum: The Environmental Turfgrass.* (Hoboken, NJ: John Wiley & Sons, 2000, 281 pages, ISBN 1-57504-141-3). An excellent source of history, culture, management and benefits of a species that is gaining increased favor in salt-affected areas.
C/H: M5, $55 – 70

Duncan, R.R., Ph.D. Co-author, *see* Carrow, R.N.

Dunn, John and Kenneth Diesburb. *Turf Management in the Transition Zone.* (Hoboken, NJ: John Wiley & Sons, 2004, ISBN 0-471-47609-9). The only book devoted entirely to this subject.
C/H: M5, $50 – 75

Elliott, Monica L., Ph.D. Co-author, *see* Schumann, Gail.

Emmons, R.D. *Turfgrass Science and Management.* (Albany, New York. Delmar Publishers 1984). Professor Emmons of the Plant Science Department of the State University of New York at Cobleskill has taught many who have been successful managers of golf courses and other large green swards.

Escritt, J.R. *ABC of Turf Culture.* (Todworth, Surrey, England: Kaye and Ward, Ltd., 1978, 248 pages, ISBN 0-7182-174-X). It covers care of sports fields including golf courses and generalized maintenance programs based upon season of the year.
C/H: M1, H2, $10 – 20

Evans, R.D.C. Co-author, *see* Hayes, P.

Everest, J.W. Co-author, *see* McCarty, L.B.

Farley, G.A. *Golf Course Commonsense.* (Cleveland Heights, OH: Farley Libraries, 1931, 256 pages). The first book on course maintenance written by a woman includes many observations and suggestions presented in a logical and down-to-earth manner. Gertrude Farley was an immensely constructive secretary to the GCSAA in its early years. She endeavored to keep her status as a woman hidden by using only her initials. Hopefully that issue has disappeared from contemporary society.
C/H – D1, C2, M4, H5, $300 – 400

Ferguson, Marvin, Ph.D. *Building Golf Holes for Good Turf Management.* (New York, NY: USGA Green Section, 1968, 55 pages, booklet). Analysis of the problems that lead to difficult and costly maintenance of golf holes when they are improperly designed and constructed, it includes an early description of USGA green construction. Dr. Ferguson became a member of the ASGCA.
C/H: D1, C3, M1, H3, $15 – 25

Finger, Joseph S. *The Business End of Building or Rebuilding a Golf Course.* (Houston, TX: Self-published, 1972, 50 pages). An engineer by training, a Texan by birth and breeding and friend of both authors of this work, Joe had strong methodical points of view. An ASGCA member, he designed many excellent golf courses and his methods are sound even thirty years later, making this rare piece worth looking for. Joe Finger was a perfectionist.
C/H: D3, C2, M1, P3, $25 – 35

Foy, John H., Director, Florida USGA Green Section. "Bermudagrass Putting Greens, Establishment and Grow-in" found in *Golf Course Design* by Robert Muir Graves and Geoffrey S. Cornish.
C/H: C2, M4, $N/A

Freeborg, R.P., Ph.D. Co-author, *see* Daniel, W.H.

Fry, Jack, Ph.D. *Applied Turfgrass Science and Physiology.* (Hoboken, NJ: John Wiley & Sons, 2004, 320 pages, ISBN 0-471-47270-0).
C/H: C2, M3, $85

Gibbs, R.J. Co-author, *see* Adams, W.A.

Grau, Fred V., Ph.D. Contributed an essay to *Grass: The Yearbook of Agriculture 1948*, see United States Department of Agriculture.

Hannon, Ed. *The Site Calculations Pocket Reference.* (New York, NY: John Wiley & Sons, 1999, 410 pages, ISBN 0-471-32435-3). A valuable, comprehensive, on-site reference guide for use in the field.
C/H: D1, C3, M2, $35 – 40

Hanson, A.A. and F.V. Juska, Editors. *Turfgrass Science.* (Madison, WS: American Society of Agronomy, 1969, 715 pages, Library of Congress Catalogue # 78-100536). One of a series of monographs in the Agronomy series with two chapters specific to golf courses in addition to essays on soil, ecology, insects, weeds and historical uses of turf under varying climatic conditions.
C/H: C2, M3, H2, $20 – 35

Hayes, P. and R.D.C. Evans and S.P. Isaac. *The Care of the Golf Course.* (West Yorkshire, England: Sports Turf Research Institute, 1992, 262 pages, ISBN 1-873431-02-3). A thorough analysis of every facet of course maintenance ranging from drainage to disease and administration to the effects of winter play. A comprehensive bibliography is included.
C/H: D3, C3, M4, H2, $20 – 40

Henderson, Peter. *Making and Maintaining Golf Links.* (New York: NY Peter Henderson & Co., 1912, 10 pages). A booklet with advice on making and repairing putting greens as well as renovating fairways. A section "Heresy" addresses heat stress and the timing of seeding.
C/H: D1, C1, M2, H5, $125 – 150

118

Henderson, Peter & Co. *Sports Turf for Golf Courses and Athletic Fields.* (New York, NY: Peter Henderson & Co., 1928). A soft cover book with a chapter on course design using Hershey Country Club, Pennsylvania, for illustration purposes. Nicely diagramed and fairly good quality pictures of courses and golfers.
C/H: D3, C3, M2, H3, $500 – 700

Hummel, Norman Jr., Ph.D. "Draft Specifications – USGA and Similar Greens, and Draft Specifications – California Greens" found in *Golf Course Design* by Robert Muir Graves and Geoffrey S. Cornish.
C/H: C3, $5 – 10

Hurdzan, Michael J., Ph.D. *Golf Greens: History, Theory, Design and Construction.* (2004, Hoboken, NJ: John Wiley & Sons, ISBN 0-471-45945-3). Intended to be a definitive text, this work is written to appeal to golfers, greenkeepers, design and construction professionals and green chairmen. Golf green development continues to evolve rapidly in response to new grasses, environmental concerns, irrigation issues, cost and long-term maintenance. This book challenges some widely held beliefs and confirms others. It also provides guidance for building greens to fit difficult sites and small budgets.
C/H: F2, D5, C5, M3, H5, P2, $60 – 95

Imperial Chemical Industries, Ltd. *The Improvement of Lawns, Golf Greens and Fairways.* (London, England: Imperial Chemical Industries Ltd, 1930, 12 pages, small format (7" x 4.5") paperback). An interesting thing about this booklet is the cover showing a basket flagstick on a green. In the United States we associate basket flagsticks with Merion Golf Club, although they are common in Europe. Imperial Chemical made "sulphate of ammonia and also a mixture of sulphate of ammonia and calcined sulphate of iron". These materials were once touted to "kill weeds and make a thicker and more uniform sward which wears well and resists drought". A very good source for those researching early maintenance practices in Europe.
C/H: M2, H3, $35 – 50

Isaac, S.P. Co-author, *see* Hayes, P.

Juska, F.V. Co-editor, *see* Hanson, A.A.

Karnok, Keith J., Ph.D., Editor. *Turfgrass Management Information Directory.* (Chelsea, MI: Ann Arbor Press, 2000, 256 pages, ISBN 1-57504-148-0). A useful compendium of information that starts with key personnel throughout the industry and moves on to seeding rates, climatic maps, conversions and calculations, web sites, poison centers, glossary and publications.
C/H: M4, $50 – 60

Krans, Jeffrey, Ph.D. *Turfgrass Biology.* (Publication pending 2005, Hoboken, NJ: John Wiley & Sons, ISBN 0-471-47263-8).

Labbance, Bob and Gordon Witteveen. *Keepers of the Green: A History of Golf Course Management.* (Chelsea, MI: Ann Arbor Press, 2002, 267 pages, ISBN 1-57504-164-2). Published for the seventy-fifth anniversary of the GCSAA, this volume traces the history of greenkeeping from its inception through the many advances of the twentieth century, highlighting the people, inventions and techniques that have improved golf course management. Intrinsically it is a history of the GCSAA.
C/H: M2, H5, P3, $40 – 50

Lees, Peter. *Care of the Green.* (New York, NY: C.B. Wilcox, 1918, 93 pages). Lees was greenkeeper at Royal Mid-Surrey in England. He came to America in 1912 to build courses for Charles Blair Macdonald, specifically Lido Golf Club on Long Island. He then built courses for other architects including A.W. Tillinghast and did some design work on his own, notably Hempstead Golf Club on Long Island and the first nine of Ives Hill Country Club, Watertown, NY.
C/H: D1, C3, M3, H5, P2, $3,500 – 4,000

Lilly, Sharon. *Golf Course Tree Management.* (Hoboken, NJ: John Wiley & Sons, 1999, 216 pages, ISBN 1-57504-117-0). Written specifically for the golf industry, this book provides readers with the tools needed to manage trees. Probably this is the first book written on tree care on golf courses. Many well-known experts contribute to its comprehensive text. It is therefore a must for course design and maintenance professionals..
C/H: D1, C1, M5, H1, $35 – 55

Liu, Haibo. *Basic Turfgrass Manual.* (Publication pending 2005, Hoboken, NJ: John Wiley & Sons, ISBN 0-471-47265-4).

Love, William R., ASGCA. *An Environmental Approach to Golf Course Development.* (*See* Love, William R., *pages 85 and 133*).

MacDonald, James. *Lawns, Links & Sportsfields.* (London, England: Country Life, 78 pages, 1923). Three chapters on golf courses are included.
C/H: D1, C1, M3, H4, $175 – 250

Macself, A.J. *Grass.* (London, England: Cecil Palmer, 1924, 204 pages). Macself wrote several books on turf and lawn care in the mid 1920s; only this one has a chapter on "Golf Links and Putting Greens".
C/H: F1, D1, C1, M2, H2, $35 – 75

Madison, J.H. *Practical Turfgrass Management.* (New York, N.Y. Van Nostrand 1971). This landmark work still exerts an impact on turfgrass science as does its companion volume *Principles of Turfgrass Culture* published the same year by the same publisher.

Maloney, Thomas R. Co-author, *see* Milligan, Robert.

Markuson, M.J. Co-author, *see* Cubbon, M.H., Ph.D.

Martin, David P. Co-author, *see* Beard, James.

McCarty, Bert, Ph.D. *Best Golf Course Management Practices.* (Upper Saddle River, NJ: Prentice Hall, 2001, 673 pages, ISBN 0-13-088359-X). This book is a compilation of articles written by turfgrass scientists from around the country with sections on best grasses, soil management practices, construction and establishment guidelines, fertilization programs, irrigation suggestions, management, pest control, pesticide and nutrient methods with accompanying charts, graphs and photos to illustrate.
C/H: D1, C3, M5, $75 – 95

McCarty L.B., Ph.D. and Grady Miller, Ph.D. *Managing Bermudagrass Turf: Selection, Construction, Cultural Practices and Pest Management Strategies.* (Hoboken, NJ: John Wiley & Sons, 2002, 221 pages, ISBN 1-57504-163-4). A reference source devoted to the subject, it is put forward with clarity and precision.
C/H: C2, M5, $55 – 65

McCarty, L.B., J.W. Everest, D.W. Hall, T.R. Murphy, F. Yelverton. *Color Atlas of Turfgrass Weeds.* (Hoboken, NJ: John Wiley & Sons, 2004 288 pages, ISBN 1-57504-142-1). With over 575 high quality color photographs, this is a critical tool that helps develop an integrated weed management program. Subjects include weed identification, prevention of weed introduction, turfgrass management and cultural practices and selection and use of herbicides, $95

McCarty, L.B., Ian R. Rodriguez, B. Todd Bunnell and F. Clint Waltz. *Fundamentals of Turfgrass and Agricultural Chemistry.* (Hoboken, NJ: John Wiley & Sons, 2004, 384 pages, ISBN 0-471-44411-1). Written in non technical language, this book conveys basic understanding and working knowledge of chemical properties that relate to turfgrass and agricultural management, $80

Mellor, David R. *Picture Perfect: Mowing Techniques for Lawns, Landscapes, and Sports.* (Hoboken, NJ: John Wiley & Sons, 2001, ISBN 1-57504151-0). A fun look at how mowing patterns can influence how a turfscape is perceived, for better or for worse. C/H: M3, $25 – 35

Metsker, Stan, CGCS. *On the Course: The Life and Times of a Golf Course Superintendent.* (Colorado Springs, CO: Metsker Publishing, 1996, 116 pages, ISBN 0-9652838-2-8). Metsker was the superintendent at Cherry Hills Country Club and other courses in Colorado. This is his story. C/H: M2, H3, P4, $25 – 35

Miller, Grady, Ph.D. Co-author, *see* McCarty, L.B.

Milligan, Robert A. and Thomas R. Maloney. *Human Resource Management for Golf Course Superintendents.* (Hoboken, NJ: John Wiley & Sons, 2004, 192 pages, ISBN 1-57504-038-7). Every aspect of course management is covered including techniques for long- and short-term planning, employee performance, training and developing new employees and increasing communication and leadership skills. $35

Moore, James Francis, Director, Construction Education Programs, USGA Green Section. "Bermudagrass Fairways, Establishment and Grow-in" found in *Golf Course Design* by Robert Muir Graves and Geoffrey S. Cornish. C/H: C3, M4, $N/A

Murphy, T.R. Co-author, *see* McCarty, L.B.

Musser, H. Burton. *Turf Management.* (New York, NY: McGraw Hill, 1950, 1962, 356 pages, Library of Congress Catalogue # 61-17144). A publication of the USGA with contributions from superintendents. A final section in the First Edition, authored by Robert Bruce Harris, ASGCA, and Robert Trent Jones, ASGCA, is specific to course design. Musser's work was the first book on turfgrass science published in America following World War II and is a landmark. Written as a general text, it nevertheless provides the information that turfgrass managers seek. C/H: D3, C2, M4, H5, $50 – 75

Musser, H.B. *See* United States Department of Agriculture.

Murray, Dr. C.M. *Greenkeeping in South Africa.* (Cape Flats, South Africa: South African Golf, 1932, 104 pages). A collection of articles that appeared in *South African Golf* magazine. Several of them assisted courses in converting from sand to grass greens. C/H: D1, C1, M2, H4, $75 – 100

121

Nickolai, Thom. *Putting Green Speed.* (Publication pending, Hoboken, NJ: John Wiley & Sons, ISBN 0-471-47272-7, $60).

Oakley, Russell A. Co-author, *see* Piper, Charles V.

Park, Eddie. *Real Golf.* (Essex, England: A. Quick & Co., 1990, 168 pages, ISBN 0-9504912-5-X). A compilation of articles by Eddie and Nicholas Park on maintenance of British courses, including agronomy, history and a discussion of how the ball is influencing design.
C/H: D2, C3, M3, H4, $75   100

Paumen, W. Gary. "Construction Methods and Equipment" found in *Golf Course Design* by Robert Muir Graves and Geoffrey S. Cornish. A chapter (Chapter 14) on course construction by contractor Paumen includes sections by seedsman Richard Elyea. Virgil Meir and Dean Mosdell describe purchase of seed and fertilizer while Christine Faulks, whose firm specializes in mixing soils, describes root zone mixes.
C/H: C3, H2, $N/A

Pennsylvania State University. *Greenkeeping.* (University Park, Pennsylvania: Department of Agriculture and Extension Education, 1981, 103 pages, AGDEX 273). A basic turfgrass textbook that provides abundant and valuable information to those working as or becoming a course superintendent.
C/H: C1, M2, $25 – 35

Piper, Charles V. and Russell A. Oakley. *Turf for Golf Courses.* (New York, NY: Macmillan Company, 1917, 1929, 262 pages). For decades this was the primary source of written information for course architects and greenkeepers throughout North America. Chapters on turfgrass identification, machinery, weeds, animal pests, soils and experimental work appeared along with an informative section of personal experiences from such luminaries as Dr. Walter S. Harban and Charles Blair Macdonald. Later editions were published.
C/H: D1, C2, M3, H5, $125 – 300

Potter, Daniel A. *Destructive Turfgrass Insects: Biology, Diagnosis and Control.* (Hoboken, NJ: John Wiley & Sons, 1998, ISBN 1-57504023-9). A wonderfully complete book on a subject of critical importance.
C/H: M4, $60 – 75

Reed, F.J. *Lawns and Playing Fields.* (London, England: Faber and Faber Ltd., 1950, 212 pages). A short chapter on golf courses emphasizes the need for a golf architect as well as a green committee and a head greenkeeper. A basic text.
C/H: M2, H2, $25 – 35

Rees, J.L. *Lawns, Greens, and Playing Fields.* (Sydney, Australia: Angus & Robertson, Ltd., 1962, 290 pages). A chapter, "Golf: Course Design," takes one through a general overview of selecting a site, course design and surveying, construction and grow-in. Another chapter on "Golf: Turf Production and Maintenance," introduces a generic approach to course maintenance as it was practiced down under in the early 1960s.
C/H: F1, D2, C1, M2, H2, $20 – 30

Rieke, P.E., Ph.D. Co-author, *see* Carrow, R.N.

Roberts, Beverley C. Co-author, *see* Roberts, Eliot.

Roberts, Eliot C., Ph.D. and Beverly C. Roberts, *Lawn and Sports Turf Benefits.* (Pleasant Hill, TN: The Lawn Institute. Pamphlet undated.) Dr. Roberts was one of the post World War II leaders in researching, teaching and consulting on golf course turf. His information was based upon the best science of the day and much of it formed the bedrock of the best management practices of the 1960s through the 1990s.

C/H: C1, M3, H3, $15 – 20

Roberts, John M. *Sports Facilities.* (McLean, VA: American Society of Landscape Architects Foundation, 1973, 80 pages, ISBN 73-92667). This booklet covers the design and construction of many outdoor sports facilities; golf one of them. It does a nice job in discussing space and safety requirements, the basics of routing golf holes, as well as strategy in design. The construction detail of tees, greens and bunkers is excellent and drainage is emphasized. The editor, the late Jot Carpenter, had a special interest in golf and course design.

C/H: D4, C3, $25 – 50

Rodriguez, Ian R. Co-author, *see* McCarty, L.R.

Sachs, Paul D. *Managing Healthy Sports Fields: A Guide to Using Organic Materials for Low-Maintenance and Chemical-Free Playing Fields.* (Hoboken, NJ: John Wiley & Sons, 2004, 256 pages, ISBN 0-471-47269-7). The chemical arsenal, once available to turf managers for pest, weed and disease control, is fast becoming restricted and regulated. As a result, alternative, non-chemical approaches to maintaining turf integrity have evolved. This work aims to liberate the modern turf manager from dependency on chemical treatments, with an array of new tactics that can be adapted to specific field types and climatic zones. Sachs covers basics of soil fertility, composting, methods of soil analysis, cultural practices and pests.

$55

Sachs, Paul D. and Richard T. Luff. *Ecological Golf Course Management.* (Chelsea, MI: Ann Arbor Press, 2002, 197 pages, ISBN 1-57504-154-5). A scholarly discussion on the use of organic products to create a healthy soil system and vibrant turf.

C/H: D1, C1, M5, H1, $45 – 55

Sanders, T.W., F.L.S. *Lawns and Greens: Their Formation and Management.* (London, England: W.H. & L. Collingridge, 1920, 116 -ages). Like most lawn and turf books of this period, it is general but still provides a wonderful look into the past of turfgrass maintenance. One chapter on "Golf Greens," covers some basic design principles as well as specifics on construction and maintenance of all golf course features.

C/H: D2, C2, M2, H4, $45 – 65

Schmidgall, Raymond S. *Superintendent's Handbook of Financial Management.* (Hoboken, NJ: John Wiley & Sons, 2004, 176 pages, ISBN 0-471-46319-1). This book, an industry standard, provides course superintendents with tools to manage daily financial operations with chapters on financial statements, course operation schedules, break-even analysis and operating budgets.

$45

Schumann, Gail L., Ph.D. and Patricia J. Vittum, Ph.D., Monica L. Elliott, Ph.D. and Patricia P. Cobb, Ph.D. *IPM Handbook for Golf Courses.* (Chelsea, MI: Ann Arbor Pres, 1998, 264 pages, ISBN 1-57504-065-4). This manual grew from courses conducted

by these scientists for the GCSAA, in which they described IPM as Intelligent Plant Management rather than Integrated Pest Management. IPM relies on proper monitoring, acceptance of threshold and tolerance levels for diseases or insects, biological and agronomic approaches to control and subsequent evaluation of effectiveness of techniques employed. All are detailed by this extraordinary quartet of scientists who have contributed enormously to the playing fields of golf.
C/H: M5, H2, $45 – 60

Scott, O.M. *Report of the Educational Conferences (Held at 1931 National Greenkeepers Association).* (Marysville, OH: O.M. Scott & Sons Co., 1931, 15 pages, small format (10" x 7"), paperback). This has historic value in that it indicates the status and concerns of the golf course industry well into the Great Depression. Of ten papers presented, the most illuminating were perhaps those by course architect Tom Winton on "Golf Course Construction in Relation to Course Maintenance" and course superintendent Jos. Williamson on "Practical Greenkeeping".
C/H: D2, M2, H4, $50 – 75

Scott, O.M. *Turf Talks.* (Marysville, OH: O.M. Scott Seed Company, 1936, 92 pages, small format (5" x 8"). This is a collection of four-page bulletins published over an eight year period, aimed specifically at the golf course and professional turf market, as opposed to lawn bulletins that Scott Seeds was also publishing at that time. One contribution of these publications is that they provide insight into how golf courses were built and maintained in the Golden Age and the Great Depression.
C/H: D1, C2, M3, H5, $200 – 250

Scott, O.M. & Sons. *The Putting Green.* (Marysville, OH: O.M. Scott & Sons Co., 1931, 39 pages). Another fine publication of Scott's, with tinted color photos and instructions on planting and care of the putting green.
C/H: C2, M2, H5, $200 – 250

Scott, O.M. & Sons. *The Seeding and Care of Golf Courses.* (Marysville, OH: O.M. Scott & Sons Co., 1922, 54 pages). A handsome small hard cover printed by the seed company with sound advice on preparing, building, planting and maintaining a golf course. Grasses are discussed, as well as pests and fertilization.
C/H: C2, M2, H5, $200 – 250

Sinclair, R.O., Editor. *The Golf Course.* (New York, NY: Peterson, Sinclair and Miller, Inc., 1917, 80 pages). A collection of "…monthly bulletins devoted to the discussion of modern methods as applied to course construction and upkeep". They were prepared in collaboration with Carter's Tested Seeds, Inc., and included at least three volumes beginning in 1916, truly a superb look into the past.
C/H: D2, C2, M2, H5, $150 – 175

Snow, James T. "Turfgrass Selection" found in *Golf Course Design* by Robert Muir Graves and Geoffrey S. Cornish. The National Director of the USGA provides a chapter on turfgrass selection for golf courses in every climate zone of the United States.
C/H: D1, C1, M4, H2, $N/A

Sprague, Howard B. *Turf Management Handbook.* (Danville, IL: The Interstate Printers, 1970, 253 pages, Library of Congress Catalogue # 74-106129). Sections on both cool season and warm season grasses and a discussion on special problems and renovating poor turf. His earlier book titled *Better Lawns* was written in 1940, a testament to his long term contributions to turf management.
C/H: M3, H1, $20 – 35

Sutton, Martin H.F. *Layout and Upkeep of Golf Courses and Putting Greens.* (London, England: Simpkin, Marshall, Hamilton & Kent, 1906, 42 pages, booklet). This was an early publication by Sutton with illustrations and advice – very rare.
C/H: D2, C3, M3, H5, $4,000 – 5,000

Sutton and Sons. *Lawns and Sports Grounds.* (Reading, England: Sutton's of Reading, 1948, 79 pages). No mention of golf but an interesting look at post World War II turf care and tools.
C/H: M2, H3, $35 – 50

Sutton and Sons. *Lawns: Garden Lawns, Tennis Lawns, Putting Greens, Cricket Grounds.* (London, England: Simpkin, Marshall, Hamilton, Kent & Co. Ltd., 1899, 40 pages). Although a chapter on putting greens is included, their construction and maintenance is blended into other chapters concerning other sports fields. Only a few pages are devoted solely to greens.
C/H: D1, C1, M1, H2, $125 – 150

Tani, Toshikazu and James B. Beard Ph.D. *Color Atlas of Turfgrass Diseases.* (Hoboken, NJ: John Wiley & Sons, 2004, 256 pages, ISBN 1-57504-021-2). With over 450 high quality color photographs of all the major turfgrass diseases, this work is a standard guide to disease diagnosis and pathogen identification. $85

Turgeon, A.J., Ph.D. *Turfgrass Management.* (Upper Saddle River, NJ: Prentice-Hall, 1980, 1985, 1991, 1996, 1999, 392 pages, ISBN 0-13-628348-9). Constantly improved and updated through five editions, this extensive reference source covers every aspect of turfgrass science for beginning students at college level together with professionals in the field. It is known as an influential work.
C/H: M4, $35 – 50

Turgeon, A.J., Ph.D. and Joseph Vargas, Ph.D. The Turf Problem Solver (*see* Appendix, page 177).

United States Department of Agriculture. *Grass: The Yearbook of Agriculture 1948.* A section, "Grass for Happier Living", describes uses of turfgrass including golf courses. Papers were prepared by the leading turfgrass scientists of the years following World War II. They included Fanny-Fern Davis, Fred V. Grau, H.B. Musser, J.A. DeFrance, G.W. Burton and Marvin H. Ferguson. Later Ferguson became a member of the ASGCA. He is also remembered as the "Father of the USGA Method for Green Construction".

Vargas, Joseph M., Ph.D. *Management of Turfgrass Diseases, Third Edition.* (Hoboken, NJ: John Wiley & Sons, Publication Pending, 2005, ISBN 0-471-474118). $60 – 80

Vargas, Joseph M., Ph.D. and A.J. Turgeon, Ph.D. *Poa Annua: Physiology, Culture and Control of Annual Bluegrass.* (Hoboken, NJ: John Wiley & Sons, 2004, ISBN 0-471-47268-9, $60).

Vittum, Patricia J., Ph.D. Co-author, *see* Schumann, Gail.

Waddington, D.V., Ph.D. Co-author, *see* Carrow, R.N.

Waltz, F. Clint. Co-author, *see* McCarty, L.B.

White, Charles B. *Turf Managers' Handbook for Golf Course Construction, Renovation and Grow-In.* (Hoboken, NJ: John Wiley & Sons, 2000, 312 pages, ISBN 1-57504-110-3). White was the agronomist for the USGA Green Section in the southeastern section and consulted on more than 100 course projects. "A poor grow-in can ruin many design features through erosion; in extreme cases, design features are lost indefinitely without major renovation," writes White.
C/H: D2, C4, M5, $50 – 65

Devil's Pulpit near Toronto by Hurdzan-Fry ranks above North America's grandest layouts

Photograph by John and Jean Henebry

Witteveen, Gordon. *A Century of Greenkeeping.* (Hoboken, NJ: John Wiley & Sons, 2001, 210 pages, ISBN 1-57504-161-8). Witteveen, a long-time superintendent, course owner and lecturer, traces the history of the profession in Ontario, featuring the personalities and camaraderie that make the region special. Often he refers to superintendents in other Canadian provinces. Witteveen is presently writing a text that covers the profession of course superintendent in all Canada.
C/H: M2, H4, P3, $25 – 35

Witteveen, Gordon. *Handbook of Practical Golf Course Maintenance (Spanish): Guia Practica para Manejo de Pastos en Campos de Golf.* (Hoboken, NJ: John Wiley & Sons, 2003, ISBN 0-471-43219-9).
C/H: C2, M5, H3, $45 – 65

Witteveen, Gordon. *Practical Golf Course Maintenance, Second Edition.* (Hoboken, NJ: John Wiley & Sons, Publication pending 2005, ISBN 0-471-47582-3).
C/H: C2, M5, H3, $50 – 65

Witteveen, Gordon and Michael Bavier. *Practical Golf Course Maintenance: The Magic of Greenkeeping.* (Chelsea, MI: Ann Arbor Press, 1998, 262 pages, ISBN 1-57504-047-6). One can tell that the two authors of this bible have not spent all their time in the library or the laboratory – they have "been there and done that". Common sense solutions abound in the illustrated text. Readers say the subtitle should have been the title of the book because of its intriguing interest.
C/H: C2, M5, H3, $35 – 50

Witteveen, Gordon. Co-author, *see* Labbance, Bob.

Yelverton, F. Co-author, *see* McCarty, L.B.

Drainage and Irrigation

"We cannot live without water. We could live better if we knew more about it."

Alfred Stefferud, editor *Yearbook of Agriculture* 1955

Barrett, James McC., Irrigation Engineer. "Golf Course Irrigation" in *Golf Course Design* by Robert Muir Graves and Geoffrey S. Cornish.
C/H: D2, C2, M3, $N/A

Barrett, James, Brian McC., Vinchesi, Bob Dobson, Paul Roche and David Zoldoske. *Golf Course Irrigation: Environmental Design and Management Practices.* (Hoboken, NJ: John Wiley & Sons, 2003, ISBN 0-471-14830-X). These distinguished irrigation designers co-author the most complete book published to date concerning course irrigation.
C/H: D3, C3, M2, $65 – 75

Cast Iron Pipe Research Association. *Golf Course Irrigation.* (Chicago, IL: Cast Iron Pipe Research Association, 1971, 22 pages, small format (6" x 9") paperback). A trade association bulletin that documents the evolution of golf course irrigation in the United States. At that point in time, Cast Iron, the mark of quality, was competing with AC (Asbestos Cement), PVC (Polyvinylchloride) and Poly (Polyethylene) pipes for a burgeoning, new market. PVC won out, but not because the Cast Iron folks weren't trying.
C/H: F1, D2, C2, H4, $20 – 25

Dobson, Bob. Co-author, *see* Barrett, James McC.

Graves, Robert Muir and Geoffrey S. Cornish. *Golf Course Design.* (New York: John Wiley & Sons, 1998, 446 pages, ISBN 0-471-13784-7). Chapter 9 by Graves and Cornish and chapter 10 by irrigation expert James Barrett are widely used references concerning golf course drainage and irrigation, respectively.
C/H: F2, D4, C4, M3, H3, $65 – 75

Huston, James. *Estimating for Landscape & Irrigation Contractors.* (Denver, CO: Smith Huston, Inc., 1994, 320 pages, ISBN 0-9628521-2-0, soft cover). This manual can help any size of business prepare an estimating budget, calculate labor burden, measure and allocate overhead costs, control equipment depreciation, account for subcontractors and present lump sum or unit price bids.
C/H: F3, D2, C2, $50 – 75

Jakobsen, Bert. Co-author, *see* McIntyre, Keith.

Jarrett, Albert R. *Golf Course & Grounds: Irrigation and Drainage.* (Englewood Cliffs, NJ: Prentice-Hall, 1985, 246 pages, ISBN 0-8359-2563-3). An in-depth treatment of each of the water management techniques commonly used on golf turf with numerous diagrams and course plans.
C/H: F1, D3, C2, M2, $25 – 35

King, F.H. *Irrigation and Drainage: Principles and Practice of Their Cultural Phases.* (New York, NY: Macmillan Company, 1898, 1899, 1902, 1907, 1913, 502 pages). Part of the Rural Science Series and edited by L.H. Bailey, this extensive work, though devoid of golf references, was the most scholarly work on the general subject for many years.

McIntyre, Keith and Bert Jakobsen. *Practical Drainage for Golf, Sportsturf and Horticulture.* (Hoboken, NJ: John Wiley & Sons, 2000, 202 pages, ISBN 1-57504-139-1). A thorough discussion of soil structure, water retention, subsoil drainage systems, surface drainage and methodology for determining soil hydraulic conductivity.
C/H: D4, C3, M3, $50 – 60

Pira, Edward. *A Guide To Golf Course Irrigation System Design and Drainage.* (Chelsea, MI: Ann Arbor Press, 1997, 434 pages, ISBN 1-57504-030-1). The reference source for planning, installing, integrating and maintaining irrigation systems. Illustrated with a wealth of charts, graphs, diagrams, schematics, sketches and photographs, this work arose from many years of teaching at the University of Massachusetts Winter School for Course Superintendents.
C/H: D4, C4, M2, $70 – 80

Roche, Paul. Co-author, *see* Barrett, James.

Vinchesi, Brian. Co-author, *see* Barrett, James.

Watkins, James A. *Turf Irrigation Manual.* (Dallas, TX: Telesco Industries, 1977, 1978, 355 pages). A comprehensive discussion of irrigation components and plans for golf course layouts, with performance results.
C/H: F1, D3, C3, M3, $15 – 25

United States Golf Association. *Wastewater Reuse for Golf Course Irrigation.* (New York, NY: Lewis Publishers, 1994 and 1997 by CRC Press LLC, 294 pages, ISBN 1-56670-090-6). Knowledgeable people recognize that the quantity and quality of irrigation water available for golf courses will become an increasingly important political, social and maintenance problem. Wisely the USGA has funded research to help mitigate those negative influences, as well as develop coping strategies. A bit dated, this is still an extremely important source manual.
C/H: F2, D2, C2, M4, H2, $75 – 100

Zoldoske, David. Co-author, *see* Barrett, James.

The Environment

"Sustainability ultimately is a matter of present commitment and priorities in light of future consequences both for the environment and for the golf course industry".

Ronald G. Dodson, President Audobon International. *Golf Course Design*, Graves and Cornish.

Balogh, James C. and William J. Walker. *Golf Course Management: Environmental Issues.* (Chelsea, MI: Lewis Publishers, 1993, 950 pages, ISBN 0-87371-742-2). An early and comprehensive source on the topic and a superb reference book summarizing the USGA sponsored environmental research through 1992. Not an easy read, but a great starting point on the environmental impact of golf course maintenance.
C/H: C2, M3, H2, $100 – 125

Bartell, Steven. *Ecological Risk Assessment for Golf Courses.* (Hoboken, NJ: John Wiley & Sons, Publication pending 2005, ISBN 0-471-472670-0).

Brennan, Anne-Maria, Ph.D. *Living Together: Golf and Nature in Partnership.* (Great Britain: The English Golf Union, 1996, 72 pages, ISBN 0901748064). A large format paperback book, it provides a holistic look at the development of golf in England, how it fits into major ecotones or eco-regions, and offers some solid advice on developing new courses to minimize environmental impact. Lots of good information amassed and organised by a scientist passionate about the environment.
C/H: F2, D3, C2, H3, $50 – 65

Center for Resource Management. *Creating a Sustainable Future: Golf and the Environment.* (Resource Management, 1996). Produced by the Salt Lake City based Center for Resource Management, this booklet sets forth "environmental principles for golf courses in the United States". Substantial portions of the text are devoted to environmental issues concerning course planning. It cites design, construction, maintenance, operations and more. The genesis of this booklet was a landmark meeting held in 1994 at Pebble Beach that brought various environmental and golf industry leaders together in a search for common ground. A diverse group of organizations worked to produce and subsequently endorse this document. Among them were the ASGCA, USGA, GCSAA, Audubon International, Club Managers Association of America, Friends of the Earth, GCBAA, LPGA, National Club Association, NGF, National Wildlife Federation and the US Environmental Protection Agency. Printing of the publication was made possible by a grant from Rain-Bird Irrigation. The project's steering committee introduces the booklet with the hope that it "will play an important role in the development or operation of your golf course and that it will help you preserve the beauty, integrity, and health of your local environment". It recommends that only qualified contractors be used in construction and that an equally qualified course superintendent be involved in the project from the beginning.
C/H: D2, C2, M2, H2, $10 – 25

Center for Resource Management. *Environmental Principals for Golf Courses in the United States.* (Salt Lake City, UT: Center for Resource Management, 1996, 15 pages, small format (5" x 8") paperback). This was the first environmental document on golf courses written and published by a collaboration of environmental and golf representatives. The intent was not to provide a set of hard guidelines to control golf course development and operations, but rather a framework from which to build those guidelines in a local area. The document was an enormous step towards bringing golf and environmental advocates into a much needed dialogue. It is similar to one prepared by the Royal Canadian Golf Association.
C/H: F1, D3, C3, M3, H5, $5 – 10

Center for Resource Management. *Environmental Siting Guide for Golf Course Development.* (Salt Lake City, UT: Center for Resource Management, 2000, 12 pages). No area of golf course development causes more emotional debate than siting of golf courses. Golf representatives see no problem with golf everywhere, while environmentalists believe that only degraded sites should be used. Of course there is a middle ground and this booklet was the agreed upon result of several years of debate among advocates of widely differing ideas. Again, there are no hard and fast guidelines or standards, but there is a mechanism with which to address issues seen as negative site impacts.
C/H: F4, D2, C1, $5 – 10

Clarke, John J. *Golf Courses and the Environment.* (Massachusetts Audubon Society, August 1999). This work acknowledges that a golf course provides a limited habitat for common species and a limited ecosystem.
C/H: D1, C1, M3, $5 – 10

Countryside Commission. *Golf Courses in the Countryside.* (Great Britain: Countryside Commission, 1993, 48 pages, ISBN 0-86170-407-X). A well done guide to planning, building and maintaining golf courses in an eco-friendly way. This booklet also helps educate planners as well as lay people on important agricultural landscapes, and how they differ. Beautifully illustrated, this is definitely a source document for designers of low impact environmental golf courses.
C/H: D4, C3, M2, $10 – 15

Diaz, Jamie and Linda Hartough. *Hallowed Ground: Golf's Greatest Places.* (Shelton, CT: The Greenwich Workshop, 1999, 154 pages, ISBN 0-86713-057-1). Write-ups with architectural mentions for the US Open courses, as well as Augusta National and the finest venues of the British Isles, coupled with celebrated artist Linda Hartough's evocative paintings.
C/H: D1, M1, $40 – 50

Dodson, Ronald G., President, Audubon International. "Designing With the Land, Not Over It" found in *Golf Course Design* by Robert Muir Graves and Geoffrey S. Cornish.
C/H: D2, C2, M3, $N/A

Dodson, Ronald G. *Managing Wildlife Habitat on Golf Courses.* (Hoboken, NJ: John Wiley & Sons, 2000, 177 pages, ISBN 1-57504-028-X). The first book written specifically for the golf industry to provide a framework for environmentally sensitive land management practices.
C/H: F2, D2, C2, M5, $40 – 50

Dodson, Ronald. G. *Sustainable Golf Courses.* (Hoboken, N. J: John Wyley and Sons, 2005, 288 pages, ISBN 0-471-465-47-X). Perhaps the most authoritative guide concerning environmental creation management of golf courses. This book was written by the founder of Audubon International. It is an increasingly valuable work. Arnold Palmer described it as, "an important guide for all who love and play the game." Dodson has been intimately involved with the dawn and development of the modern environmental Srewardship movement for golf courses. In this book he explains the concept of sustainability as understood by the environmental purists as well as how to effectively conduct pre-design resources inventories, design concepts to preserve and enhance environments, ideas on construction and maintenance to support environmental management, along with some case studies.
CH: F3,D3,C2,M5, $60-70

Durden, Dusty. *A Field Guide to Oldfield.* Okakie, SC, 9 Oldfield, 29909-4024. A unique and attractive booklet written by a naturalist, outlining in words and graphics the history of the vines, shrubs, ornamentals, oaks, shade trees, animals and birds that inhabit this golf course and its surroundings. Caution: A reader charmed by the presentation should not overlook its important message, namely, that it reflects the lore of what is left of the American wilderness on the East Coast.
$25 - 35

European Golf Association Ecology Unit. *An Environmental Strategy for Golf in Europe.* (Great Britain: Pisces Publications, 1995, 42 pages, ISBN 1-874537-09-9). One of the first golf publications from the European Golf Association composed of twenty-six countries. All agree that golf courses have special opportunities and obligations toward the environment. This was written as the first step to unifying environmental philosophies of all EGA members. It clearly spells out an agenda and subsequent steps to obtain it.
C/H: D1, C1, M2, $16 – 25

European Golf Association Ecology Unit. *The Committed to Green Handbook for Golf Courses.* (Oxford, England: European Golf Association Ecology Unit, 1997, 36 pages, ISBN 1-874357-13-7). A remarkably easy to follow planning guide that should allow golf courses to maximize their environmental potential. It covers all Europe. Accordingly, it is a bit general, but without doubt it is a primary resource for seeing it can be done.
C/H: F2, D3, C2, M3, $15 – 25

Evans, M. Co-author, *see* Harker, D.

Evans, S. Co-author, *see* Harker, D.

Gillihan, Scott W. *Bird Conservation on Golf Courses.* (Hoboken, NJ: John Wiley & Sons, 2000, ISBN 1-57504113-8). Written by the Forested Ecosystems Program Coordinator for the Colorado Bird Observatory, this is a comprehensive manual for the design and sustainability of bird habitat on golf courses. An important book for anyone engaged in producing an environmentally friendly golf course.
C/H: F1, D4, C4, M4, $25 – 45

Gould, David and Center for Resource Management. *A Collaboration Guide.* (Salt Lake City, UT: Center for Resource Management, 2000, 46 pages.) The Golf and Environment Initiative hired well-known writer David Gould to craft a document

that would explain the wisdom and rationale of course developers, communities and environmentalists for working together for every one's benefit. This final work was approved by most major golf and environmental organizations. The booklet is thin on details and standards because that was not the intent, but rather to simply show how working together benefits all.
C/H: D2, C2, M2, H3, $5 – 10

Harker, D., S. Evans, M. Evans and K. Harker. *Landscape Restoration Handbook.* (Boca Raton, FL: Lewis Publishers, 1993, 563 pages, ISBN 087371-952-2). Described as an "ecological call to arms", this work includes lists of plant species suitable for restoring many environments in the United States including golf courses.
C/H: D2, C2, M4, $80 – 90

Harker, K. Co-author, *see* Harker, D.

Hartough, Linda. Co-author and artist, *see* Diaz, Jamie.

Hurdzan, Michael J., Ph.D. "Minimizing Environmental Impact by Golf Course Development: A Method and Some Case Studies" in *Handbook of Integrated Pest Management for Turf and Ornamentals.* Edited by Anne R. Leslie. (Chelsea, MI: CRS Press, 1994).
C/H: F1, D2, C2, M2, $N/A

Jacoby, Martin. *The Wildlife of Valderrama.* (London, England: Jamie Ortiz-Patino, 1999, 32 pages, ISBN 0-9526131-4-X). A beautifully written and illustrated booklet that features Valderrama Golf Course and the diverse and abundant wildlife it attracts and sustains. Mr. Ortiz-Patino is an active and determined environmentalist who has the resources and desire to showcase just how good an environment a golf course can be. The booklet identifies nine separate sanctuaries on the golf course and the critters, creatures and plants that can be found there. A superior model and example of how courses can help educate golfers and non-golfers on environmental issues.
C/H: D2, C1, M4, H3, $25 – 50

Klemme, Michael. *A View From the Rough.* (Chelsea, MI: Sleeping Bear Press, 1995, 136 pages, ISBN 0-886947-06-6). Mike Klemme's photos are some of the best in golf, and in this book he captures strong images of courses and wildlife. Although several course architects are quoted for environmental concepts, it is the Klemme photos that deliver the message.
C/H: D2, C2, M4, H2, $30 – 40

L.A. Group. (S. Jeffrey Anthony, Barbara B. Beall and Kevin J. Franks). "The Team Approach to the Design, Permitting, and Construction Monitoring of Golf Projects" found in *Golf Course Design* by Robert Muir Graves and Geoffrey S. Cornish.
C/H: F2, D3, C3, $N/A

Leslie, Ann, Editor. *Handbook of Integrated Pest Management for Turf and Ornamentals.* (Chelsea, MI: 1989, 660 pages, ISBN 0-87371-350-8). The editor, Ann Leslie, was an administrator for the US Environment Protection Authority concerned with Integrated Pest Management and turf and ornamentals. The contributors are all luminaries of turf and ornamental science with emphasis on environment. An excellent research source.
C/H: F2, D2, C3, M2, $115 – 140

Libby, Gary, Ronald. F. Harker, & Kay Harker with Jean Mackay. *Managing Wetlands on Golf Courses.* (Hoboken, N.J: John Wyley and Sons, 2004, 210 pages, ISBN 0-471-4723-5). An important how-to-do book with loads of valuable and practical information. This book is thorough and well written and easy to understand.
CH: D1, C3, M5. $50 - 60

Lilly, Sharon. *Golf Course Tree Management.* (Chelsea, MI: Ann Arbor Press, 2001, 216 pages, ISBN 1-57504-117-0). The science of trees is the basis for this discussion of protecting course aesthetics while properly managing the horticulture of trees. (*See Section II*).
C/H: D1, C1, M5, H1, $35 – 50

Love, William R., ASGCA. *An Environmental Approach to Golf Course Development.* (*See entry page 85*, Love, William R.). (Chicago, IL: American Society of Golf Course Architects, 1992, 43 pages; 1999, 45 pages). An informative and "go to" source for the design process of a golf course within environmental guidelines. This booklet has served as a model for communities writing environmental regulations for golf courses and contains many case studies of successful projects.
C/H: F4, D4, C1, M2, $20 – 30

Mackay, Jean. *A Guide to Environmental Stewardship on the Golf Course.* (Hoboken, NJ: John Wiley and Sons. ISBN 0-471-47273-5.) Written in cooperation with the USGA, Audubon International and The National Fish and Wildlife Foundation, this is an immensely important work relating to the creation of golf courses and their contribution to our environment.
C/H: F2, D2, C1, M3, $60

Mackay, Jean, Editor. *A Guide to Environmental Stewardship on the Golf Course.* Second Edition. Selkirk, NY: Audubon International, 2002. The Director of Educational Services of Audubon International has edited a comprehensive and valuable book, now in its second printing, with contributions from leading environmentalists and those involved in the maintenance of turfgrass. An introductory paperback text that explains the basic outline for environmental stewardship for golf courses, but without much detail.
C/H: F2, D1, C1, M3, $25

National Association of Audubon Societies. *Golf Clubs as Bird Sanctuaries.* (New York, NY: National Association of Audubon Societies, 1925, 64 pages). This well illustrated booklet details how golf courses can attract and protect birds and their habitats. Serving on the Audubon committee at that time was Robert Tyre Jones Jr. (Bobby Jones) and famed writer Grantland Rice. Very rare and it is difficult to find.
C/H: D1, C1, M3, H1, $500 – 1000

Nature Conservancy Council. *On Course Conservation: Managing Golf's Natural Heritage.* (Great Britain: Nature Conservancy Council, 1989, 46 pages, ISBN 0 86139 594 8). An early and still reliable resource book on how to make golf courses better friends to the environment. Chapters deal with resources available, management guidelines for various types of areas of the course, water features and "location, design and recreation" of natural areas.
C/H: D2, C2, M2, $15 – 25

Dunarave Golf Course on Prince Edward Island, Canada celebrates its linkage to the Brudnell River with some spectacular golf holes that buffer it. (Hurdzan/Fry Golf Course Design)

Goals of environmental course architecture include designing and building a course that requires the low inputs of water, fertiliser, pesticides and fossil fuels to produce a marketable golf product. The more the designer understands the complexity of the ecosystem he is working in, the more he can apply emerging technology to reduce maintenance inputs
(The Heritage at Westmoor, Westminster, Colorado; Hurdzan/Fry Golf Course Design)

Nature Conservancy Council. *Your Course: Preparing a Conservation Management Plan.* (Great Britain: Nature Conservancy Council, 1990, 16 pages, ISBN 0-86139-692-8). This is a step by step workbook of how to develop habitat or conservancy areas on a golf course. It shows how to identify potential areas for enhancement as well as develop management strategies. It is a very simple yet complete way to establish and sustain habitat on the golf course.
C/H: D1, C1, M3, H3, $10 – 15

Royal Canadian Golf Association. *Environmental Guidelines for Canadian Golf Clubs.* (Oakville, Ontario, Canada: Royal Canadian Golf Association, 1993, 12 pages, small format (5" x 8")). Environmentally, Canadians have in some ways led the way towards regulations and they have been good stewards of the land and environment. This publication preceded

Bill Love, ASGCA, produced a work of profound importance while Jeremy Pern EIGCA returned to the University of Wales to write The Nature of Golf. *The National Golf Foundation has been prolific in publishing works relevant to course development*

the American equivalent by three years. It is presented in much stronger terms, owing in part to fewer and less diverse environments than the US contends with. This is an exceedingly well thought through and an intensely valuable statement of principles.
C/H: F1, D3, C3, M3, H5, $5 – 10

Shoeman, Russell. Co-author, *see below.*

Stewart, Thomas P. and Russell Shoeman. *The Nature of Golf: Exploring the Beauty of the Game.* (Pinehurst, NC: Thomas P. Stewart, 1999, 434 pages, ISBN 0-9625276-2-9). A gorgeous book that features case studies of golf projects around the country that were not only successfully integrated into the environment, but enhanced both it and the ecology of the region.
C/H: D2, C1, M3, H1, T3, $65 – 75

Walker, William J. Co-author, *see* Balogh, James.

Wogan, Philip, A. ASGCA. *Golf Courses and the Environment.* (A white paper, ASGCA 1977). The seminal paper concerning golf courses and the environment, said by some to be confrontive, served to introduce the important subject of the environment and golf courses. They continue to occupy an increasingly vast acreage worldwide.

A Selection of Additional Books with Informative Passages Concerning Golf Course Design

In preparing this selection, the authors acknowledge making abundant references to impressive bibliographies by Donovan and Murdoch, Grant and Daniel Wexler's guide to golf literature.

Campbell, Malcolm. *The Encyclopedia of Golf.* (London, Dorling Kindersley, 1991. Revised 1994 and 2001. US Edition: *Random House International Encyclopedia of Golf,* Random House, 1991, 336 pages, $40.00.)

Campbell, Malcolm. *The Scottish Golf Book.* (Chicago, IL: Sports Publishing, 1999, 224 pages, $35.00.)

Dalrymple W., Editor. *Golfer's Guide to the Game and Greens of Scotland.* (Edinburgh, W.H. White, 1894, 208 pages, $600.00.)

Darwin, Bernard. *Bernard Darwin and Aberdovey.* (Droitwich, Grant Books, 1996, 81 pages, $50.00.)

Darwin, Bernard. *Darwin on the Green.* (London, Souvenir, 1986, 240 pages, $25.00.)

Dobereiner, Peter. *For the Love of Golf.* (London, Stanley Paul, 1981 and US Edition, Atheneum, 1981, 256 pages, $25.00.)

Getmapping. *Golf Courses.* (London, Harper Collins, 2002, 128 pages, $25.00.)

Green, Robert. *Golf: An Illustrated History of the Game.* (London, Willow, 1987, 208 pages, $25.00.)

Jenkins, Dan. *Fairways and Greens.* (New York: Doubleday, 1994 and London: Collins Willow, 1995, 247 pages, $25.00.)

Laidlaw, Renton. *The Royal and Ancient Golfer's Handbook.* (London, 1899 and continuing.) The contemporary edition of the long published *Golfer's Handbook.* $43.00. (Early Edition $175.00; Postwar Edition $50.00.)

Lambrecht, Lawrence Casey. *Emerald Gems: The Links of Ireland* (Westerly, RI: Lambrecht Photography, 2002, 209 pages, $99.00.)

Lawrenson, Derek. *The Complete Encyclopedia of Golf:* London, Carlton, 1999, 648 pages. $45.00.)

Lonsdale, The Earl of (Editor). *The Lonsdale Library: The Game of Golf:* (London, Seeley, Service & Co., 1931, 251 pages, $75.00.)

Macleod, John. *A History of the Royal Dornoch Golf Club, 1877-1999.* (Elgin: Moravian, 2000, 120 pages, $32.00.)

Matux, Roger. *Sports Golf.* (Detroit, MI: Visible Ink Press, 1997, 640 pages.)

McLean, Stuart. *South African Golf Courses: A Portrait of the Best.* (Cape Town, Struik, 1993, 144 pages, $45.00.)

Oliver, Darius. *Australia's Finest Golf Courses.* (Sydney, New Holland, 2003, 160 Pages. $45.00.)

Pennink, Frank. *Frank Pennink's Golfer's Companion.* (London, Cassell, 1962, 311 pages, $30.00.)

Pennink, Frank. *Frank Pennink's Choice of Golf Courses.* (London, A and C Black, 1976, 293 pages, $30.00.)

Ramsey, Tom. *Discover Australia's Golf Courses* (Melbourne, Dent, 1987, 231 pages, $30.00.)

Ramsey, Tom. *Great Australian Golf Courses.* (Sydney, Weldon, 1990, 384 pages, $30.00.)

Redmond, John. *The Book of Irish Golf.* (Dublin, Gill and Macmillan, 1997, 159 pages, $40.00.)

Shapiro, Mel, Editor. *Golf: A Turn-of-the-Century Treasury.* (Secaucus, NJ: Castle, 1986, 467 pages, $25.00.) First US Edition, D. Appleton, 1902.

Trebus, Robert S. and Richard C. Wolffe, Jr. *Baltusrol 100 Years.* (Baltusrol Golf Club, 1995, 166 pages, $65.00.)

Various Authors. *Twentieth Century Golf Chronicle.* (Lincolnwood, IL: Publications International, 1998, 608 pages, $25.00.)

Winter, Grant. *Guide to Southern African Golf Courses.* (Cape Town, Struik, 1996, 278 pages, $30.00.)

Many outstanding club histories have appeared that give credit to the architects

A Selection of Books relating to
The Old Course, St Andrews

Passages describing the Layout of The Old Course
and its Worldwide Impact on Course Design

Compiled by H.R.J. Grant

The creation of the universe and everything in it was incidental to the creation of the Old Course at St Andrews, according to many golfers. Indeed, the authors of this work wonder if its playing qualities can be adequately described in words and illustrations while its glorious landscapes, characterized by changing winds together with differing light and shade effects as the day advances, provide a unique and indescribable mystique to each hole.

Our publisher, H.R.J. Grant, has undertaken to select the books he feels best describe its architecture and impact on our art form worldwide.

Michael J. Hurdzan

Geoffrey S. Cornish

★ ★ ★

The Old Course at St Andrews has exerted the greatest impact of any course on golf architecture, while few course architects if any have not trodden its hallowed turf.

The land, bordered by the North Sea and the Firth of Forth, was created by the receding sea. With scant vegetation surviving on the grazed, sandy soil, it was ideal for golf. The turf was firm while the rough was bordered by gorse, bright yellow in spring. With other species taking a hand, the turf has flourished but remained short. The course is not long by modern standards, but the little pot bunkers and others in the most unlikely places are terrifying. Originally twenty-two holes, but now eighteen, little has changed over the years, although length has been added to ensure that the bunkers continue to punish wayward shots. The weather is always a factor and it is rare for the day to be still and the flags drooping. More often there is a stiff breeze, which can turn into a gale and change a 6-iron shot into a 3-wood. Golfers love it or hate it.

Much has been written about the Old Course and the matches and championships that have been played over it, but there has never been a detailed history of its original design and layout, although many books touch on the subject, some in greater detail than others. However New Zealander Scott Macpherson, based in Edinburgh and having spent three years studying the layout and its literature, has recently published what is claimed to be the most comprehensive book yet. Its title is *The Evolution of the Old Course* (publication pending, late 2005, see page 87).

Adamson, Alistair. *Allan Robertson: His Life and Times.* (Worcestershire: Grant Books, 1985. 92 pages, illustrated). Part 1: Allan Robertson, Golfer: His Life and Times; Part 2: Allan Robertson's Album. This is an important addition to the history and development of golf.
H2, $60 - $80

Balfour, James. *Reminiscences of Golf on St. Andrews Links.* (Edinburgh: David Douglas, 1887. 68 pages, wrappers. Classics of Golf reprint, 1987). This rare little book tells of playing the Old Course at a time when there were few golfers. It is of great interest because it provides a first hand account of how the course played in the nineteenth century.
E2, H1, $6,000 - $8,000; Reprint $30 - $40

The History of the Royal and Ancient Golf Club in Three Volumes:

This trilogy, published for The Royal and Ancient Golf Club by Grant Books, is perhaps the most detailed and researched of any club history. It tells both the history of the Club and the evolution of golf implements and rules. It also contains a detailed description of how the Old Course, which is public, came to be run by the R&A in conjunction with the St Andrews Links Committee.
D2, C2, H5, P3, $100 per volume in cloth
The St. Andrews Editions are bound in Morocco and with slipcases, $400 per volume

Behrend, John and Lewis, Peter N. *Challenges and Champions: The Royal and Ancient Golf Club 1754-1883.* (St Andrews, The Royal and Ancient Golf Club, 1998. 266 pages, extensively illustrated in colour and mono).

Behrend, John; Lewis, Peter N. and Mackie, Keith. *Champions and Guardians: The Royal and Ancient Golf Club 1884-1939.* (St Andrews, The Royal and Ancient Golf Club, 2001. 286 pages, illustrated in colour and mono). John Behrend died in 2000 after completing the first half of the book.

Steel, Donald and Lewis, Peter N. *Traditions and Change: The Royal and Ancient Golf Club 1939-2004.* (St Andrews, The Royal and Ancient Golf Club, 2004. 328 pages, illustrated in colour and mono).

The Behrend, Mackie, Steel and Lewis trilogy recounting the history of the R&A is important to the literature of the game

Bennett, Andrew. *The Book of St Andrews Links, Containing Plan of Golf Courses, Description of the Greens, Rules of the Game, By-Laws of the Links, Regulations for Starting, Golfing, Rhymes, etc.* (Edinburgh: J. Menzies, 1898. 80 pages and a folding map). An important book and the first to give some detailed descriptions of the courses in the early nineteenth century.
D3, H4. First Edition $4,000 plus. Ellesborough Press Reprint. $250 - 300

Clark, Robert. *Golf: A Royal and Ancient Game.* (Edinburgh, 1875. 285 pages, illustrated). The first Trade Edition; subsequent editions appeared in 1893 and 1899. The book gathers together important literature that had been previously published and is one of the masterpieces of golf literature.
H4. First Edition $3,000 - $4,000; subsequent editions $300 - $600; 1975 Reprint $50 - $60

Everard, H.S.C. *A History of the Royal and Ancient Golf Club, St Andrews from 1754-1900.* (Edinburgh: William Blackwood, 1907. 306 pages, illustrated in colour and mono). The first history of the most renowned golf club, beautifully produced. It has been partly superseded by the recently published three-volume history of The Royal and Ancient Golf Club by Steel and Lewis (*see above*).
H2, $1,500 - $2,000

Farnie, H.B. *Handy Book of St Andrews.* (Joseph Cook & Son [Nd. c. 1859] 138 pages. Double page plan of St Andrews). There is a chapter on golf which includes reference to the "Nine Holes," comments on Allan Robertson, "the best player who ever lived", and other historical information.
D1, H3, $1,500 - $2,500

Hackney, Stewart. *Bygone Days on the Golf Course.* (Dundee: Ravensbury Communications, 1990. 59 pages). A somewhat amateurish production, but nevertheless interesting and with valuable historical information.
H3, $30 - $40

Hutchinson, Horace G., et al. *British Golf Links: A Short Account of the Leading Golf Links of the United Kingdom and Ireland.* (J.S. Virtue, 1897. 331 pages, illustrated). A beautiful and elaborate production.
D1, C1, H3. First Edition $1,500 - $ 2,500; 2005 Reprint $85

Jarrett, Tom. *St Andrews Golf Links: The First Six Hundred Years.* (Edinburgh: Main Stream, 1995. 192 pages, illustrated). Of historical interest, it also includes two chapters dealing with physical changes of the links holes and bunkers of the Old Course.
B1, H2, $40 - 50

Taylor, Dawson. *St Andrews Cradle of Golf.* (New Jersey: A.F. Barnes & Co., 1976, and subsequent reprints. 207 pages, illustrated in mono). An illustrated guide to the courses and the historical tournaments.
D1, H2, $30 - $40

Tulloch, W.W. *The Life of Tom Morris With Glimpses of St Andrews and Its Golfing Celebrities.* (London, 1908. 334 pages, illustrated. USGA reprint, 1992). One of the great biographical works in the history of golf and the only one on the cult figure of Old Tom Morris.
D1, H3, $1,500 - $2,000; Reprint $250 - $300

Wilson, John H. *Nature Study Rambles Round St Andrews.* (London, 1909. 258 pages with 14 full page plates of a variety of flora and also geological formations). It is an interesting publication. The author has studied the natural history of the district around St Andrews including the Links, the Eden Estuary and the areas surrounding it. Chapters on links deal with their formation from sand hills, dunes and grasses together with the plants to be found on them.
D3, C2, $80 - $100

As the oceans receded sandy fields or links formed. Golf was first played on them. The glorious playing fields of the game tell their own story, yet that story is enhanced by the written word

Desert Highlands, Arizona, a Jack Nicklaus production. Vertical lines of the mounds are similar to those of the mountain in the background

Part IV

Arrangement of Large Collections

... book collecting is the most
exhilarating sport of all

A *Book Hunter's Holiday*, p. 106 – A.S. Wolf Rosenbach

143

Cape Cod National Golf Club, Brewster Massachusetts, by Brian M. Silva, ASGCA

Le Baron Hills, Lakeville, Massachusetts, by Mark Mungeam, ASGCA. Partners Silva and Mungeam have been active nationwide and abroad in producing new courses and restoring older ones including Olympia Fields near Chicago for the 2003 US Open Championship

Arrangement of Large Collections

A SUBSTANTIAL LIBRARY not only symbolizes accumulated knowledge; it also speaks to the depth of passion that the owner of that library has for the subject matter. But the best ones are "working libraries", which means they are used as source documents to research a topic, and are not there just to look pretty. Moreover there may be tens, if not hundreds of books, pamphlets, booklets and related ephemera, that deal with a particular subject, in whole or in part, that should naturally be grouped together; especially in a working library. Arranging these materials into a functional system, that has room to expand with added items, requires some thought and organisation.

The key terms are "functional" and "organisation", especially for an avid collector with the potential for a large library. There are no specific rules for arranging a library, so it comes down to individual preference. In addition one must remember that books can have different dollar values as well as a difference in the significance of the information they contain. For example Mackenzie's *Golf Architecture* can be valued at close to $1,000, but be less informative on a particular topic than Cornish and Graves book *Golf Course Design* that costs less than $100.

Some books may have fabulous pictures that inspire design concepts, yet give no clue on how to achieve them. Still others give no architectural insights but are interesting to read such as biographies of famous designers or club histories.

A personal method of arranging books is by subject matter and shelf. We first group books by their principal subject in sections for (1) design, (2) construction and maintenance, (3) drainage and irrigation, and (4) environmental. Then within each section, we place books on "shelves" based upon the importance of the material they contain. Since this book focuses on golf course design, so does our section and shelf system. Think of this system of consisting of five shelves, and on each one are placed publications related to a topic or section.

"First or top shelf" would be reserved for publications that provide "answers" (e.g., Cornish and Graves) or are considered "primary sources" such as Colt and Alison, Mackenzie, Thomas, etc. These books are timeless, with information on design, history, important personalities or research resources. Every course architect should or would like to have them at his disposal, as should all those interested in the subject.

If the "top shelf" provides answers, then the "second shelf" provides ideas and insights. On the second shelf, we placed publications with magnificent pictures and personality profiles, descriptions of extraordinary places as well as anything that may spark a design idea. These materials should supplement primary or top shelf sources.

The "third shelf" is for publications of ancillary information or of lesser importance. This could be catalogues, research reports, *USGA Green Section Record,* or interesting articles. Also included might be publications concerning environmental and research information, maintenance issues, history, personalities and travel, related to golf course design not offering critical information.

The "fourth shelf" is for "interesting or leisure reading". It includes stimulating information not critical to professional practice. Examples are club histories and travel guides. This shelf also includes older publications whose information has been transcended by emerging technology, or has been updated by new publications. For example, Jones and Rando's 1974 ULI booklet has been replaced by others in later versions, with the newest version on the top shelf.

Finally we suggest a "locked" bookcase for "rare treasures" that the searcher may never find or afford (or one may be lucky enough to stumble across a special piece and not know what it is). Examples of "rare treasures" are brochures by Stanley Thompson, William Langford and the American Park Builders. Fifty years ago one of the authors found Alister Mackenzie's 1920 book for sale. Paying 75¢ for it, he was told, "We should be paying you for getting it out of here, it has been in stock for years". The lesson is that times change.

Notwithstanding the foregoing recommended arrangement, we suspect that if one's library contains fewer than a couple of hundred books, or thereabouts, alphabetical arrangement by author is the most convenient.

Primary Source

Top shelf should be for publications that are primary sources of information. This shelf is divided into sections by topic, and the materials included on each section or shelf is the personal selection of Michael Hurdzan

Michael Hurdzan

1 Design – (Top Shelf)
Original or Reprint

Balfour, James. *Reminiscences of Golf on St Andrews Links* (reprint)

Bauer, Aleck. *Hazards, Those Essential Elements in a Golf Course Without Which the Game Would be Tame and Uninteresting* (reprint)

Braid, James. *Advanced Golf*

Brown, J. Lewis. *Golf at Glen Falls*

Campbell, Sir Guy. *Golf for Beginners*

Colt, H.S. and C.H. Alison. *Some Essays on Golf Course Architecture* (reprint)

Cornish, Geoffrey. *Eighteen Stakes on a Sunday Afternoon*

Cornish, Geoffrey and Ronald E. Whitten. *The Architects of Golf*

Cornish, Geoffrey and Ronald E. Whitten. *The Golf Course*

Cornish, Geoffrey and William Robinson. *Golf Course Design…An Introduction*

Daley, Paul. *Golf Course Architecture: A Worldwide Perspective, Volume I*

Daley, Paul. *Golf Course Architecture: A Worldwide Perspective, Volume II*

Daley, Paul. *Links Golf: The Inside Story*

Daley, Paul. *The Sandbelt: Melbourne's Golfing Heaven*

Doak, Tom. *The Anatomy of a Golf Course*

Elliott, Mal. *Perry Maxwell's Prairie Dunes*

Graves, Robert Muir and Geoffrey S. Cornish. *Golf Course Design*

Graves, Robert Muir and Geoffrey S. Cornish. *Classic Golf Hole Design: Using the Greatest Holes as Inspiration for Modern Courses*

Hawtree, Fred. *Aspects of Golf Course Architecture (1889 – 1924)*

Hawtree, Fred. *Elements of Golf Course Layout and Design*

Hawtree, Fred. *The Golf Course: Planning, Design, Construction and Maintenance*

Hunter, Robert. *The Links* (reprint)

Hurdzan, Michael Ph.D. *Building a Practical Golf Facility*

Hurdzan, Michael Ph.D. *Golf Course Architecture: Design, Construction and Restoration*

Hurdzan, Michael Ph.D. *Golf Course Architecture: Evolution in Design, Construction and Restoration Technology*

Hutchinson, Horace. *Golf Greens and Green-Keeping* (reprint)

Klein, Bradley S. Ph.D. *Discovering Donald Ross: The Architect and His Golf Courses*

Low, John L. *Concerning Golf* (reprint)
Mackenzie, Dr. Alister. *Golf Architecture: Economy in Course Construction and Greenkeeping* (reprint)
National Golf Foundation. *Golf Course Design and Construction*
Nicklaus, Jack with Chris Millard. *Nicklaus by Design: Golf Course Strategy and Architecture*
Park, Willie Jr. *The Game of Golf* (reprint)
Richardson, Forrest L. *Routing the Golf Course: The Art and Science that Forms the Golf Journey*
Shackelford, Geoff. *Grounds for Golf – The History and Fundamentals of Golf Course Design*
Shackelford, Geoff. *The Golden Age of Golf Design*
Sutton, Martin A.F. *Golf Courses: Design, Construction and Upkeep* (reprint)
Thomas, George C., Jr. *Golf Architecture in America: Its Strategy and Construction* (reprint)
Tillinghast, A.W. *Gleanings From the Wayside*
Tillinghast, A.W. *Reminiscences of the Links*
Tillinghast, A.W. *The Course Beautiful*
Travis, Walter J. *Practical Golf*
Wethered, H.N. and T. Simpson. *The Architectural Side of Golf* (reprint)

2 Construction & Maintenance – (Top Shelf)
Original or Reprint

Beard, James B., Ph.D. *Turf Management for Golf Courses*
Brede, Doug Ph.D. *Turfgrass Maintenance Reduction Handbook*
Hurdzan, Michael J., Ph.D. *Golf Greens: History, Theory, Design and Construction*
Labbance, Bob and Gordon Witteveen. *Keepers of the Green: A History of Golf Course Management*
McCarty, Bert, Ph.D. *Best Golf Course Management Practices*
McCarty, Bert, Ph.D. and Grady Miller. *Managing Bermudagrass Turf: Selection, Construction, Cultural Practices and Pest Management Strategies*
Piper, Charles V. and Russell A. Oakley. *Turf for Golf Courses*
Schumann, Gail L. et al. *IPM Handbook for Golf Courses*

3 Drainage & Irrigation – (Top Shelf)
Original or Reprint

Barrett, James et al. *Golf Course Irrigation: Environmental Design and Management Practices*
McIntyre, Keith and Bent Jakobsen. *Practical Drainage for Golf, Sportsturf and Horticulture*
Pira, Edward. *A Guide to Golf Course Irrigation System Design and Drainage*

4 The Environment – (Top Shelf)
Original or Reprint

Dodson, Ronald G. *Sustainable Golf Courses: A Guide to Environmental Stewardship*
Dodson, Ronald G. *Managing Wildlife Habitat on Golf Courses*
Gillihan, Scott W. *Bird Conservation on Golf Courses*

Harker, D.S., et al. *Landscape Restoration Handbook*
Leslie, Ann. *Handbook of Integrated Pest Management for Turf and Ornamentals*
Love, William R. *An Environmental Approach to Golf Course Development*
United States Golf Association. *Wastewater Reuse for Golf Course Irrigation*

Pictures, Personalities, Places or Ideas

Second Shelf is reserved for publications that provide pretty pictures, detailed information on personalities or places, and materials that may inspire ideas or new application of old ideas. These publications should be seen as supplements to the primary sources.

1 Design – (Second Shelf)
Original or Reprint

Adams, John. *The Parks of Musselburgh*
Allen, Sir Peter. *The Sunley Book of Royal Golf*
Bahto, George. *The Evangelist of Golf: The Story of C.B. Macdonald*
Barclay, James A. *The Toronto Terror*
Barton, John et al. *Golf Digest's Places to Play*
Butler, William. *The Golfer's Guide*
Doak, Tom et al. *The Life and Work of Dr. Alister Mackenzie*
Dunn, Paul and B.J. *Great Donald Ross Golf Courses You Can Play*
Dye, Pete with Mark Shaw. *Bury Me in a Pot Bunker*
Fay, Michael. *Golf, As It Was In The Beginning: The Legendary British Open Courses*
Fay, Michael. *Golf, As It Was Meant To Be Played*
Fazio, Tom with Cal Brown. *Golf Course Designs*
Fazio, Tom with Cal Brown. *Golf Course Designs by Fazio*
Ferrier, Bob. *The World Atlas of Golf Courses*
Gilliland, Robert J. and Peter Macdonald. *Prairie Dunes: The First Fifty Years*
Gordon, John. *The Great Golf Courses of America*
Gordon, John. *The Great Golf Courses of Canada*
Hawtree, Fred. *Colt & Co. Golf Course Architects*
Hurdzan, Michael and Dana Fry. *Selected Golf Courses of Hurdzan/Fry: Photos and Essays, Volume I*
Jacobs, Timothy. *The Golf Courses of Jack Nicklaus*
Jacobs, Timothy. *Great Golf Courses of the World*
Jenkins, Dan. *Sports Illustrated's – The Best 18 Golf Holes in America*
Jones, Robert Trent, Jr. *Golf by Design: How to Play Better Golf by Reading the Features of a Course*
Kato, Shunsuke. *What Makes a Golf Course Good*
Kirk, John and Timothy Jacobs. *The Golf Courses of Robert Trent Jones, Jr.*
Kroeger, Robert. *The Golf Courses of Old Tom Morris*
Labbance, Bob. *The Old Man: The Biography of Walter J. Travis*
Macdonald, Charles Blair. *Scotland's Gift – Golf* (reprint)
Machat, Udo. *Poppy Hills, Pebble Beach, CA*

Miller, Michael and Geoff Shackelford. *The Art of Golf Design: Landscapes by Michael Miller and Essays by Geoff Shackelford*

Moreton, John F. *The Golf Courses of James Braid*

Morgan, Brian. *A World Portrait of Golf*

Muirhead, Desmond with Tip Anderson. *St Andrews, How to Play the Old Course*

National Golf Review. *Golfer's Yearbook, 1938*

Peper, George et al. *The 500 World's Greatest Golf Holes*

Quirin, Dr. William L. *America's Linksland: A Century of Long Island Golf*

Quirin, Dr. William L. *Golf Clubs of the MGA: A Centennial History of Golf in the New York Metropolitan Area*

Rathbun, Mickey. *Double Doglegs and other Hazards: The Life and Work of Larry Packard*

Ross, Donald. *Golf Has Never Failed Me*

Scarth, John. *Round Forever*

Shackelford, Geoff. *Masters of the Links: Essays on the Art of Golf and Course Design*

Shackelford, Geoff. *The Captain: George C. Thomas, Jr. and His Golf Architecture*

Steel, Donald. *Classic Golf Links of England, Wales and Ireland*

Strawn, John. *Driving the Green*

Thompson, Stanley. *About Golf Courses, Their Construction and Upkeep* (reprint)

United States Golf Association. *Golf: The Greatest Game*

Ward-Thomas, Pat et al. *The World Atlas of Golf*

Whitten, Ron with Theres Airey. *Gentlemen Joe Lee, Fifty Years of Golf Design*

2 Construction & Maintenance – (Second Shelf)

Original or Reprint

Arthur, Jim. *Practical Greenkeeping*

Beard, James B., Ph.D. *Turfgrass: Science and Culture*

Carrow, R.N., Ph.D., and R.R. Duncan, Ph.D. *Salt-Affected Turfgrass Sites*

Carrow, R.N., Ph.D., et al. *Turfgrass Soil Fertility and Chemical Problems*

Casler, M.D., Ph.D., and R.R. Duncan, Ph.D. *Turfgrass Biology, Genetics and Breeding*

Christians, Nick, Ph.D. *Fundamentals of Turfgrass Management*

Christians, Nick, Ph.D., and Michael Agnew. *Mathematics of Turfgrass Maintenance*

Crockford, Claude. *The Complete Golf Course: Turf and Design*

Dernoeden, Peter H., Ph.D. *Creeping Bentgrass Management: Summer Stresses, Weeds and Selected Maladies*

Hayes, P. et al. *The Care of the Golf Course*

Karnok, Keith J., Ph.D. *Turfgrass Management Information Directory*

Mead, Daniel and Joseph Reid Akerman. *Contract Specifications and Engineering Relations*

Musser, Burton H. *Turf Management*

Sachs, Paul D. and Richard T. Luff. *Ecological Golf Course Management*

Turgeon, A.J. *Turfgrass Management*

White, Charles B. *Turf Manager's Handbook for Golf Course Construction, Renovation and Grow-in*

3 Drainage & Irrigation – (Second Shelf)
Original or Reprint

Huston, James. *Estimating for Landscape and Irrigation Contractors*

Jarrett, Albert R. *Golf Course and Grounds: Irrigation and Drainage*

King, F.H. *Irrigation and Drainage: Principles and Practices of Their Cultural Phases*

Watkins, James A. *Turf Irrigation Manual*

4 The Environment – (Second Shelf)
Original or Reprint

Balogh, James C. and William J. Walker. *Golf Course Management and Construction: Environmental Issues*

Brennan, Anne-Maria, Ph.D. *Living Together: Golf and Nature in Partnership*

Center for Resource Management. *Creating a Sustainable Future: Golf and Environment*

Center for Resource Management. *Environmental Principles for Golf in the United States*

Countryside Commission. *Golf Courses in the Countryside*

European Golf Association Ecology Unit. *An Environmental Strategy for Golf in Europe*

European Golf Association Ecology Unit. *The Committed to Green Handbook for Golf Courses*

Gould, David and Center for Resource Management. *A Collaboration Guide*

Center for Resource Management. *Environmental Siting Guide for Golf Course Development*

Lilly, Sharon. *Golf Course Tree Management*

Jacoby, Martin. *The Wildlife of Valderrama*

Nature Conservancy Council. *Your Course: Preparing a Conservation Management Plan*

Royal Canadian Golf Association. *Environmental Guidelines for Canadian Golf Clubs*

Research Information, Catalogues, and Secondary Resource Materials

These publications may provide insights or answers but are not an important reference source related to golf course architecture. This shelf can be thought of to contain "nice to know" information that is not really critical or significant.

1 Design – (Third Shelf)
Original or Reprint

Arterburn, Todd A. *Public-Private Partnerships in Golf Courses.*

Bartlett, Michael. *The Golf Book*

Bennett, Roger. *Golf Facility Planning*

Bendelow, Stuart W., Sr. *Tom Bendelow 1868 – 1936: The Johnny Appleseed of American Golf*

Browning, Robert. *A History of Golf*

Caner, George C., Jr. *History of Essex Country Club 1893 – 1993*

Cappers, Elmer Osgood. *Centennial History of The Country Club 1882 – 1982*

Darwin, Bernard. *Golf*

Darwin, Bernard. *James Braid*

Darwin, Bernard. *The Golf Courses of the British Isles* (reprint)

Doak, Tom. *The Confidential Guide to Golf Courses*

Donovan, Richard and Joseph S.F. Murdoch. *The Game of Golf and the Printed Word 1566 – 1985*

Ginny, A.E. and M.E. Benson. *Golf Courses and Country Clubs: A Guide to Appraisal, Market Analysis, Development and Financing*

Grant, Donald. *Donald Ross of Pinehurst and Royal Dornoch*

Grant, H.R.J. and J.F. Moreton. *Aspects of Collecting Golf Books*

Henderson, I.T. and D.I. Stirk. *Golf in the Making*

Heuer, Karla L. and Cecil McKay, Jr. *Golf Courses: A Guide to Analysis and Evaluation*

Hurdzan, Michael J. Ph.D. *Evolution of the Modern Green*

Johnston, Alastair J. and James F. Johnston. *The Chronicles of Golf: 1457 – 1857*

Jones, Rees and Guy Rando. *Golf Course Developments*

Jones, W. Pete. *A Directory of Golf Courses Designed by Donald Ross*

Kains, Robert. *Golf Course Design and Construction*

Klein, Bradley S., Ph.D. *Cultural Links: An International Political Economy of Golf Course Landscapes*

Klein, Bradley S. Ph.D. *Rough Meditations*

Klemme, Michael. *A View From the Rough*

Mackenzie, Dr. Alister. *The Spirit of St Andrews*

McMillan, Robin. *The Golfer's Home Companion*

Moss, Richard. *Golf and the American Country Club*

Murdock, J.S.F. *The Library of Golf 1743 – 1966*

National Golf Foundation and McKinsey & Co. *A Strategic Perspective on the Future of Golf*

Orians, G.H. et al. *Adapted Minds*

Ortiz-Patino, Jamie. *Valderrama the first Ten Years 1985 – 1995*

Phillips, Patrick L. *Developing with Recreational Amenities, Golf, Tennis, Skiing, Marinas*

Price, Charles. *The American Golfer*

Price, Robert. *Scotland's Golf Courses*

Riddell, Gervase Carre. *Practical Golf Course Design and Construction*

Sato, Akiro. *The History of Golf Course Development Worldwide*

Scarth, John and Neil Crafter. *The Treasury of Australian Golf Course Architects*

Sheehan, Lawrence. *A Commonwealth of Golfers*

Steel, Donald, Peter Ryde and H.W. Wind. *Encyclopedia of Golf*

Stimpson, Edward S. III. *Forty-One Years from Intervention to Convention*

Taylor, J.H. *Taylor on Golf*

Taylor, Joshua. *The Art of Golf*

Tulloch, W.W. *The Life of Old Tom Morris* (reprint)

Vardon, Harry. *How to Play Golf*

Vardon, Harry. *The Complete Golfer*

Wethered, H.N. *The Perfect Golfer*

Wethered, H.N. et al. *The Game of Golf, The Lonsdale Library Volume IX*

Wexler, Daniel. *The Missing Links*

Whigham, H.J. *How to Play Golf*

2 Construction & Maintenance – (Third Shelf)

Original or Reprint

Adams, W.A. and R.J. Gibbs. *Natural Turf for Sport and Amenity: Science and Practice*

Baker, S.W., Ph.D. *Sands for Sports Turf Construction and Maintenance*

Barron, Leonard. *Lawns and How to Make Them, Together with The Proper Keeping of Putting Greens*

Beale, Reginald. *Lawns for Sports: Their Construction and Upkeep*

Beale, Reginald. *The Practical Greenkeeper*

Campbell, John. *Greenkeeping*

Escritt, J.R. *ABC of Turf Culture*

Daniel W.H., Ph.D. and R.P. Freeborg, Ph.D. *Turf Manager's Handbook*

Hannon, Ed. *The Site Calculations Pocket Reference*

Hanson, A.A., Ph.D. and F.V. Juska, Ph.D. *Turfgrass Science*

Henderson, Peter. *Making and Maintaining Golf Links*

Lilly, Sharon. *Golf Course Tree Management*

MacDonald, James. *Lawns, Links and Sportsfields*

Macself, A.J. *Grass*

Mellor, David R. *Picture Perfect: Mowing Techniques for Lawns, Landscapes and Sports*

Metsker, Stan, CGCS. *On the Course: The Life and Times of a Golf Course Superintendent*

Morrison, J.S.F. *Around Golf*

Murray, Dr. C.M. *Greenkeeping in South Africa*

Park, Eddie. *Real Golf*

Pennsylvania State University. *Greenkeeping*

Reed, F.J. *Lawns and Playing Fields*

Roberts, Eliot C. and Beverly C. Roberts. *Lawn and Sports Turf Benefits*

Sanders, T.W., F.L.S. *Lawns and Greens: Their Formation and Management*

Sprague, Howard. *Turf Management Handbook*

Vargas, Joseph M., Ph.D. and A.J. Turgeon, Ph.D. *Poa annua: Physiology, Culture and Control of Annual Bluegrass*

Witteveen, Gordon. *A Century of Greenkeeping*

Witteveen, Gordon and Michael Bavier. *Practical Golf Course Maintenance: The Magic of Greenkeeping*

3 Shelf Drainage & Irrigation Section – (Third Shelf)

Original or Reprint

Cast Iron Pipe Research Association. *Golf Course Irrigation*

4 The Environment – (Third Shelf)

Original or Reprint

Klemme, Michael. *A View From the Rough*

Libby, G., D.F. Harker and K. Harker. *Managing Wetlands on Golf Courses.*

Stewart, Thomas P. and Russell Shoeman. *The Nature of Golf: Exploring the Beauty of the Game*

Publications Related to Golf Course Design for Interesting Leisure Reading

These may include brochures, outdated catalogues, travel or history books, stories about championships and courses they are played. Such books add depth to a library and the reader but are only casually involved with golf course design.

1 Design – (Fourth Shelf)

Original or Reprint

Allen, Sir Peter. *Play the Best Courses*

Allen, Sir Peter. *Famous Fairways: A Look at the World of Championship Golf*

Bamberger, Michael. *To the Linksland*

Barclay, James A. *Golf in Canada: A History*

Barkow, J. et al. *Applied Mind*

Brummer, Andy. *Tech TV's Guide to the Golf Revolution: How Technology is Driving the Game*

Colville, George M. *Five Open Champions and the Musselburgh Golf Story*

Cotton, Sir Henry. *Golf in the British Isles*

Cousins, Geoffrey and Paul Kegan. *Golf in Britain*

Cousins, Geoffrey and Don Pottinger. *An Atlas of Golf*

Cronin, Tim. *The Spirit of Medinah: 75 Years of Fellowship and Championships*

Curtiss, Frederic H. and John Heard. *The Country Club 1882 – 1932*

Darwin, Bernard. *A History of Golf in Britain*

Darwin, Bernard. *Golf Between Two Wars*

Davis, William H. *The World's Best Golf*

Davis, William H., et al. *Great Golf Courses of the World*

DiPerna, Paula and Vicki Keller. *Oakhurst: The Birth and Rebirth of American's First Golf Course*

Dobereiner, Peter. *The Glorious World of Golf*

Dobereiner, Peter. *The World of Golf: The Best of Peter Dobereiner*

Dunn, John Duncan. *Natural Golf*

Edmund, Nick. *Classic Golf Courses of Great Britain and Ireland*

Fall, R.C. et al. *Golfing in South Africa*

Finnegan, James W. *A Centennial Tribute to Golf in Philadelphia*

Finnegan, James W. *All Courses Great and Small: A Golfer's Pilgrimage to England and Wales*

Finnegan, James W. *Pine Valley Golf Club*

Forse, Ronald. *Classic Golf Courses and the Master Architects*

Gallagher, Donald. *Woodland Golf Club*

Garrity, John. *America's Worst Golf Courses*

Govedarica, Tom. *Chicago Golf: The First 100 Years*

Graffis, Herb. *The PGA*

Grimsley, Will. *Golf: Its History, People and Events*

Harber, Paul. *The Complete Guide to Golf on Cape Cod*

Harrison, Mike. *The Official Guide to Jack Nicklaus Computer Golf*

Haultain, Arnold. *The Mystery of Golf*

Hawtree, Fred. *Triple Baugé*

Hecker, Genevieve. *Golf for Women*

Hill, David and Nick Seitz. *Teed Off*

Hitch, Thomas K. and Mary I. Kuramoto. *Waialae Country Club: The First Half Century*

Hopkins, Frank. *Golf Holes They Talk About*

Hoteling, Neal. *Pebble Beach Golf Links: The Official History*

Huck, Barbara and Doug Whiteway. *One Hundred Years at St Charles Country Club*

Hutchinson, Horace. *Golfing*

Johnson, Joseph. *The Royal Melbourne Golf Club: A Centenary History*

Jones, Robert Trent, Sr., with Larry Dennis. *Golf's Magnificent Challenge*

Kroeger, Robert. *To the 14th Tee: A Pilgrimage to the Links of Scotland*

Labbance, Bob and David Cornwell. *The Maine Golf Guide*

Lafaurie, Andre-Jean. *Great Golf Courses of the World*

Lee, James P. *Golf in America* (reprint)

Leigh-Bennett, E.P. *Some Friendly Fairways*

Machat, Udo with text by Cal Brown. *The Golf Courses of the Monterey Peninsula*

Mahoney, Jack. *The Golf History of New England*

Martin, H.B. *Fifty Years of American Golf*

Massy, Arnand, translated by A.R. Allinson. *Golf*

McCarthy, John Francis. *The Beauty of Golf in New York*

McCord, Robert R. *The Best Public Golf Courses in the United States, Canada, the Caribbean and Mexico: A Complete Guide to 617 Courses*

McCord, Robert R. *The Quotable Golfer*

Miller, Dick. *America's Greatest Golfing Resorts*

Moone, Theodore. *Golf From a New Angle*

Mulvoy, Mark and Art Spander. *Golf: The Passion and the Challenge*

Pace, Lee. *Pinehurst Stories: A Celebration of Great Golf and Good Times*

Pennink, Frank. *Home of Sport: Golf*

Peper, George. *Golf Courses of the PGA Tour*

Peter, Thomas H. *Reminiscences of Golf and Golfers*

Pilley, Phil. *Heather and Heaven: Walton Heath Golf Club 1903 – 2003*

Player, Gary with Michael McDonnell. *To Be the Best*

Price, Charles. *The World of Golf: A Panorama of Six Centuries*

Quirin, Dr. William L. *The Garden City Golf Club Centennial Anniversary*

Rawson, Chris. *Where Stone Walls Meet the Sea: Sakonnet Golf Club, 1899 – 1999*

Ray, Edward. *Driving, Approaching, Putting*

Ray, Edward. *Inland Golf*

Rees, J.L. *Lawns, Greens, and Playing Fields*

Roberts, John M. *Sports Facilities*

Robertson, James K. *St Andrews – Home of Golf*

Rubenstein, Lorne. *A Season in Dornoch: Golf and Life in the Scottish Highlands*

Seagram Distillers Company. *Seagram's Guide to Strategic Golf*

Seelig, Pat. *Historic Golf Courses of America*

Shackelford, Geoff. *The Good Doctor Returns*

Shackelford, Geoff. *The Riviera Country Club: A Definitive History*

Sheehan, Lawrence with Michael Carroll. *A Commonwealth of Golfers: A Centennial Tribute to the Game and its Players*

Sheehan, Lawrence. *A Passion for Golf*

Smith, Douglas LaRue. *Winged Foot Story: The Golf, the People, the Friendly Trees*

Soutar, Daniel G. *The Australian Golfer*

Steel, Donald. *Golf Facts and Feats*

Taylor, Dawson. *St Andrews, Cradle of Golf*

Tolhurst, Desmond. *St Andrew's Golf Club: The Birthplace of American Golf*

Tufts, Richard S. *The Scottish Invasion*

Two of His Kind. *The Six Handicap Golfer's Companion*

Tyler, Lee. *The Case of the Missing Links – A Golf Mystery*

Tyler, Lee. *The Teed Off Ghost*

Weeks, Edward. *Myopia, A Centennial Chronicle, 1875 – 1975*

Wexler, Daniel. *Lost Links, Forgotten Treasures of Golf's Golden Age*

Wind, Herbert Warren. *Following Through*

Wind, Herbert Warren. *The Story of American Golf*

Wind, Herbert Warren. *The Complete Golfer*

Windeler, Robert. *Links With a Past: The First 100 Years of the Los Angeles Country Club, 1897 – 1997*

Wright, Harry. *A Short History of Golf in Mexico and the Mexico City Country Club*

2 The Environment – (Fourth Shelf)

Original or Reprint

Clarke, John J. *Golf Courses and the Environment*

Diaz, Jamie and Linda Hartough. *Hallowed Ground: Golf's Greatest Places*

Old and Rare Publications of High Value

If these rare treasures are not isolated, they seem to be easily forgotten or lost, and your library is poorer for it. Fewer volumes in a separate space are easier to monitor and protect.

1 Rare Books – (Fifth Shelf)

Balfour, James. *Reminiscences of Golf on St Andrews Links*

Bauer, Aleck. *Hazards, Those Essential Elements of a Golf Course Without Which the Game Would be Tame and Uninteresting*

Bendelow, Tom. *Golf Courses by the American Park Builders*

Clark, Robert. *Golf, A Royal and Ancient Game*

Colt, H.S. and C.H. Alison. *Some Essays on Golf Course Architecture.* (original)

Crawford, MacGregor & Camby. *Stepping Stones to a Golf Course*

Darwin, Bernard. *The Golf Courses of the British Isles*

Darwin, Bernard. *The Golf Links of France*

Darwin, Bernard. *A Round of Golf on the L(ondon) & N(orth) E(astern) R(ailway)*

Finger, Joseph S. *The Business End of Building or Rebuilding a Golf Course*

Forbes, Ross. *The Most Influential Golf Course Architects in the History of the Game*

German Railway System. *Golf in Germany*

Hotchkin, S.V., Col., M.C. *The Principles of Golf Architecture*

Hunter, Robert. *The Links*

Hutchinson, Horace. *British Golf Links*

Hutchinson, Horace. *Golf Greens and Green-Keeping*

Imperial Chemical Industries Ltd. *The Improvement of Lawns, Golf Greens and Fairways*

Jones, Rees. *Bethpage Black Course: Field Notes*

Jones, Robert Trent. *Golf Course Architecture,*

Kerr, John. *The Golf Book of East Lothian*

Kladstrup, Donald M. *The Evolution of a Legacy*

Langford, William B. *Golf Course Architecture in the Chicago District*

Leach, Henry. *The Happy Golfer*

Lee, James P. *Golf in America: A Practical Manual*

Low, John. *Concerning Golf*

Macdonald, Charles Blair. *Scotland's Gift – Golf*

Mackenzie, Dr. Alister. *Golf Architecture: Economy in Course Construction and Greenkeeping*

Park, Willie Jr. *The Game of Golf*

Peter, Thomas H. *Reminiscences of Golf and Golfers*

Robertson, Kolin. *Some Yorkshire Golf Courses*

Scott, O.M. *Report of the Educational Conferences (held at 1931 National Greenkeepers Association)*

Scott, O.M. *Turf Talks*

Sinclair, R.O., Editor. *The Golf Course*

Smith, Garden. *The World of Golf*

Sorensen, Gary L. *The Architecture of Golf*

Sutton and Sons. *Lawns: Garden Lawns, Tennis Lawns, Putting Greens, Cricket Grounds*
Sutton and Sons. *Lawns and Sports Grounds*
Sutton, Martin A.F. *Golf Courses: Design, Construction and Upkeep*
Sutton, Martin A.F. *The Book of the Links: A Symposium on Golf*
The Golfer's Year Book. *The Golfer's Yearbook 1930*
Thomas, George C., Jr. *Golf Architecture in America: Its Strategy and Construction*
Thompson, Stanley. *About Golf Courses, Their Construction and Upkeep*
Tillinghast, A.W. *Planning a Golf Course*
Tull, A.H. *The Relationship of the Design of Golf Courses to Low Maintenance Cost*
Tulloch, W.W. *The Life of Old Tom Morris*
Uzzell, Thomas. *Golf in the Oldest Mountains*
Wethered, H.N. and T. Simpson. *The Architectural Side of Golf*
Whigham, H.J. *How to Play Golf*

2 Construction and Maintenance – (Fifth Shelf)
Cubbon, M.H., Ph.D. and M.J. Markuson. *Soil Management for Greenkeepers*
Farley, G.A. *Golf Course Commonsense*
Ferguson, Marvin, Ph.D. *Building Golf Holes for Good Turf Management*
Lees, Peter. *Care of the Green*
Scott, O.M. & Sons. *The Putting Green*
Scott, O.M. & Sons. *The Seeding and Care of Golf Courses*
Sutton, Martin H.F. *Layout and Upkeep of Golf Courses and Putting Greens*

3 The Environment – (Fifth Shelf)
National Association of Audubon Societies. *Golf Clubs as Bird Sanctuaries*

Part V

Resources

... determination to realise
a world that shall be better
is the prevailing characteristics
of the modern spirit

The Greek View of Life – Goldsworthy L. Dickinson

Devil's Pulpit near Toronto by Hurdzan and Fry, ASGCA, epitomizes the magnificence of golf holes

Resources

Societies of Golf Course Architects

The American Society of Golf Course Architects

THE ASGCA was formed officially in 1947, although it resulted in part from informal get-togethers in Toronto during Prohibition. In turn, that very early concept of a professional society came from the formation in London, England of the *International Society of Golf Course Architects* in the 1920s. Never incorporated, the latter disappeared during Depression and War. The ASGCA publishes a monthly newsletter for members only. Brochures concerning relevant subjects are available from the Society as is the important *Building a Practical Golf Facility.*

125 North Executive Drive, Suite 106, Brookfield, WI 53005
Phone: (262) 786-5960. Fax: (262) 786-5919. E-mail: info@asgca.org
Website: http://www.asgca.org

The British Association of Golf Course Architects

Formed in 1971, the association later became the *British Institute of Golf Course Architects (BIGCA)*. The *French Association (AFAG)* was founded in 1983 and the *European Society of Golf Course Architects (ESGA)* in 1989. The three European groups were merged in 2000 to become the *European Institute of Golf Course Architects (EIGCA)*. The European Institute publishes a yearbook in English.

The European Institute of Golf Course Architects (EIGCA)

The European Institute of Golf Course Architects represents Europe's most qualified and experienced golf course architects. Members of the Institute have shown through their skill, experience and training that they are able to design and supervise the construction of golf courses to the highest standards.

The Institute aims to enhance the status of the profession, to increase opportunities for its members to practice throughout the world and to develop the role of education.

In addition the Institute's main objectives are:

- To advance the study of golf course architecture, planning and development.
- To promote the technical and artistic development of golf courses and to encourage the highest standards of design and construction.
- To define and demand ethical and responsible professional conduct among its members and to qualify those members through education, examination and practical experience.
- To teach any subjects relating to golf course architecture, to educate students through its own diploma course and to provide continuing professional training for its members.
- To initiate, watch over and petition authorities and governments in relation to measures affecting, or likely to affect, golf course developments.

EIGCA consider environmentally friendly and sensitive design to be the cornerstone of their members professional work.

The Institute has three main categories of membership: Members, Associates and Graduates. Presently there are a total of eighty-four members for all categories.

Head Office: Chiddingfold Golf Club, Petworth Road, Chiddingfold,
Surrey GU8 4SL, UK
Phone/Fax: (44) 01428 681528
E-mail: info@eigca.org
Website: http://www.eigca.org

Japanese Society of Golf Course Architects

The Society was established for those engaged in the golf course design.

The aims are: to heighten members' capabilities, improve design skills, keep up to date with current trends, to contribute to the growth of the golf industry and uphold the best in the culture of golf.

According to legend, a four hole course was laid out by a Scot on a mountain top in Japan in 1888. By 1901, a nine hole course was in play near Kobe and in 1906 a private club was opened in Yokohama. The 100th anniversary of golf in Japan was celebrated in 2001 with the *Japanese Society of Golf Course Architects (JSGCA)* playing a prominent role. Apparently the four hole layout was not considered to be sufficiently documented to be considered Japan's first layout.

Kinya Fujita, 1889-1964, of Kasumigaseki Golf Club fame, was among the first Japanese born course architects. He was in part a protégé of Charles Alison, with whom he worked in Japan and later visited in Great Britain. Alison made a short visit to Japan in 1914 and returned for an extended stay in the 1930s to create or remodel a dozen layouts. His impact on course design in Japan can be compared to that of his former partner, Dr. Alister

Mackenzie, in Australia and New Zealand, who made a shorter but significant visit to those countries in 1926. Torakichi "Pete" Nakamura, 1915-, three times winner of the Japanese Open, entered the practice of course design in 1963 with a dozen or more courses to his credit, while Shunsuke Kato laid out Japan's first links style course in Setonaikai in 1991.

In 2001, memorial events were held to mark the 100th anniversary of golf in Japan. The JSGCA contributed two projects including a booklet, *Golf Courses in Japan Designed by Course Architects From Overseas,* and a par 3 design contest. The booklet is significant in that many non-Japanese course architects have practiced in Japan with both the architects and their creations generously received. The group's publication, *GCA Journal,* appears annually in Japanese and English.

2-7-17-5F Kita-aoyama, Minato-ku, Tokyo 107-0061
Phone: +81-3-6821-3501   Fax: +81-3-5772-6580   E-mail: infobox@jsgca.com
Website: http://www.jsgca.com

Society of Australian Course Architects

Ratho Golf Club in Tasmania was laid out between 1822 and 1842 by Alexander Reid from Leith, near Edinburgh, with help from neighbors all hailing from the links of Scotland. It is still in existence almost in its original form, making it one of the oldest existing courses outside the United Kingdom and Ireland.

Since the arrival around 1850 of David Robertson, older brother of Scotland's famous Allan, Australia has provided an impressive contribution to course design. Sadly, the first Scottish professional to follow Robertson with golf business and course design in mind, namely David Strath of North Berwick fame, died at sea in 1879 en route to Australia. In 1903, Daniel G. Soutar, 1882-1939, arrived from Carnoustie. Soon he was competing in the game and course design with his boyhood friend Carnegie Clark. Soutar authored *The Australian Golfer.*

Conversely, two Australian expatriates, Walter Travis, 1862-1927, and Greg Norman, renowned contemporary professional, have contributed to course design in North America. Although Travis designed no courses in his homeland, Greg Norman is active in Australia.

Course designer, Irish born Charles H. Readhead, 1874-1944, became New Zealand's most prolific designer before World War II while Michael A. Morcom (-1937) and his son H. Vernon Morcom (-1972), descendants of David Robertson on the maternal side and both greenkeepers, were perhaps the most prolific course designers in Australia. *A Round Forever* by John Scarth Lovell describes their careers and lists their courses.

Dr. Alister Mackenzie made a three to four month visit to Australia and New Zealand starting in 1926. He planned several courses, most completed by

Australian architect Alex Russell. Those courses exerted a monumental impact on course design in those countries. Still, the magic and mystery of courses in Australia and New Zealand appears to flow from designers based there. The *Society of Australian Golf Course Architects* was formed in the 1980s. It publishes *Golf Architecture.*

ABN 40 913 055 171

Golf Australia House, 153-155 Cecil Street, South Melbourne,
Victoria 3205, Australia

Website: http://www.sagca.org.au

Groups Honoring Individual Course Architects of the Past

The James Braid Golfing Society

This organization celebrates the life of one of the most prolific architects ever.

Golf Road, Brora, Sutherland, Scotland KW9 6QS

Phone: 01408 621 252   Fax: 01408 621 181

E-mail: braidatbrora@btinternet.com

Joe Lee Scholarship Foundation

A book, *Gentleman Joe Lee: Fifty Years of Golf Design* showcases many of Lee's designs and colorful language, while contributing to his favorite causes.

P.O. Box 1270, Boynton Beach, FL 33425

The Alister Mackenzie Society

The Alister Mackenzie Society is a non profit organization founded and sustained by member clubs that (a) were designed by Dr. Alister Mackenzie; (b) wish to promote his design principles through the work of current and future generations of architects; (c) seek to preserve and share information about his design ideas and methods; and (d) restore his work when neglected. The organization meets annually at one of the participating clubs and sponsors a competition for the Mackenzie Cup among teams from attending clubs. The Society also supports the annual Alister Mackenzie "Lido" Competition in Golf Course Architecture, and awards cash prizes to non-architects who submit winning hole designs. Competitors may request entry forms from:

Green Hills Country Club, End of Ludeman Lane,
Millbrae, CA 94030

Seth Raynor Society

Founded by Doug Stein and King Oemig as a gathering place for enthusiasts of the work of Charles Blair Macdonald, Seth Raynor and Charles Banks.

P.O. Box 5246 Chattanooga, TN 37406

Website: http://www.sethraynorsociety.org

164

Donald Ross Society
The group traces its beginning to 1988, when members at the circa 1926 Ross-designed Wampanoag Country Club in West Hartford, Connecticut decided to return their layout to its original design. In mid-May of each year, the Donald Ross Society holds a meeting in Pinehurst. Scholarships are announced and honorees acknowledged.

    Michael J. Fay, Executive Director, 66 Hillsboro Drive, West Hartford, CT 06107

    Phone: (860) 930-0676

Stanley Thompson Society
Founded in 1998 to research, record and publicize the life and works of Canada's Stanley Thompson, who some say created the world's most impressive courses, this Society publishes *Dormie*, a quarterly newsletter, holds an annual Stanley Thompson Society golf tournament and has republished Thompson's booklet, *Golf Courses, Their Design, Construction and Upkeep*.

    Bev. Peck, 908-505 Consumers Road, North York, On. M2J 4V8

    Phone: (416) 626-2101   Fax: (416) 497-9610   E-mail: bevpeck@onaibn.com

Tillinghast Association
Honoring golf course architect A.W. Tillinghast. According to Rees Jones, "Tilly" was a genius. Obviously he created several of the world's greatest courses and wrote abundantly. Many of his essays are combined into three volumes by Wolffe, Trebus and Wolffe (entered in the Bibliography under Tillinghast).

    Ken Stofer

    E-mail: STOFAORK@aol.com   Website: http://www.tillinghast.net

The Walter J. Travis Society
Founded in 1994, the Society includes member clubs designed by Travis as well as individual memberships. A biography, *The Old Man* by Bob Labbance, was commissioned by the Society.

    Archivist/Treasurer Ed Homsey, 24 Sandstone Drive, Rochester, NY 14616

    Phone: (716) 663-6120   E-mail: ebhomsey@frontiernet.net

Allied Organizations

Audubon International
  46 Rarick Road, Selkirk, NY 12158-2104
  Phone: (410) 583-7653   e-mail: info@aereps.com

Canadian Golf Course Superintendents Association
A national organization of Canadian course superintendents, this group publishes *The Greenmaster,* a monthly magazine directed to superintendents.
  5580 Explorer Drive, Suite 509, Mississauga, Ontario, LAW4Y1
  Phone: (800) 387-1056   Fax: (905) 602-1958
  Website: http://www.golfsupers.com

Club Managers Association of America
A network of administrators who run golf clubs in America. The body holds an annual meeting with education and interaction among its members, and certifies managers who have advanced their standing through courses and published papers.
  1733 King Street, Alexandria, VA 22314
  Phone: (703) 739-9500   Fax: (703) 739-0124   Website: http://www.cmaa.org

Environmental Institute for Golf
This organization, established under the auspices of the GCSAA, is of profound importance in this era of environmental awareness and is sure to play an increasing role in management of water, plant, wildlife, site selection, energy and waste management.
  Michael Hurdzan, Ph.D, Chairman
  1421 Research Park Drive, Lawrence, KS 66049-3859
  Phone: (785) 841-2240 or 1 (800) 472-7878   Fax: (785) 832-4448

The British Golf Collectors Society
The British Golf Collectors' Society was formed in 1987, with the aim of fostering an interest in the history and traditions of golf, and the collection of artefacts associated with that history.

The Society organises a number of meetings on both a national and regional basis, offering opportunities to share collecting experiences at the same time as enjoying a round of golf. Members often use hickory-shafted clubs and wear period dress. Competitions are held at Gullane, Rye and Aberdovey for the respective annual national hickory championships of Scotland, England and Wales and increasingly, the Society is asked to field a hickory team against clubs celebrating their centenaries.

The quarterly magazine, *Through the Green*, is produced to a high standard, covering news and book reviews, and carrying well-illustrated articles on a wide range of subjects, including historical developments in golf architecture.

The British Golf Collectors' Society has a membership of over 650 from all five continents, but principally Europe and North America. Further details can be obtained from the Society's web-site, britgolfcollectors.wyenet.co.uk or from the Honorary Secretary, 22 Cherry Tree Close, Brinsley, Nottinghamshire NG16 5BA. Tel: 01773 780420; email: anthonythorpe@ntlworld.com

Golf Collectors Society
This society, important to this bibliography, was founded in 1970 by Joseph Murdoch and Robert Kuntz, who shared a passion for collecting golf memorabilia. Joe, a writer, sought the written word in every nook and cranny of America, while Bob, a tinkerer, was lured to the vast array of weaponry that golfers had used through centuries. Later Joe authored several books on the subject of collecting golf books, including a seminal volume, *The Library of Golf 1743-1966*, while Bob concentrated on club repair and restoration and wrote *Antique Golf Clubs: Their Restoration and Preservation* in 1990.

The Bulletin, edited by Bob Labbance, a twenty-four page quarterly publication, features news of events and meetings, suggestions on collecting, in-depth explorations of golf history and opportunities to buy, sell and trade memorabilia.

Over the years, the world's foremost authorities and also sophisticated collectors have joined and have shared their knowledge of collecting, while using the network to advance their own collections. Dr. Gary Wiren, an early member, has built an extensive collection that includes a large number of golf instruction devices while writing and producing videos that educate collectors of every persuasion. Dick Donovan co-authored *The Game of Golf and the Printed Word* with Joe Murdoch. Course architects Ben Crenshaw, Keith Foster and Mike Hurdzan are members with large collections, while Mel Lucas, a former president of the GCSAA and the CGS possesses an extensive collection including many greenkeeping items.

Karen Bednarski, executive director, P.O. Box 3103, Ponte Vedra Beach, Florida 32004-3103
Phone: (904) 825-2191   Fax: (904) 810-5301   Website: www.golfcollectors.com

Golf Course Association
1470 Ben Sawyer Blvd., Mount Pleasant, SC 29464
Phone: (843) 881-9956   Fax: (843) 881-9958   E-mail: ngcoa@awod.com

Golf Course Builders Association of America
Founded in 1970 with nine members, this association of contractors has grown to include over 200 certified and other members. The organization meets twice annually. It bestows its prestigious Donald Rossi award and offers educational sessions. It publishes an annual directory of members and a quarterly newsletter.
727 O Street, Lincoln, NE 68508
Phone: (402) 476-4444   Fax: (402) 476-4489   E-mail: gcb@aol.com
Website: http://www.gcbaa.org

Golf Course Superintendents Association of America
An international association of course superintendents that offers a comprehensive educational program, an annual meeting, extensive resources and a library and archive at its Kansas headquarters. Its membership exerts an impressive impact on course maintenance worldwide, while its monthly publication, *Golf Course Management*, is heralded for its integrity and interest.
Steve Mona, Executive Director.
1421 Research Park Drive, Lawrence, KS 66049-3859
Phone: (785) 841-2240   Fax: (785) 832-4448   E-mail: gcsaacom@gcsaa.org
Website: http://www.gcsaa.org

Golf Development Council
This association offers services, in the United Kingdom, similar to the National Golf Foundation in the United States.
The Quadrant, Richmond, Surrey, England TW9 1BY

Ladies Professional Golf Association
2570 Volusia Avenue, Suite B, Daytona Beach, FL 32114
Phone: (904) 254-8800

National Club Association
A source of information and a voice on legal legislative and regulatory matters.
1120 20th Street, Northwest, Suite 725, Washington, DC 20036-3459
Phone: (202) 822-9822

National Golf Course Owners Association
An international association of course owners that has grown to include the majority of daily fee courses in the United States. It publishes *Golf Business*, a monthly magazine for its members concerning the industry, and joined the GCSAA in 2004 in producing that organization's annual show.
1470 Ben Sawyer Boulevard, Suite 18, Mount Pleasant, SC 29464
Phone: (843) 881-9956   Fax: (843) 881-9958
E-mail: bailey@awod.com or ngcoa@ngcoa.com   Website: http://www.ngcoa.com

National Golf Foundation
For decades, the NGF has disseminated information about every phase of the golf industry from architecture to finance, while tracking rounds played and new course construction. Founded by Herb and Joe Graffis of *Golfdom* magazine in the 1930s, it is one of the most important groups in the business world of golf.
As the clearing house for golf, the Foundation provides assistance for all in the business world of golf with brochures, booklets and text books. Periodically it provides a catalogue.
1150 South US Highway One, Suite 401, Jupiter, FL 33477
Phone: (561) 744-6006   Fax: (561) 744-6107   Website: http://www.ngf.org

PGA of America
100 Avenue of the Champions, P.O. Box 109601, Palm Beach Gardens, FL 33418
Phone: (561) 624-8400   Fax: (561) 624-8448

Public Golf Management Association
8030 Cedar Avenue, Suite 215,   Minneapolis, MN 55425
Phone: (612) 854-7272

Royal Canadian Golf Association
The governing body for golf in Canada. This dynamic and immensely resourceful association is involved with all aspects of the game in Canada.
1333 Dorval Drive, Oakville, ON LBJ 423, Canada
Phone: (905) 849-9700   Fax: (905) 845-7040   e-mail: golfhouse@rcga.org

The Royal and Ancient Golf Club of St Andrews

The Royal and Ancient Golf Club of St Andrews holds a unique position in golf. Established in 1754, it evolved through two and a half centuries as a leading authority in the world game. As the Club celebrated its 250th anniversary in 2004, it devolved responsibility for the administration of the Rules of Golf, the running of The Open Championship and other key golfing events, and the development of the game in existing and emerging golfing nations, to a newly formed group of companies collectively known as The R&A. As a separate entity The Royal and Ancient Golf Club of St Andrews remains a private golf club with a worldwide membership of 2,400. It has an impressive Golf Library.

Peter Dawson, Secretary
The Royal and Ancient Golf Club of St Andrews, Fife, KY16 9JD
Phone: 01334-460000   Fax: 01334-460001
Website. www. theroyalandancientgolfclub.org

The R&A

Prior to 2004, The Royal and Ancient Golf Club was responsible for administering the Rules of Golf, running The Open Championship and other key golfing events and funding and encouraging the development of the game around the world. In January 2004, these responsibilities were devolved to The R&A. The work of The R&A is carried out with the consent of over 125 national and international, amateur and professional organisations from 109 countries and on behalf of an estimated twenty-six million golfers in Europe, Africa, Asia and the Americas.

Peter Dawson, Chief Executive
The R&A, St Andrews, Fife, KY16 9JD
Phone: 01334-460000 Fax: 01334-460001   Website. www.randa.org

The Sports Turf Research Institute

STRI has been a leading publisher and supplier of turfgrass titles since 1929 when it was established in Bingley, West Yorkshire, England.

Five years ago STRI launched the first specialist on-line mail order book service, which now supplies over 250 turfgrass titles collected from publishers around the world, the widest range of titles available for the turfgrass industry, from a single source.

The on-line catalogue includes dedicated lists covering all aspects of golf including golf course architecture and design, golf course ecology and golf course construction and maintenance.

STRI, St Ives Estate, Bingley, BD16 1AU, UK
Go to www.stri.co.uk/bookshop for further details or telephone 01274 518908

United States Golf Association

The ruling body of golf in the United States. The USGA shares world responsibility for the game with The R&A. Its immense library and museum has the world's largest collection of golf related books and relevant material.

David Fay, Executive Director
Golf House, P.O. Box 708, Far Hills, NJ 07931
Phone: (908) 234-2300   Fax: (908) 234-9687   e-mail: usga@usga.org

USGA Green Section

This section of the United States Golf Association serves as a clearing house for information regarding turfgrass science and its application to golf course management. It retains turfgrass scientists in every region of the nation to consult with member clubs and courses and publishes the *USGA Green Section Record* six times a year. The important Green Section of the USGA also sponsors turfgrass research and includes a division devoted to course construction under the direction of agronomist James Moore. Founded in 1921, the Green Section published a monthly bulletin "to promote the betterment of golf courses" called *The Bulletin of the Green Section of......* It was published into the Great Depression and was a modest publication as those times allowed. Eventually it became the *Green Section Record*. The Bulletin included many essays from course architects of those days.

Jim Snow, Director, P.O. Box 708, Far Hills, NJ 07931-0708
Phone: (908) 234-2300   Fax: (908) 781-1736   E-mail: jsnow@usga.com
Website: http://www.usga.org

Urban Land Institute

This prestigious group publishes *Urban Land* twelve times a year for its members, often including essays on course development. It has also published leading books on course development.

1025 Thomas Jefferson Street, N.W., Suite 500, West Washington, DC 20007
Phone: (202) 624-7000   Fax: (202) 624-7140   E-mail: ull.org@1997

Libraries and Museums

Public and university libraries, together with the USGA, the R&A and the RCGA maintain large libraries of books on golf as do some state golf associations.

Amateur Athletic Foundation

The AAF operates the largest sports research library in North America, the Paul Ziffren Sports Research Center. When the Ralph Miller Golf Library, with its huge library and reference center, left the City of Industry, it found a home at AAF. The state of the art AAF research facility and learning center is dedicated to the advancement of sports knowledge and scholarship. The Foundation also maintains a sizable collection of historic sport art and artefacts. The AAF is a private, non profit institution that has committed over $100 million since 1985 to accomplish its mission to serve youth through sport and to increase knowledge of sport and its impact on people's lives.

2141 W. Adams Boulevard, Los Angeles, CA 90018
Phone: (323) 730-4600   Main Fax: (323) 730-9637
Library Phone: (323) 730-4646   Library Fax: (323) 730-0546
Main e-mail: info@aafla.org   Library e-mail: library@aafla.org
Website: http://www.aafla.org

British Columbia Golf Museum
The British Columbia Golf Museum, established in 1987, is a non profit organization dedicated to the preservation and promotion of golf history in British Columbia. It provides resources for research and education, and promotes an active interest in golf, recognizing the achievements of British Columbian golfers and others who have contributed to the game's development in the province.

2545 Blanca Street, Vancouver, B.C.V, 6R 4N1

Phone: (604) 222-4653 (GOLF) Fax: (604) 222-4654 E-mail: mashie@intergate.ca

The British Golf Museum
A visit to the British Golf Museum transports one down a pathway of surprising facts and striking feats during 500 years of golf history. Using diverse displays and exciting exhibits, the Museum traces the history of the game, both in Britain and abroad, from the Middle Ages to the present day. A library is also available to researchers. The museum is located adjacent to the Old Course at St Andrews.

Peter N. Lewis, Director

Bruce Embankment, St Andrews, Fife, KY16 9AB Scotland

Phone: 01334-460046   Fax: 01334 – 460064   E-mail: samgroves@randagc.org

Canadian Golf Hall of Fame and Museum
The Canadian Golf Hall of Fame preserves and honors the traditions of golf from its early European origins to the present day's modern equipment and superstar players. A walk through the Canadian Golf Hall of Fame mirrors a stroll over an 18 hole golf course, with each "hole" representing a significant element in the game's history, from its genesis to the champions of the modern game. The Royal Canadian Golf Association also supports turfgrass research in Canada through the Canadian Golf Foundation. It is the intent of the Foundation to raise funds to support research which addresses questions and issues facing the Canadian turfgrass industry. By striving to continually improve cultural practices and turfgrass species it hopes to reduce maintenance requirements and enhance the environment. Annually the Golf Hall of Fame inducts people into the Canadian Golf Hall of Fame and sponsored historian James Barclay's monumental *Golf in Canada*. The Hall of Fame includes a library of golf books.

Suite 1 – 1333 Dorval Drive, Oakville, ON L6M 4X7, Canada

Phone: (800) 263-0009

Colorado Golf Historical Center
The story of the Colorado PGA Section and professional golf in Colorado is revealed in this new Historical Center that shares a building with the Colorado PGA Section offices.

Scott Wellington, Executive Director

The Golf Club at Bear Dance, 6630 Bear Dance Road, 2nd Floor

Larkspur, CO 80118   Phone: (303) 681-0742

German Golf Museum
In June 2007, golf in Germany will celebrate its centennial. In anticipation of the event, a history center was established in July 2000.

Website: http://golfarchiv.dshs-koeln.de/index.htm

Given Memorial Library / Pinehurst Town Library, see Tufts Archive.

Massachusetts Golf Association

One of the oldest state golf associations, it published *A Commonwealth of Golfers* in 2002, a magnificent centennial tribute to the game and players, edited by eminent writer Larry Sheehan, with illustrations by Mike Carroll. Sponsored by the Massachusetts Golf Association Centennial Commission, headed by former executive director of the MGA, Richard D. Haskell and Thomas E. Landry, current director, the book provides superb accounts of the courses of the Commonwealth and their architects. The Massachusetts Golf Association publishes a quarterly magazine, entitled *MassGolfer.*

   300 Arnold Palmer Blvd., Norton, MA 02766-1365

   Phone: (800) 356-2201   Website: http://www.mgalinks.org

Francis Ouimet Library (at the same address)

Honors the rich tradition of golf in Massachusetts and the individuals who have shaped the game over the past century, the Massachusetts Golf Museum opened its doors to the public on 29 October 2002. The Museum pays tribute to the people and moments, both past and present, that have created the Commonwealth's rich golf heritage. It features interactive kiosks, multimedia quizzes, a replica of the Francis Ouimet Library, Hall of Trophies and a video tribute to the game of golf in Massachusetts.

Michigan State University Libraries

Maintains extensive collections including a growing collection of plans of course architects.

   100 Library, East Lansing, MI 48824-1048

   Phone: (517) 355-2341   Fax: (517) 432-3532

   E-mail: hakac@pilotmsu.edu   Website: www.lib.msu.edu/tgif

Michigan State University Turfgrass Information Center

Eminent scientist and author Dr. James B. Beard donated his immense collection of turfgrass information to Michigan State University's Turfgrass Information Center (TIC), which now contains the most comprehensive collection of turf-grass educational materials publicly available in the world. TIC has over 76,000 records in its primary database (TGIF – the Turfgrass Information File). Dr. Beard's donation and the rest of the library can be used on-line by subscription. Visit *http://tic.msu.edu/subs.htm* for details. *Turfgrass Bibliography 1672-1972* (*see* Beard, James B.), authored by Dr. Beard, Harriet J. Beard and David P. Martin is the most complete book covering turfgrass science.

   The TIC also includes the O.J. Noer Collection. During his career, turfgrass scientist O.J. Noer accumulated books, journals and conference proceedings related to the science, culture and maintenance of turfgrass. Upon his death, this legacy fell to turfgrass scientist Charles Wilson and later the O.J. Noer Research Foundation, which was formed to honor his name in support of turfgrass research and education. To assure universal availability to turfgrass students, the collection was transferred to Michigan State University at the behest of Dr. James B. Beard, then of the Department of Crop and Soil Science and Dr. Richard E. Chapin, then Director of Libraries. Beginning in 1968, the O.J. Noer Memorial Turfgrass Collection served to expand the existing collection of literature which had evolved during a concentrated effort to increase the MSU Libraries' turf holdings through the 1960s, a cooperative effort of both teaching and library faculty.

Other private contributions included collections from Dr. James Watson, Mr. Thomas Mascaro, Dr. John Gallager and Dr. James B. Beard. Valuable books and publications were solicited by Charles G. Wilson and James Latham on behalf of the O.J. Noer Foundation. Subsequent major donations have included materials from the USGA Green Section, GCSAA, Dr. William Daniel, Dr. Kenyon T. Payne, and Mr. Fred Opperman. In 2003, the Michigan State program was expanded to include representative plans of a growing number of course architects and a biographical profile of each. The program is known as *"The Architect's Gallery"*.

   Phone: (517) 365-2341   E-mail: hakac@pilot.msu.edu
   Website: http://www.tic.msu.edu/subs.htm

Museum of Virginia Golf History

Time and tradition have intersected magnificently at the Museum of Virginia Golf History located in Independence Golf Club's Charles House clubhouse. The museum and clubhouse blend artefacts and memorabilia as well as 200 pieces of artwork and photographs, which help to retell and continue to celebrate Virginia's rich history of golf. Inside the museum, display cases house all VSGA championship trophies and feature exhibits and memorabilia from Virginia clubs and founding organizations. Artefacts were gathered from Washington Golf and Country Club and the golf museum at James River Country Club. One of the display cases features the 1566 Scottish Acts of Parliament, courtesy of James River Country Club. The museum is the first and oldest dedicated to preserving the game.

   Andrew Blair, Communications Manager
   Phone: (804) 378-2300, extension 12   E-mail: vsgacomm@earthlink.net
   Website: http://www.vsga.org

PGA of America Historical Center

The PGA of America operated the PGA World Golf Hall of Fame in Pinehurst, North Carolina from 1984 to 1993. At that time the Association loaned many pieces of memorabilia to the World Golf Hall of Fame near St Augustine, Florida. Now the collection has been installed at the PGA Historical Center in Florida.

The Center's showcase is the Probst Library, one of the world's premier golf collections of both periodicals and hardbound books. In addition, the Center presents memorabilia from throughout golf history and displays that honor many of the Association's premier professionals and events.

   PGA Village, Port St Lucie, FL
   Phone: (561) 624-8400

Tufts Archives

The founding family of Pinehurst started a collection chronicling the growth, development and daily life of Pinehurst Resort, the Village of Pinehurst and the surrounding area. In 1970, the photos, promotional materials, artefacts and logbooks were archived and stored in the rear wing of the Given Memorial Library, in the Village of Pinehurst. The Archives are open to the public weekdays from 9.30 a.m. to 5.00 p.m.; Saturdays 9.30 a.m. to 12.30 p.m., and are a must-see for all visitors.

Librarians can also help researchers access the materials. There are no fees for usage, but donations are greatly appreciated.

    Tufts Archives at Given Memorial Library, Audrey Moriaty, Curator
    P.O. Box 159, Pinehurst, NC 28370
    Phone: (800) ITS-GOLF or (910) 235-8553   Fax: (910) 295-9053
    E-mail: tuftsarchives@earthlink.net   Website: under construction.

USGA Golf House

The largest collection of golf material in North America and the world with an extensive library, photo and video archives, ephemera, correspondence, equipment, medals, trophies and unique items. It is said that a golfer who has never visited Golf House is akin to the student of American government who has never visited Washington, DC. The long line of distinguished curators and archivists at the USGA, including Janet Seagle, Karen Bednarski, Andrew Mutch and Rand Jerris have also contributed immeasurably to collecting and cataloging golf books.

    Rand Jerris, Museum Curator
    P.O. Box 708, Far Hills, NJ 07931
    Phone: (908) 234-2300

World Golf Village Hall of Fame

The on-site World Golf Village Hall of Fame is a repository of facts and personal possessions of the greatest golfers in history, displayed in an interactive and educational setting.

    500 S. Legacy Trail, St Augustine, FL 32092
    Phone: (904) 940-8000   Website: http://www.worldgolfrenaissance.com

Sources for Books and Facsimile Editions

David Berkowitz

    Golf's Golden Years
    PO Box 842 Palatine, IL 60079-0842
    Phone: 1-847-934-4108   Fax: 1-847-934-4107
    Email: dave@golfsgoldenyears.com   Website: http://golfsgoldenyears.com

The Booklegger

    P.O. Box 2626, Grass Valley, CA 95945-2626
    Phone: (530) 272-1556   Fax: (530) 272-2133

The Classics of Golf

In 2002, Carala Ventures, Ltd. obtained both the Classics of Golf and its related spin-off, Flagstick Books, and began reissuing previous golf titles in these series while adding new and exciting examples of early golf literature. Under the direction of publisher Michael Beckerich and editor Gary Wiren, the new Classics of Golf will carry on the same mission, reprinting important golf books from the early days of the game, but with an even greater emphasis on quality. The Classics of Golf originated in the early 1980s, with the reproduction of thirty-eight early golf books carefully selected by Herbert Warren Wind, the dean of American golf writing. No new titles have been added to the series since Wind's retirement in 1995, though Flagstick Books offered twenty-two additional titles.

    Phone: (800) 483-6449   Website: http://www.classicsofgolf.com

Dick Donovan
A rare book dealer with expertise in golf collectibles. His volume, *The Game of Golf and the Printed Word (1566-1985)*, written with Joe Murdoch, is the most comprehensive source to the thousands of golf books available. No longer publishing catalogues of used books, Donovan concentrates more on auctions and appraisals for individual customers.

305 Massachusetts Avenue, Endicott, NY 13760-5609

Phone: (607) 785-5874

GCSAA Book Store
Maintains a large and valuable collection of contemporary books on design, construction and maintenance.

Golf Course Superintendents Association of America

1421 Research Park Dr., Lawrence, KS 66049

Phone: 1-800-379-8812   Fax: 1-800-868-5506   Website: www.gcsaa.org

Golf Classics
Book dealer John Bonjernoor issues an on-line catalogue multiple times each year with a substantial listing of rare and out-of-print books.

P.O. Box 250, St Clair Shores, MI 48080-0250

Phone: (313) 886-8258   Fax: (313) 886-6126   Cell: (313) 506-9607

E-mail: jbonjernoor@comcast.net

Golf Gap
1055 Bay Street, #1109, Toronto, Canada, M55 3A3

Phone: (416) 485-5316

The Golf Shopper (Phil Mason's)
Claims a wide collection of golf books.

403 Stringtom Road, Williamsbury, KY 40769

Phone: (606) 549-4827

Grant Books
This partnership of H.R.J. (Bob) and Shirley Grant was established in 1971. In the decades since, Grant Books has published dozens of new golf titles, offered many comprehensive catalogues of out-of-print volumes, as well as engaging in publishing many reprints of classic British golf books. Grant has built up a unique role in golf book sales, publishing and distribution, becoming one of the most respected sources of written golf material in Europe and the entire world.

The Coach House, New Road, Cutnall Green, Droitwich,

Worcestershire WR9 0PQ, United Kingdom

Phone: (0) 1299 851 588   Fax: (0) 1299 851 446*

E-mail: golf@grantbooks.co.uk   Website: www.grantbooks.co.uk

Quarto Book Shop situated on Golf Place, St Andrews, almost overlooking the eighteenth green of the Old Course. Quarto Book Shop always has a fine collection of golf books, old and new and also Scottish and local history. Margaret Squires, the proprietor, will always give you a warm welcome. It is a delightful place to have a browse after a day on the links.

8 Golf Place, St Andrews, Fife, KY16 9JD, United Kingdom. Phone (0) 1334 474 616)

Rhod McEwan

Rhod McEwan is the leading Scottish dealer in antiquarian, second-hand and elusive golf books. His golf website is devoted to the game of golf and its written word. He lives in Scotland on Royal Deeside in the heart of the Scottish Highlands and sells golf books via an occasional mail order catalogue and by phone. He maintains a comprehensive and interactive website.

Rhod McEwan Bookseller
Glengarden, Ballater, Aberdeenshire, AB35 5UB Scotland
Phone: (0) 13397-55429   Email: teeoff@rhodmcewan.com
Website: http://www.rhodmcewan.com

Brian Siplo Antiquarian Books

A book dealer with a comprehensive knowledge of both British and American golf titles. Although he no longer issues regular catalogues, Brian Siplo may be able to locate hard to find titles through a worldwide network of booksellers.

18 Robin Lane, Pepperell, MA 01463
Phone: (978) 433-2414   Fax: (978) 433-2033   E-mail: briansiplo@charter.net

John Wiley and Sons, Inc.

Customer Care Center, 1 Wiley Drive, Somerset, NJ 08875-1272
Phone: 1-800-225-5945   Fax: 1-732-302-2300
Email: custserv@wiley.com   Website: www.wiley.com

Peter Yagi Golf Books

For the past ten years Peter Yagi has published one of the few remaining American catalogues of out-of-print books. The Fall 2003 issue featured more than 1,400 items, from the most common title to the finest collectible literature of the game.

Peter Yagi Golf Books
16149 Redmond Way, #187, Redmond, WA 98052
Phone: (425) 562-6660   Cell: (206) 551-4853   Fax: (425) 562-3411
E-mail: pete@moneytolend.com

*For US to call UK, dial 011 44, drop "0" then dial complete number.

NOTES: Remember, Buyer Beware! Never pay more for an item than you can afford to lose. If there is any question, do not buy unless it is from a reputable dealer. This list is by no means inclusive. There are many other excellent sources of books. It just may be we are not familiar with them.

Appendix

Recent publications and other books notified after completion of the bibliography

Bendelow, Stuart, W. Jr. *Thomas "Tom" Bendelow (1868-1936) "The Johnny Appleseed of American Golf".* (Williams and Company, Savanah, Georgia, publication pending). Tom Bendelow was truly a founding father of golf course design and development in North America. Touring the continent from British Columbia to Florida and from Montreal to Mexico he laid out some 700 courses including renowned Medinah and the South Course of Olympia Fields in the Chicago area. Stuart Bendelow presents an eloquent book concerning his grandfather who played an important role in the development of golf and its playing fields in North America.

de St. Jorre, John and Anthony Edgeworth. *Legendary Golf Links of Ireland.* (Wellington, Florida. Edgeworth Editions 2006, 400 pages, ISBN pending). The third in the series, it covers sixteen great links courses.
$100

Edward, Ian. *The Aberdeen Golfers: 225 Years on the Links.* (Worcestershire, UK. Grant Books, November 2005, pages 228). Founded in 1780 it is a classic links course. Published in a limited edition of 1000 copies.
$55. Leather edition $220

Stephen, Walter. *Willie Park Jr: The Man who took Golf to the World.* (Edinburth, Luath Press, 2005, pages 317)
$40

Stewart, John W. *William Clark Fownes, Jr. The Man, The Golfer, The Leader.* (Fredericksburg, VA. Sheridan Books, 2003, 106 pages. Printed for private circulation by Mackenzie Investment Corporation, Lutherville MD). The Fownes family were intimately connected to Oakmont.

Turgeon, A.J. and Joseph M. Vargas. *The Turf Problem Solver.* (Hoboken, NJ: John Wiley & Sons, Inc., 2005, 256 pages, ISBN 0-471-73619-8). Two celebrated American experts and educators in turfgrass science have written a practical guide to problem solving. The case studies are relevant and the solutions are reasonable. The book addresses problems involving the environmental (climate, shade, moisture, etc.), cultural (mowing, fertilizing, irrigation, rolling, etc.), pests and pesticides (weeds, insects, and diseases), and a good bit more.
C/H: M-4, $70

177

Short Title Index

In such indexes, although small pricks to their
subsequent volumes, there is seen the baby figure of
the giant mass of things to come at large

Troilus and Cressida, Act 1, Scene 3, Line 343 – Shakespeare

182

187

Index
Authors, Associations, Resources

Every moment dies a man,
every moment one is born

The Vision of Sin – Alfred Lord Tennyson

192